Phila-Nipponica:

An Historic Guide to Philadelphia & Japan

フィラデルフフィアと日本を結ぶ歴史的絆

Copyright © 2015 by the
Japan America Society of Greater Philadelphia
200 South Broad Street, Suite 910
Philadelphia, PA 19102
japanphilly.org

ISBN-13: 978-0692349472
ISBN-10: 0692349472

Edited by Linda H. Chance & Tetsuko Toda
Cover illustration by Matthew Meyer

Foreword
序文

"Phila-Nipponica"(フィラ・ニッポニカ)という名称は、ペンシルバニア大学に属するウィリアム・ラフラー、カール・コーラー、そしてリンダ・チャンス先生たちの会話から誕生した偶然の産物といえる。

1990年代中頃、この3人は会議に参加するために雨の中の高速道路を1台の車に乗り合わせていた。その時、フィラデルフィアと日本が、いかに深い歴史的な繋がりを持っているかについて話が盛り上がった。その話を聞いた当時フィラデルフィア美術館客員研究員であった筑波大学の今井雅晴先生が、さらなる研究を重ねられた結果、確かに歴史的な繋がりがあることが明らかになっていったのである。

ギリシャ語で愛を意味する"philia"から生まれた"Philadelphia"(フィラデルフィア)という都市名に、"ニッポン"(日本)を足して"フィラ・ニッポニカ"という造語が誕生したわけであるが、名付け親たちは決してスローガンを目指していたわけではなかった。しかし、いったんこの名称が生まれると、驚くほど多くのプロジェクトに使用されるようになった。

1996年から始まった毎年日本を訪れる地域教育者のための研修名「フィラ・ニッポニカ：フィラデルフィア地域の学校に日本研究を紹介」が、まず登場する。その後、同名のシンポジウムを開催しようという案が出たが、日本とフィラデルフィアの歴史的な繋がりの再発見を記録したガイドブックを出そうというアイデ

"Phila-Nipponica" was a happy coinage from the fertile mind of William R. LaFleur, in the company of Karl Kahler and Linda Chance, all from the University of Pennsylvania. While cruising a rainy highway to a conference in the mid–1990s, their conversation turned to the many historic ties between Philadelphia and Japan, then being brought to light by the eager research of Masaharu Imai of Tsukuba University.

The group was not particularly searching for a slogan, but once born the name—incorporating the Greek word for love (*philia*) that is the source of 'Philadelphia,' and a traditional native pronunciation for Japan (*nippon*)—attached to many projects. It became the title for a series of trips to Japan by Philadelphia educators that began in 1996, "Phila-Nipponica: Bringing Japanese Studies to Philadelphia Area Schools." Discussions proceeded for a symposium under the name, but ultimately the idea of a written guide focusing on rediscovered histories captured the imagination of sponsors.

With Felice Fischer of the Philadelphia Museum of Art as the Editor and Catherine Nagel, the first Executive Director of the Japan America Society of Greater Philadelphia, spearheading production, everything and everyone came together. The first volume, *Phila-Nipponica: An Historic Guide to Philadelphia and Japan*, published in 1999, and this expanded second edition, are

アに、企業のスポンサーが最終的に興味を示した。

かくして、フィラデルフィア美術館学芸員フェリス・フィッシャー女史とフィラデルフィア日米協会初代専務理事キャサリン・ネーゲルが本の出版に向けて活動を開始する。その後は自然の成り行きで、全てが一挙に動き始めたという表現がぴったりであろう。初版「フィラ・ニッポニカ:フィラデルフィアと日本を結ぶ歴史的絆」はこうして1999年に出版された。その後15年を経て、1世紀半に及ぶ歴史的関係の記録をさらに追記した改訂版が、今年ここに出版されるに至ったのである。

本書の出版は、フィラデルフィア日米協会20周年記念事業の一環でもある。過去35年余りをフィラデルフィアで過ごした私にとって、今回この改訂版プロジェクトチームに参加できたことは非常に名誉なことである。生涯の思い出となることを、ここに深く感謝申し上げたい。

チューニ一美
2014年11月

the sum of Philadelphia's Japanophilia and Japanese attraction to Philadelphia that have linked our two regions for over a century and a half.

This publication is also part of the Japan America Society's 20th year anniversary celebration. As a Japanese living in Philadelphia for the past 35 years, having been part of the second edition production team is an honor and privilege that I will cherish for many years to come.

Kazumi Teune
November 2014

A Note on Names

Names of Japanese persons appear in Japanese order, with the family name first and the given name second (Oguri is the family name, Kōzukenosuke is the personal name, and a.k.a. Tadamasa indicates an alternate given name). Those who made a practice of presenting their names in western order when publishing in the United States appear in western order (Masaharu is the personal name, Imai is the family name). In any case, the family name is the one we use when referring to the person by a single name. Art names (Eitokusai) and tea names indicate significant attainment in a pursuit.

CONSULATE GENERAL OF JAPAN
299 PARK AVENUE
NEW YORK. N. Y. 10171
(212) 371-8222

[Phila-Nipponica 改訂版　出版によせて]

２０１４年１１月

　１９９４年に創立されたフィラデルフィア日米協会２０周年にあたる本年、「Phila-Nipponica: An Historic Guide to Philadelphia & Japan：フィラデルフィアと日本を結ぶ歴史的絆」の改訂版が出版されますことを、心よりお喜び申し上げます。

　フィラデルフィアと日本の関係は、江戸末期に始まります。徳川幕府より派遣された万延元年遣米使節団が侍の衣装で市内をパレードした際には何万人もの観客が熱狂的な歓迎をしたと記録されております。その後、明治時代から昭和初期までの間に、後の日本の近代化を支えた多くの日本人指導者たちがフィラデルフィアに滞在し、医学、科学、建築、近代ビジネスなどの分野で最先端の知識を日本に持ち帰りました。

　明治時代初期において、多くのクエーカー教徒が、フィラデルフィアに滞在していた日本人に対して個人的な支援を熱心に行っていたことは、日本のみならず地元でもほとんど忘れられていると伺っております。今回の改訂版に、現在、多くの日本人子弟が通っている日本語補習校のキャンパスになっている屋敷の持ち主であったメアリー・モリス氏を含め、フィラデルフィアにて当時の日米の交流に尽力した多くの人物の貢献が追記されていることは、フィラデルフィアと日本の歴史に対する再評価とも言える大きな貢献であると思います。

　フィラデルフィア日米協会の過去２０年にわたる日米交流への貢献を土台として、今後ともフィラデルフィアと日本の関係がさらに深まっていくことを祈念します。

在ニューヨーク日本国総領事・大使

4

CITY OF PHILADELPHIA

MICHAEL A. NUTTER
Mayor

Greetings!

The City of Philadelphia and the Island Nation of Japan have enjoyed a rich and reciprocal friendship that dates as far back as 1872, the year the first official Japanese delegation visited Philadelphia. The Japanese historian Kume Kunitake wrote in his *True Account of a Tour of America and Europe* (Tokumei Zenken Taishi Bei-O Kairan Jikki - published in 1878) that "The American people are peaceful in their dealings with others, and Philadelphians are especially cordial, friendly and energetic. The fact that Americans are filled with friendship is probably based on the way of thinking in Philadelphia."

These warm sentiments have persisted through the years as the relationship between Philadelphia and Japan continues to thrive. As this 2nd Edition of the Phila-Nipponica illustrates, the Philadelphia-Japan nexus spans many years and takes many forms, proving to be a vital bridge between our two peoples.

Today, Japan and Philadelphia are as connected as ever. Since 1986, Philadelphia and Kobe, Japan have had an official partnership through the Sister Cities program. Philadelphia's own Temple University has had a branch campus in Tokyo since 1982—making it not only the oldest, but also the largest foreign university in Japan.

One of Philadelphia's newest and most beautiful traditions is the Subaru Cherry Blossom Festival, which is inspired by the Japanese appreciation of these lovely blossoms. The Festival has its roots in a tree planting effort organized by the Japan America Society in 1998 that echoed a gift of 1,600 cherry trees from the Japanese government to Philadelphia in 1926. Over the years, the Festival has grown into a celebration of all forms of Japanese culture, drawing thousands to Fairmount Park each year. The Festival has created the opportunity for an exciting cultural exchange and serves as a reminder of our rich shared history.

It is my privilege to have contributed a proud chapter to this storied relationship. On behalf of the City of Philadelphia, I join in this salute to 150 years of rewarding exchange between Philadelphia and Japan and offer my heartfelt hopes that we will continue to grow in friendship and mutual appreciation for yet another 150 years.

Sincerely,

Michael A. Nutter
Mayor

Contents
目次

The 19th Century: Early Contacts and Diplomacy
最初の出会い

1. Diplomatic Beginnings
外交と交流の始まり

Learning from Each Other: Commerce and Art
モノや文化の交流

2. Philadelphia Expo and Museum
万国博覧会＆商業博物館

3. Exchanges in Arts and Literature
芸術と文学の交流

Learning From Each Other: People-to-People
人の交流

4. Japanese in Philadelphia
フィラデルフィアに来た日本人

5. Philadelphians in Japan
日本に来たアメリカ人

Continuing Connections
現代につながっている交流

6. Benjamin Franklin's Descendents and Japan
フランクリンの子孫たちと日本

Introduction

フィラデルフィア、日本、近代世界

フィラデルフィアと日本の関係からは、近代史のもう１つの側面が見える。一般的に近代史は冷酷なヨーロッパの台頭として語られるが、『フィラ・ニッポニカ』のプリズムを通した近代史からは、近代文明の生成過程における日本とアメリカの重要性が見えてくる。同時に、グローバル都市としてのフィラデルフィアの意義もよく分かる。

かつてヨーロッパが劇的変化を遂げ世界の中心に躍り出たように、19世紀のアメリカと日本は遅れて世界の国際舞台に登場したにもかかわらず、同様に目覚しい変化を遂げた。主にヨーロッパからやって来た3000人のお雇い外国人に助けられて、日本は1868年には封建制度から脱した。アメリカは1830年代には世界でも有数の捕鯨国に、そして1861年には世界で最大の海運国となり、19世紀初頭の太平洋において脅威な存在であった。アメリカの捕鯨船があの有名な漂流者、ジョン・万次郎を助けたのは1841年のことだった。ペリー提督の率いる海軍は、イギリスとフランスが中国でとった行動に倣って、封建制度の下にあった日本に門戸を開くように迫った。

ペリー提督による日本開国は、アメリカの産業発展においてフィラデルフィアが重要な役割を果たしていたことを示してくれる。ペリー提督の旗艦はアメリカで最初の蒸気フリゲート艦で、1842年にフィラデルフィア海軍造船所で造られたものだった。フィラデルフィアの16番通りにあったノリス機関車工場は、ペリー

Philadelphia's ties with Japan offer a striking alternative glimpse at the history of the modern world. Typically a tale of the inexorable rise of Europe, modern history from a "Phila-Nipponica" prism accentuates the importance of Japan and the United States in the creation of modern civilization. It highlights, in turn, Philadelphia's significance as a global city.

Although newcomers to the world stage, nineteenth century U.S. and Japan underwent transformations as dramatic as those that had catapulted Europe to the center. Modern Japan rose from feudalism after 1868, aided by over three thousand foreign advisers, principally from Europe. But as the world's pre-eminent whaling nation by the 1830s and with the largest merchant marine by 1861, the U.S. enjoyed a formidable presence in the early nineteenth century Pacific. An American whaler rescued celebrated Japanese castaway John Manjirō in 1841. And it was the American navy under Commodore Perry that opened feudal Japan to modern trade in 1853 following British and French precedent in China.

Perry's mission highlights Philadelphia's pivotal place in American industrialization. Philadelphia Naval Shipyard launched the commodore's flagship, America's first steam frigate, in 1842. And Norris Locomotive Works on Sixteenth Street dominated American locomotive manufacturing and

11

提督が日本に寄贈した4分の1サイズの蒸気機関車の実用模型を製作した会社である。この模型をつくったとき、ノリス社はアメリカの機関車業界を支配し、大手として最初に蒸気機関車の輸出を手掛けた会社であった。

近代日本における最初の大使節団（岩倉使節団）や政治活動家の馬場辰猪、写真家の小川一真、優秀な学生であった柴四朗（ウォートン）、野口英世（ペンシルベニア大学）、新渡戸稲造（フレンズ外国伝道協会）、津田梅子（ブリンマー大学）、有島武夫（ハバフォード大学）などがフィラデルフィアにやって来たことは、19世紀日本の大いなる開化熱を物語るばかりでなく、フィラデルフィアが世界の政治や文化、産業のハブとして有名で、その名声が日本にも届いていたことを表わしている。

アメリカ独立100周年記念万国博覧会（1876）と、独立150周年記念万国博覧会（1926）の開催地として、フィラデルフィアは一躍、世界的な産業都市として知名度を上げた。さらに万国博覧会を2回開催し、仁王門（寺の山門）をフェアモント公園に移築したことにより、フィラデルフィアは19世紀後半に世界を席巻した日本の芸術と文化への熱狂（ジャポニズム）に対して大いに貢献したのである。

第1次世界大戦後、日本との繋がりのおかげで、アメリカはヨーロッパの経済や政治、文化の覇権を覆すことができた。フィラデルフィア商業博物館の日米友好人形大使（1927）とフィラデルフィア美術館の茶室（1928）は、戦間期に日米の文化的繋がりが発展していたことを物語る。

was the first major exporter of American locomotives when it built a quarter scale model for Perry to present to Japan. The Philadelphia sojourn of modern Japan's first large-scale embassy (the Iwakura Mission), political activist Baba Tatsui, photographer Ogawa Kazumasa, and distinguished students Shiba Shirō (The Wharton School, University of Pennsylvania), Noguchi Hideyo (University of Pennsylvania), Nitobe Inazō (Friends Foreign Missionary Society), Tsuda Umeko (Bryn Mawr College), and Arishima Takeo (Haverford College) together attest to the enormous reformist zeal of nineteenth century Japan and to Philadelphia's renown as a world political, cultural, and industrial hub. Centennial (1876) and sesqui-centennial (1926) expositions catapulted Philadelphia to the rank of a global industrial city. And both expos, together with the arrival of Niō-mon Temple Gate to Fairmount Park (1905), confirm the city's critical contribution to the craze for Japanese art and culture that swept the latter nineteenth century world (Japonism).

Ties with Japan helped the U.S. displace European economic, political, and cultural hegemony after World War I. A Japanese Friendship Doll, Miss Saga, at the Commercial Museum of Philadelphia (1927) and teahouse at the Philadelphia Museum of Art (1928) signaled growing interwar cultural links. Japanese rehabilitation after World War II owed largely to unprecedented bilateral intimacy facilitated by the U.S.-Japan Security Alliance and a formidable new American physical presence in Japan—including Philadelphia Quaker Elizabeth Gray Vining, tutor to the Japanese crown prince. And Japan's gift of a villa to Fairmount

第2次世界大戦後の日本復興は、前例がないほど緊密な日米相互関係によって達成された。それは日米安全保障同盟と新たに来日した多くのアメリカ人—その中には皇太子の家庭教師となったフィラデルフィア・クエーカー、エリザベス・グレイ・バイニングも含まれる—によって可能となったのである。そして、日本がフェアモント公園の山荘（松風荘）を寄贈（1958）したことや、フィラデルフィア管弦楽団の日本演奏旅行（1967）、テンプル大学東京校の開設（1982）は、「奇跡の経済復興」を遂げた日本の経済力を示す出来事だった。同様に、これらの出来事は、世界大国アメリカにおいてフィラデルフィアが重要な都市であり続けていることを示している。

フレデリック・R・ディッキンソン
戸田徹子 訳

Park (Shōfūsō, 1958), the Philadelphia Orchestra's 1967 tour of Japan, and a Temple University branch campus in Tokyo (1982) spotlight the power of Japan's postwar "economic miracle." They hint, in turn, at the continuing importance of Philadelphia to American global stature.

Frederik R. Dickinson

The 19th Century:
Early Contacts and Diplomacy

最初の出会い

1

Diplomatic Beginnings

外交と交流の始まり

1.1 *Hyōson kiryaku* (**Drifting to the Southeast**): The Story of Manjirō

フィラデルフィアにあるジョン万次郎の本：『東南漂流記』

1841年、ペリーの船が江戸に近い浦賀湾に入る12年前、14歳の少年と4人の仲間が日本の南の小島で座礁し、助けられた。救助した船はジョン・ハウランド号で、ウィリアム・H・ホイットフィールドが船長を務めるアメリカの捕鯨船であった。少年の名は万次郎（後の中浜万次郎、1827‐1898）といい、乗組員からジョン・マンという英語名をつけられた。船がハワイに入港した時、4人の仲間はそこに留まることにしたが、万次郎は捕鯨船で働くことを選んだ。船がマサチューセッツ州ニュー・ベッドフォードに戻ると、万次郎はフェアヘイブンの近くにあるホイットフィールド船長の家に連れて行かれた。万次郎はそこから学校に通い、漁に出たりしながら、アメリカで約10年間生活した。

1851年、万次郎は日本へ戻ったが、幕府は1年半にわたり万次郎を拘束して取り調べをした。当時まだ鎖国状態であった日本に、万次郎が危険な外国の思想を持ち込むことがないかを確かめるためであった。1852年末、万次郎は自由の身となり、土佐（現在の高知県）の家族の元に帰った。その後、万次郎は河田小龍（1824‐1898）の庇護下に置かれた。河田は土佐藩主に仕える武士だったが、学者で、芸術にも造詣が深かった。河田は万次郎の取り調べをした役人の1人であり、万次郎の海外体験をすべて書き留めていた。（万次郎自身は日本語の読み書きができなかった。）

『漂巽記畧＜東南漂流記＞』と題された

In 1841, twelve years before Perry's ships entered Uraga Bay near Edo (now Tokyo), a fourteen- year-old boy and four companions were picked up after a shipwreck on a small island south of Japan. The rescue ship was the *John Howland*, an American whaling schooner under the command of Captain William H. Whitfield. The boy's name was Manjirō, and he was given the English name John Mung by the ship's crew. While his four companions stayed in Hawaii when the ship entered port there, Manjirō opted to work on the whaling schooner, and after its return to New Bedford, Massachusetts, Manjirō was taken to live in the home of Captain Whitfield near Fairhaven. Manjirō lived in the United States for approximately ten years, spending part of the time in school and part of the time at sea. In 1851, Manjirō returned to Japan, where he was detained and examined by the authorities for over a year and a half to be sure that he would not introduce dangerous foreign ideas to the still "closed" country. He was then freed and reunited with his family, the Nakahamas, in Tosa (present-day Kōchi Prefecture, on the island of Shikoku) in late 1852. At that time Manjirō came under the patronage of Kawada Shōryū (a.k.a. Shōryō; 1824–1898), an artist, scholar and samurai in the service of the Lord of Tosa Province. Kawada had been one of the officials who examined Manjirō and wrote down all of Manjirō's experiences abroad (Manjirō himself could not yet read or write Japanese). The four

全4巻の本には、万次郎の口述に基づいて描かれた水彩画の挿絵が50点以上も収められている。河田の手になる元本は土佐の藩主に贈呈されたが、何冊かの写本が作られ、その中には万次郎用の写本もあった。現在、フィラデルフィアのローゼンバック博物館・図書館に収蔵されているのは、万次郎用の写本と思われる。その写本には54ヶ所の挿し絵があり、肖像画、地図、その他捕鯨船や鯨などの題材が水彩絵の具できれいに描かれている。また海軍の制服、列車、硬貨といったアメリカの「珍品」や、ニュー・ベッドフォード、オアフ、日本など

volumes, entitled *Hyōson kiryaku* (Drifting to the Southeast), included over fifty watercolor illustrations based on Manjirō's descriptions. The original manuscript by Kawada was presented to the Lord of Tosa. Several copies of the manuscript were made, including one for Manjirō himself. This latter edition of the manuscript is believed to be the one now in the collection of The Rosenbach Museum & Library in Philadelphia. It is beautifully illustrated with fifty-four watercolor portraits, maps, and other subjects including whaling ships and whales; American "curiosities" such as naval uniforms, trains, and coins; and views of places as diverse as New Bedford, Oahu, and Japan. Most of the illustrations are by Kawada Shōryū, but ten are signed "John Mung," that is, by Manjirō himself, in English. Other additions to this manuscript by Manjirō testify to his efforts to master the English alphabet and vocabulary. The *Hyōson kiryaku* manuscript became widely known among the feudal lords, many of whom were eager to learn about foreign lands and their technology.

Because of his direct knowledge of these subjects, Manjirō was employed by the Lord of Tosa as a teacher and adviser to the young samurai of the province. Then, in July 1853, the arrival of four black ships of the American navy, led by Commodore Matthew Perry, again changed Manjirō's life dramatically. He was summoned to Edo to the service of the shogunal government and was sent to the United States anew in 1860 as an interpreter aboard a Dutch-built ship, the *Kanrin Maru*, which sailed across the Pacific Ocean from Japan under the command of an American captain to

Nakahama Manjirō. *[Hyōson kiryaku].*
The Story Five of Japanese:
A very Handsome Tails [sic]: MS, 1852.
The Rosenbach Museum & Library, Philadelphia

の様々な場所の風景の挿し絵もある。ほとんどの挿絵は河田小龍の手になるものであるが、10点の挿絵には万次郎が英語で「ジョン・マン」と署名している。他にも万次郎がこの原稿に書き加えた個所があり、それを見ると彼が英語のアルファベットや言葉を習得しようと努力したことが良く分かる。『漂巽記畧』の原稿は、海外の国々や技術について知りたいと切実に願っていた藩主たちに、広く知られるようになった。

万次郎は外国や技術を直に知っていたため、若い武士たちの指南役として土佐の大名に雇われた。1853年7月にマシュー・ペリー提督率いるアメリカ海軍の4隻の黒船が到着すると、万次郎の生活は再び劇変した。万次郎は江戸に呼び出され、幕府に仕えた。1860年には、オランダ建造船「咸臨丸」に通訳として乗船し、再びアメリカへ渡るように命じられた。アメリカ人船長の指揮下で日本の船乗りたちに長期航海の訓練を施すため、「咸臨丸」は日本を出港し太平洋を渡った。万次郎は、その後1870年にも再びアメリカとヨーロッパに派遣された。

万次郎は波乱の人生を精一杯生きた。1868年の明治維新の後は、東京帝国大学の前身校の教授に任命され、初期の日米交流において重要な役割を果たした。偶然にも、万次郎とアメリカとの最初の出会いの記録は、フィラデルフィアにあるローゼンバック博物館・図書館に収蔵されているのである。

ローゼンバック博物館・図書館
今井元子/戸田徹子 訳

train the Japanese seamen for long-distance voyages. Manjirō was sent to the United States and Europe once more in 1870.

Manjirō (1827–1898) lived a full and distinguished life. After the Meiji Restoration in 1868, he received an appointment as professor at the forerunner of the Tokyo Imperial University. He played an important role in improving early communications between Japan and America. It is indeed fortuitous that the record of his first encounters with America has ended up in a distinguished Philadelphia collection.

By The Rosenbach Museum & Library

Selected References: Fumiko Mori Halloran, *Humanity Above Nation: The Impact of Manjiro and Heco on America and Japan* (Honolulu: Japanese Cultural Center of Hawaii and The Joseph Heco Society of Hawaii, 1995), pp. 1–17; Kawada Shoryo, *Drifting Toward the Southeast: The Story of Five Japanese Castaways, A complete translation of Hyoson kiryaku,* trans. Junya Nagakuni and Junji Kitadai (New Bedford, MA: Spinner Publications, 2003).

If you go: The Rosenbach Museum & Library, 2008–2010 Delancey Place, Philadelphia PA 19103.

1.2　U.S.S. *Mississippi*: Perry's Flagship to Japan
蒸気船ミシシッピ号：日本に来航したペリーの旗艦

1842年1月のある日、マシュー・カルブレイス・ペリー提督（1794‐1858）が注意深く見守る中、アメリカ海軍の最新軍鑑ミシシッピ号はデラウェア川に進水した。ペリーは海軍で最も技術的経験が豊かな将校として、海軍の有名な造船技師サミュエル・ハンフリーズやジョン・レンソールと緊密に協力し合って、外輪蒸気船を設計した。ミシシッピ号は、フィラデルフィア海軍造船所（当時はサウスワーク地区のフェデラル通りの端にあった）で建造されたアメリカ初の「外洋蒸気船」だった。

外輪は直径28フィート（約10メートル）、長さは229フィート（約70メートル）あり、一時は海軍で最長の船だった。また、メリック・アンド・タウン社製のゴシック様式の装飾がついた最新エンジンを搭載し、最速10ノットで進むことができ、10門の大砲を積んでいた。

蒸気力が伝統的な帆船や木造船に実験的に使われているだけの頃、ミシシッピ号は「ヤンキーの創造力」を象徴し、アメリカが世界列強に名を列ねようと、軍事力を拡大しつつあることを表わしていた。ペリーの「お気に入りの旗艦」のため、議会は56万9670.70ドル出費した。ミシシッピ号はまた、南北戦争以前の大型軍鑑の標準モデルとなった。その巨大なエンジンは「鉄の地震」などと描写されたが、ペリーはその船の働きぶりを「我らがミシシッピ号は、メキシコ湾を航行した時と同様に頑強で調子が良い。サスケハナ号に勝り、時化（しけ）に

The newest U.S. Navy warship, *Mississippi*, was launched at Philadelphia into the Delaware River under the watchful eyes of Commodore Matthew Calbraith Perry (1794–1858), on a January day in 1842. As the Navy's most technologically-experienced officer, Perry worked closely with the legendary naval constructors, Samuel Humphries and John Lenthall of Philadelphia, in the design of this side-wheel steamer. Built at the Philadelphia Navy Shipyard (then located in the Southwark section of the city at the foot of Federal Street), *Mississippi* was designated as the nation's first "sea steamer."

Her paddle wheels measured twenty-eight feet in diameter, and she was for a time the Navy's longest vessel (229 feet in length). She boasted the latest engine decorated "in the Gothic style," built by Merrick and Towne of Philadelphia, which could propel her at a maximum speed of ten knots per hour, and she carried ten guns.

At a time when steam power was experimentally applied to traditional sails and wooden-hull ships, *Mississippi* symbolized "Yankee ingenuity" and represented the nascent military presence of the U.S. in its bid for world power. Perry's "favorite Flagship" cost $569,670.70 and became the standard model for subsequent naval warships prior to the Civil War. Her massive engines were described as "iron earthquakes," but Perry

Scroll depicting the arrival of the United States Naval Expedition to Japan, MS, 1854.
The Rosenbach Museum & Library, Philadelphia

あってもサスケハナ号ほど揺れず、石炭の消費量は3分の1少ない」と誇らしげに、1853年に香港から書き送った。

ミシシッピ号はメキシコ戦争でペリーの旗鑑としての役割を果たした後、ペリーの日本への「外交的な遠征」に使用された。日本はヨーロッパ人やアメリカ人から利益の上がる市場になりそうだとみられていたが、2世紀にわたる鎖国政策により、国を挙げて外国船舶の停泊を拒んでいたので、彼らは日本に近付くことができないままだった。アメリカの海軍省は「無理強いしてでも、おだててでも、なんとしても国家間の友好関係に日本を引きずり込む機が熟した」と考えた。そこでミシシッピ号は1852年11月、バージニア州ノーフォークを出航し、新しい蒸気船サスケハナ号、そしてスループ船(一本マストの縦帆装船)の軍艦、サラトガ号とプリマス号に合流した。小さくとも威嚇的なミシシッピ号は、1853年7月8日浦賀に到着した。おそらく、これは、地元の人たちが初めて目にした蒸気船だったと思われる。

wrote proudly from Hong Kong of her performance in 1853, "Our *Mississippi* is as staunch and fit as when she was in the Gulf (of Mexico), beating the *Susquehanna*, making better weather and consuming one-third less coal."

After serving as Perry's flagship in the U.S.–Mexican War, *Mississippi* carried Perry on a "diplomatic expedition" to Japan. The Japanese empire was seen by Europeans and Americans as a potentially lucrative market but remained inaccessible to them because of its two-century-old measures refusing harborage to foreign shipping. The U.S. Navy Department felt that "the time was ripe for either forcing or flattering Japan into the brotherhood of nations," and in November 1852, *Mississippi* left Norfolk, Virginia to be joined by the new steamer *Susquehanna* and the sailing sloops of war, *Saratoga* and *Plymouth*. This small but menacing squadron arrived off the shore of Uraga on July 8, 1853. These were perhaps the first steamships ever seen by the local population.

50年後、下田のある老人は、地元住民たちが煙突から上る黒煙を最初、船火事と勘違いしたと回想している。侵略だという噂が広まり、パニックから、「泰平の 眠りを覚ます 蒸気船 たった四杯で夜も眠れず」という風刺歌が作られた。（厳密に言えば、4隻の船のうち2隻だけが「湯気をたてるカップ」だった。）ペリーは日本の役人をミシシッピ号の船上に迎え入れた。役人たちはそこで、アメリカの技術力を目の当たりにしたのである。提督は探りを入れたり、それとなく脅しをかけたりした後、ミラード・フィルモア大統領からの国書を浦賀奉行に手渡した。ペリーは幕府の返事をもらうために、翌年に再訪すると告げた。

1854年1月、ペリーは前回より大きな艦隊で来航した。その艦隊は、蒸気船のポウハタン号、サスケハナ号、ミシシッピ号、そしてスループ船の軍艦プリマス号、サラトガ号、マセドニア号、バンダリア号、物資輸送船のサプライ号、レキシントン号、サウサンプトン号で編成されていた。この威嚇的な艦隊のおかげで、アメリカは条約締結にこぎつけたのである。反対派が是が非でも日本の鎖国する権利を守ろうとしていたにもかかわらず、幕府の老中たちはアメリカとの条約を批准した。これにより2つの「条約で定められた港」—下田と函館—が、アメリカの商船と水夫たちを受け入れることになった。ミシシッピ号は日本との永遠の別れの前に、墨田川の水上で蒸気を短くあげた。その同じ場所で、1866年、日本の新しい造船所が、蒸気を動力とする最初の軍艦を進水させたのであった。

日本政府は、フィラデルフィアで建造された旗艦ミシシッピ号が出航してから

Fifty years later, an old man of Shimoda recollected that at first the residents took the black smoke rising from the funnels to be ships on fire. Rumors of an invasion spread and the panic inspired a "satirical song of that time which went like this: 'What a joke the steaming teapot fixed by America—Just four cups, and we cannot sleep at night!'" (Technically only two of four ships were "steaming cups.") Perry received Japanese officials aboard *Mississippi* where they witnessed the Americans' technological might first-hand. The Commodore presented his credentials and a letter from President Millard Fillmore to the Imperial Government's local representative after making a combination of overtures and tacit threats. Perry announced that he would return the following year for the Government's reply.

In January (1854), Perry arrived with a larger squadron consisting of the steamers *Powhatan*, *Susquehanna*, and *Mississippi*, the sloops of war *Plymouth*, *Saratoga*, *Macedonia*, and *Vandalia*, and the store-ships *Supply*, *Lexington*, and *Southampton*. This intimidating fleet secured a treaty with the U.S. that was ratified by the Shogun's ministers in spite of opposition within Japan that sought to maintain the empire's sovereign right to seclusion at any cost. The treaty's main article protected and welcomed American merchant ships and sailors in two specified "treaty ports," Shimoda and Hakodate. Before departing Japan forever, the *Mississippi* steamed briefly up the waters of the Sumida River. Twelve years later, in 1866, a new Japanese shipyard launched its first steam warship in the very same waters.

The Flagship *Mississippi* from Philadelphia

数ヶ月のうちに、海軍の方針を決定し
ようとしていた。日本政府は2つの海軍
訓練所を創立し、帝国海軍の中核とな
る4隻の船を手に入れた。日本で建造
され、日本人乗組員を乗せた巡洋艦清
輝号（1897トン）は、1878年、ヨーロッ
パの海上に初めて日本の旗を掲揚し
た。1882年には30隻の巡洋艦と12隻
の水雷艇の建造計画が承認され、日本
は近代の列強国の地位を確保したので
あった。

F・マイケル・アンジェロ
今井元子/戸田徹子 訳

helped inspire the Japanese government
to begin its bid to control its maritime fate
within months of the ship's departure. Two
seamen's training schools were established
and four vessels were acquired, forming the
core of the new Imperial Navy. In 1878, a
Japanese-built and Japanese-staffed cruiser,
Seiki (1,897 tons), first flew the flag of Japan
in European waters. A program to construct
thirty cruisers and twelve torpedo boats was
approved in 1882, securing for Japan the
status of a modern world power.

By F. Michael Angelo

Selected References: Matthew Calbraith
Perry, *The Japan Expedition, 1852–1854: The
Personal Journal of Commodore Matthew C.
Perry*, ed. Roger Pineau (Washington, DC:
Smithsonian Institution Press, 1968); Oliver
Statler, *The Black Ship Scroll: An Account
of the Perry Expedition at Shimoda in 1854
and the Lively Beginnings of People-to-People
Relations Between Japan & America* (Rutland,
VT: Tuttle, 1964).

If you go: Site of the first Philadelphia Navy
Yard (1801–1876) near Front Street and
Federal Street, Philadelphia, PA.

Plans and prints of the *Mississippi* held by
Independence Seaport Museum, 211 South
Columbus Boulevard, Philadelphia PA
19106.

1.3　A Steam Locomotive Built in Philadelphia: Perry's Present to the Emperor
ペリーが天皇に贈呈した蒸気機関車

19世紀半ば、アメリカの主な蒸気機関車製造会社のうち2社が、フィラデルフィアの16番通りとスプリング・ガーデン通りの交差地点を基点として、16番通りの両側にあった。リチャード・ノリス機関車会社とボールドウィン機関車会社が南に数ブロックにわたり広がっていた。

1840年から10年間、リチャード・ノリス機関車会社はロシアのニコライ皇帝、オーストリアの皇子、フランスのルイ・フィリップ王などへの贈り物として、自社の機関車の、縮尺4分の1サイズの実際に動く模型を製作した。ルイ・フィリップ王の機関車は、パリの工芸学校に現在も展示されている。

1853年、ノリス社はアメリカ大統領から日本の天皇への贈り物として、第4番目の縮尺4分の1の機関車模型を作った。　その後、ノリス社の機関車と炭水車、そして別の会社が製作した客車が、1854年の初め、ペリーの黒船艦隊と共に日本に到着した。その実演走行のために横浜近くに用意された小さな環状線路で、日本人は極東で初めて、列車に乗る体験をしたのである。その出来事をペリー総督は次のように記している。

「この後、いよいよ大統領から天皇への贈呈品の検分が始まった。目玉は磁性電信機と丸い軌道を走る機関車の実演である。これらは実演の後に、ほかの品々とともに正式に授与が行われることになっていた。日本人は贈呈品の披露に

In the middle of the nineteenth century, two of the leading manufacturers of steam locomotives in the U.S. were located in Philadelphia, on Spring Garden Street on either side of Sixteenth Street. The properties of Richard Norris and Company and the Baldwin Locomotive Works extended several blocks south.

During the decade of the 1840s, Richard Norris and Company built quarter-scale operating models of its locomotives for presentation to Tsar Nicholas of Russia, the Archduke of Austria, and Louis-Philippe, King of France. Louis-Philippe's locomotive is still exhibited at the Conservatoire des Arts et Métiers in Paris.

In 1853, Richard Norris and Company built a fourth quarter-scale model of a current locomotive for presentation by the President of the United States to the Emperor of Japan. The locomotive and its tender and a passenger car made by another firm arrived in Japan with Perry's squadron of black ships in early 1854. The Japanese experienced the first train ride in the Far East on a small circular track built near Yokohama for the presentation. Commodore Perry described the event:

This being over, we now proceeded to examine the presents sent by the President to the Emperor, and particularly to witness the operations of the magnetic telegraph and the movements of

Delivery of the American presents at Yokohama, 1854.
The Japan America Society of Greater Philadelphia

も受領にも同じように形式張っていて、儀式はなかなか終わらないのだった」。

「小さな炉から蒸気が上がり、客車が接続され、委員の一人の秘書官がおっかなびっくり客車の屋根にまたがった。一方ダンビー氏は炭水車にまたがり、片手で石炭をくべながらもう片方の手で機関を操作する。美しい小さな機関車が、甲高い汽笛で空気を震わせながら円を描いて走ると、集まった大勢の人々は驚喜したものだ。次いで最後にもう一度電信機の実演が行われた」。

「委員たちはまた数々の農具を見学し、その使い方の簡単な説明を受けたが、その後美作守が委員たちの代表となって、大統領の贈呈品受領の儀式を執り行った。こちらでは、贈呈に関する同様

the locomotive engine around its circumscribed track, preparatory to these and other articles being formally presented and received. The Japanese being equally formal in the presentation and receiving of presents, the ceremony was yet to come off.

Steam had been raised in the little furnace, the car attached, and the secretary of one of the commissioners, not a little alarmed, was placed upon the roof of the car whilst Mr. Danby sat upon the tender feeding the fire with one hand and managing the engine with the other. The beautiful little machine whirled round the circle filling the air with its shrill steam whistle, to the astonishment and delight of the immense crowd

の全権はアダムス参謀長に与えてあったので、贈呈品の授受は両者が形式張って五、六回もお辞儀をしあうことでようやく終わった」。(ロジャー・ピノー編、金井圓訳『ペリー日本遠征日記』〈新異国叢書第II輯、雄松堂出版、1989〉、206-207頁)

その後、日本側は、その機関車を東京の海軍兵学校に納めたが、兵学校は1868年に火事にあい、アメリカから日本への最初の贈り物は焼失してしまった。

クインシー・ウィリアムズ
今井元子/戸田徹子 訳

collected. After this the telegraph was for the last time put in operation, and the commissioners having also seen the numerous agricultural implements and their various uses being briefly explained to them, the prince of Mimasaka was deputed on the part of the commissioners to go through the form of accepting the President's gifts. Captain Adams received the same authority from me to present them, which was done by a half-dozen formal bows on both sides.

Subsequently, the Japanese housed the locomotive in the Naval Academy in Tokyo. In 1868, a fire destroyed the school and this first gift of the United States to Japan.

By Quincy Williams

Selected References: Matthew Calbraith Perry, *The Japan Expedition, 1852–1854: The Personal Journal of Commodore Matthew C. Perry*, ed. Roger Pineau (Washington, DC: Smithsonian Institution Press, 1968), pp. 176–80; 194–98.

If you go: The site of the former Richard Norris and Company property is presently part of the campus of the Community College of Philadelphia, 1700 Spring Garden Street, Philadelphia, PA 19103.

1.4 The 1860 Diplomatic Mission to the United States: Iron and Gold

万延元年遣米使節：徳川幕府が派遣した使節団

アメリカへ

万延元年（1860）1月、日米修好通商条約批准書交換と先進国アメリカを仔細に視察する目的の遣米使節、正使新見豊前守正興、副使村垣淡路守範正、目付小栗豊後守忠順（のち上野介）の3人に従者も含め、77人が米艦ポウハタン号で出航した。江戸（現在の東京）・ハワイ・サンフランシスコ・パナマ。パナマ鉄道で東に出るとロアノーク号でカリブ海を渡りワシントンに上陸し、ホワイトハウスでブキャナン大統領に条約批准書を渡した。その名がよく知られている咸臨丸は使節の随行船で、日本・サンフランシスコ・ハワイ・日本を往復した。

日本ブーム

ワシントンではペンシルベニア通りを馬車の大パレードで進み、ウィラード・ホテルまでの沿道は黒山の人だかり。街路樹に登って見る者もいた。初めは珍しい

In January of 1860, Chief Ambassador Shinmi Buzen-no-Kami Masaoki, Vice-Ambassador Muragaki Awaji-no-Kami Norimasa, Special Censor Oguri Bungo-no-Kami Tadamasa (later known as Oguri Kōzukenosuke), and their attendants, seventy-seven passengers in all, embarked for America on the U.S.S. *Powhatan*. Their mission was to ratify the US-Japan Treaty of Amity and Commerce and to make the first official diplomatic visit to America. They traveled from Edo (now Tokyo) to Hawaii to San Francisco to Panama. From Panama they made their way east by train and then crossed the Caribbean Sea on the U.S.S. *Roanoke*, finally arriving in Washington. At the White House they presented President Buchanan with the treaty. The famous Japanese warship *Kanrin Maru* was sent as an escort—from Japan to San Francisco to Hawaii and back to Japan.

In Washington, the delegation took part in a grand carriage-led parade down Pennsylvania Avenue, the road lined with large crowds of spectators all the way to the Willard Hotel. Some climbed trees to watch. At first they came to see the strange visitors from the Orient, but as soon as word spread of the exquisiteness and fine quality of their

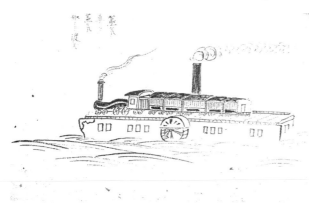

The ferry Maryland, Satō Tōshichi,
A Record of Crossing the Sea. Tōzenji Temple
「メリーランド号」佐藤藤七 「渡海日記」 東善寺所蔵

The Japanese Mission presenting the treaty to President Buchanan at the
White House, June 2, 1860. Tōzenji Temple 東善寺所蔵

東洋の客人と見ていたが、衣服や持物の精緻な織物や工芸品、武士の礼儀正しい文化教養を感じさせる振舞いが報じられ、たちまち日本ブームが起き、どの街でも大歓迎のパレードが繰り広げられた。

鉄の国アメリカ
一行は「ホテルの垣根はすべて鉄」「鉄の橋がいくつも河にかかっている」と鉄があふれるアメリカに圧倒され、サスケハナ河では汽車ごとフェリー・メリーランド号で渡って、すぐに走り出す様子に驚嘆した。日本をこうした近代文明の国にするため、一行は海軍造船所、造幣局、裁判所、国会、博物館、鉄工場、学校、砲台などを積極的に見学し、好奇心と進

clothes and possessions, and the samurai dignity and civility with which they carried themselves, the popularity of the Japanese exploded. It seemed as if a parade was being held on every street to welcome the visitors.

Astonished at the abundance of iron to be found in America, the delegates noted "the fences of the hotel are all made of iron" and "a number of iron bridges span the rivers." They marveled at how a train could go onto the ferry *Maryland*, which would cross the Susquehanna River, allowing the train to continue on the other side. With the goal of developing Japan into a modern country, the delegation eagerly toured and studied facilities and institutions such as a navy yard,

取性に富む日本人を印象づけた。

「彼らは財布をはたいて、あらゆる種類の反物、金物、火器（銃）、宝石類、ガラス器、光学機器、そのほかわれわれの創意と工夫を示す無数のものを買う。我が国と日本との通商の道が十分に開放されれば、これらの物品はそっくり真似され改良されて、我が国に戻ってくるに違いない」と、『ニューヨーク・タイムズ』紙 は将来の日米関係を洞察した記事で賞賛した。

フィラデルフィア

駅に着くと、30万人の人出で街中が日の丸と星条旗で覆われるような歓迎であった。パレードはブロード通りを北上→ ウォルナット通りで左折し→ 19番通りを右折→ アーチ通りで右折→ 3番通りで右折→ チェスナット通りで右折→公園前を通り→ 最後に市役所を大きく一周して、コンチネンタルホテルに案内された。6月10日から16日まで1週間滞在し、毎日押しかける見物人や花火大会、タイマツ行列、消防の実演などで歓迎された。独立記念館、市議会、税関、小学校から大学までの学校や孤児院、病院、劇場、刑務所、工業機械会社などた

The ferry *Maryland* near the Susquehanna River.
Courtesy of Richard Sherill

a mint, courts of law, the Congress, museums, ironworks, schools, and military batteries. The curious and industrious Japanese were quite impressed.

In a laudatory and insightful article, *The New York Times* wrote of future US-Japan relations:

> *They appear to have reserved their spare cash for outlay here, and invest in all manner of dry goods, hardware, firearms, jewelry, glass ware, optical instruments and innumerable other evidences of our ingenuity and art — doubtless when our commerce with Japan is fully opened, to be returned to us in the shape of duplicate imitations and improvements. OGURE-BUNGO-NO-KAMI is said to be greatly in favor of introducing American improvements in Japan.*

When they arrived at the train station in Philadelphia, the delegation was welcomed by a huge crowd of 300,000 people beneath the Japanese Hinomaru flag and the Stars and Stripes. They participated in a parade that went north up Broad Street, turned left onto Walnut Street, made a right onto Nineteenth Street, another right onto Arch Street, right again at Third Street, made a final right turn onto Chestnut Street, proceeded past a park, and finally after making a giant circle around the City Hall, arrived at the Continental Hotel.

The Japanese Mission at Washington Naval Yard, April 5, 1860. Oguri, who was inspired by the shipyard, is in the front row, second from right. Tōzenji Temple 東善寺所蔵

くさんの鉄工場、ガラス工場、船具工場、綿布工場、ガス工場、石版印刷工場、気球を見学し、本屋で天文学や数学、自然科学の書籍に関心を示した。アセネウムのチェス・クラブに招かれ、展示品の日本の将棋を説明し、実際にやってみせるというエピソードもあった。そして、使節団を派遣した井伊大老が桜田門外の変で暗殺されたニュースを最初に知ったのが、ここフィラデルフィアの新聞であった。

金貨の分析実験
この頃、日米通貨の交換比率の不釣り合いから、外国人は日本でメキシコドル銀貨と換えた一分銀貨を小判金貨に換え、国外に持ち出して交換すると、はじ

They stayed there for one week, from June 10 to June 16, every day encountering onlookers and being welcomed to such events as fireworks displays, torchlight processions, and firefighting demonstrations. They toured Independence Hall, the City Council, the Customs House, schools from elementary level to university, orphanages, hospitals, theaters, prisons, all manner of industrial machine manufacturers and ironworks, glass factories, chandlers, clothiers, gasworks, and lithographic print shops, and watched hot air balloons. At bookshops they expressed interest in texts on astronomy, mathematics, and the natural sciences. Several of the samurai were also invited to the Athenaeum Chess Club, where they demonstrated and

めのドルが3倍に増える状況が生まれていた。外国人は争って小判を持ち出し、日本は金貨の「濫出」状態で混乱が生じていた。使節はフィラデルフィアの造幣局で両国金貨の分析実験を要求、その場を離れない集中心と忍耐力、熱意と知性、鋭敏さが感銘を与えた。結果はドルも小判も金貨どうしはほぼ同じ価値を有することが証明され、その小判をアメリカ人がメキシコドル銀貨を使って、3分の1の値段で買っているのはおかしいと納得させる結果が出た。その先の交換比率改定交渉は使節に権限がないとして、ここまでとなったが、通貨まるごとの全量分析を強硬に主張した小栗は、のちに「ノーと言った最初の日本人」と評される。

日本人初の世界一周
ニューヨークでも警護の軍隊8000人というパレードで大歓迎を受けた。帰路はナイアガラ号で、ニューヨーク・大西洋・アンゴラのルアンダ・インド洋・インドネシアのバタビヤ ・香港・日本と航海し、日本人初の世界一周で11月10日に帰国した。

村上泰賢

参考文献:
『万延元年遣米使節史料集成 全7巻』（風間書房、1961）
服部逸正『77人の侍アメリカへ行く』(講談社、1974)
村上泰賢『小栗上野介 ―忘れられた悲劇の幕臣―』(平凡社新書、2010)

played shogi with members. It was also in Philadelphia that the delegation first learned of the Sakuradamon incident and the assassination of Chief Minister Ii Naosuke, who had dispatched the delegates to America. This was reported by a Philadelphia newspaper.

Because of the imbalance of the Japanese-American currency exchange rate at the time, foreigners in Japan had begun exchanging Mexican silver dollars for Japanese silver quarters and then gold *koban* coins, which when exported abroad could be exchanged once again at triple the original value. As foreigners scrambled to export *koban* coins, Japan experienced an economic crisis resulting from this massive outflow of gold coinage. Thus, at the Philadelphia Mint, the envoys insisted on a test comparing the gold coins of both countries. The delegation's patience, zeal, intelligence, and acuity impressed the Americans, and as the results of the test affirmed the approximately equal value of the gold dollar and the *koban*, they conceded the ridiculousness of being able to buy a Japanese koban at one third the price of a Mexican silver dollar. (Oguri has since been described as "the first Japanese person to say 'no,'" due to his insistence that the total weights of the *koban* and the gold dollar be tested despite the fact that the Japanese delegation had previously not been granted the authority to negotiate exchange rate reform.)

The officials of the diplomatic mission to America were also warmly received in New York City with a parade accompanied by 8,000 military guards. Returning home they traveled on the U.S.S. *Niagara* from New

York, across the Atlantic Ocean to Luanda in Angola, across the Indian Ocean to Batavia (now Jakarta) in Indonesia, to Hong Kong, and back to Japan. On November 10 they arrived home as the first Japanese to travel around the world.

By Taiken Murakami
Translated by Paul Schuble

Selected References: "The Japanese in New-York," *New York Times*, June 22, 1860); James D. Johnston, *China and Japan: Being a Narrative of the Cruise of the U.S. Steam-Frigate Powhatan, in the Years 1857, '58, '59, and '60* (Philadelphia: Charles Desilver, 1860; reprint, London: Ganesha Publishing, 2003).

If you go: The Athenaeum of Philadelphia, 219 S. 6th St., Philadelphia, PA 19106. The Chess Room is on the second floor.

1.5　Oguri Kōzukenosuke: "The Father of Meiji"
小栗上野介忠順：「明治の父」となった徳川の幕臣

明治の父

万延元年遣米使節一行が帰国した日本は、井伊大老の暗殺で狂気の攘夷熱が吹き荒れ、アメリカでの貴重な体験を語ることがはばかられる風潮にあった。その中で自身の見聞を活かし日本近代化に貢献した人物が、フィラデルフィアの造幣局で通貨の全量分析を求めた小栗忠順（1827‐1868）だった。

作家の司馬遼太郎は、万延元年遣米使節団の中で日本近代化に貢献した人物として、小栗と咸臨丸の福沢諭吉、勝海舟の3人を挙げ、小栗を「明治の父」と称えた。帰国後8年間に小栗が実施あるいは構想したものは、横須賀造船所建設の推進・洋式陸軍制度（歩兵・騎兵・砲兵）の採用・横浜のフランス語学校設立・群馬の中小坂（なかおさか）鉄山開発・日本最初の株式会社（兵庫商社）設

Oguri Kōzukenosuke (a.k.a. Tadamasa; 1827–1868) was one of the main contributors to the modernization of Japan in the Meiji era. He was a member of the 1860 Japanese diplomatic mission to the United States. While the mission was in Philadelphia, the envoys went to the U.S. Mint and insisted on a test comparing the gold coins of both countries. The results of the test affirmed the approximately equal value of the U.S. gold dollar and the Japanese *koban*.

Ii Naosuke was a prominent daimyo who signed the Harris Treaty with the United States in 1858, granting access to ports for trade to American merchants and seamen and extraterritoriality to American citizens. In March of 1860 (while the Japanese diplomatic mission was still visiting the United States), he was attacked and killed by a band of seventeen young samurai loyalists. When the delegation returned to Japan the following November, society was in chaos. The desire to exclude foreigners from Japan raged on and there was a general reluctance to discuss the valuable experiences the mission had in the United States.

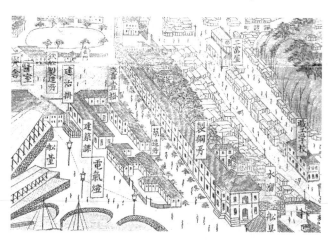

Rope factory in Yokosuka Shipyard.
Tōzenji Temple 横須賀造船所内 ロープ工場. 東善寺所蔵

Calligraphy of the five Confucian virtues by Tōgō Heihachirō. Tōzenji Temple
東郷平八郎 書. 東善寺所蔵

立・布施（おぶせ）の船会社・江戸の築地ホテル建設、提案としてガス灯設置・郵便電信制度の開設・新聞発行・鉄道建設・金札発行など金融経済の立て直し・郡県制度・森林保護と、まさに日本改造とも言うべき多岐にわたり、ほとんどが明治4年（1871）岩倉使節団の米欧視察前後に実行されている。「明治の近代化は小栗上野介の敷いたレールの上になされた」と言われるゆえんである。

幕府の運命、日本の運命
なかでも特筆すべきは横須賀造船所の建設である。当時にあって、造船所とは総合工場ともいうべきもので、ワシントン海軍造船所の見学は最大の収穫だった。そこは蒸気機関を原動力として、鉄の塊を熔解し蒸気機関の釜、シャフト、パイプ、大砲やライフル銃も砲弾も作り、組み立てるネジ、船室のドアノブまであらゆる鉄製品を造船所で製造している。当時の黒船は木造で船体、船室、階段を木工所で作り、蒸気機関と帆走を併用するから、製帆所もロープ工場もある。造船所はすべての製品が１つの工場内で補い合って生産され、「船も」造る総合工場であった。

During the eight years following Oguri's return to Japan, he planned, promoted, and brought about the construction of the Yokosuka shipyard, the adoption of the Western Army system (infantry, cavalry, and artillery), and the establishment of the French School at Yokohama. Oguri also aided in the development of the Nakaosaka ironworks in Gunma Prefecture and the genesis of Japan's first corporation (Hyogo Trading Company), a shipping company (Obuse), and the Tsukiji Hotel construction. In addition, he promoted the installation of gas lighting, the establishment of a postal telegraph system, railway construction, newspaper publishing, reformation of financial and economic matters such as the introduction of the bank note, the organization of county and prefectural units, and environmental conservation efforts. Indeed, Oguri's efforts could be referred to as a "remodeling of Japan," most of which occurred shortly before or after he went abroad on the Iwakura Mission in 1871. It is for this reason that the saying, "The modernization of Meiji Japan occurred on the rails that Oguri laid," became a common figure of speech in Japan.

Tsukiji Hotel, woodblock triptych by Kunishige. Shimizu Corporation
築地ホテル. 清水建設所蔵

帰国後の小栗の提案で建設された横須
賀製鉄所（造船所）もやはり最初から蒸
気機関を原動力とする日本初の本格的
な総合工場であった。小栗の造船所建
設提案に時期尚早、金が無い、など様々
な反対論が渦巻いた時、小栗は「幕府
の運命に限りがあるとも、日本の運命に

A beautiful picture of the stump-tailed cows which supply the inhabitants of New York with fresh milk. Sketched from life by the artist of the Japanese Embassy.

Cartoon from U.S. press showing Japanese taking
memos all the time. Tōzenji Temple 東善寺所蔵

The Yokosuka Steel Plant and Shipyard was built at Oguri's suggestion. It was Japan's first full-scale comprehensive plant to utilize the power of the steam engine. Its construction played a pivotal role in the fate of the *bakufu* (the Shogun's government) and of Japan itself. Oguri's design of the Yokosuka Shipyard was greatly inspired by a tour he took of the Washington Naval Yard. At Yokosuka, the steam engine facilitated the melting of iron and thus enabled the production of iron shafts, pipes, cannons, rifles, shells, and guns as well as assembly screws, cabin doorknobs, and other iron products. Before then, the production of

Tomioka Silk factory,
1873 woodblock by Asataka.
Tōzenji Temple 富岡製糸. 東善寺所蔵

wooden ships required that a ship's hull, cabin, and stairs be constructed at a woodworking shop, while the steam engine and sails were produced by specialists, and rope shops provided the necessary rope. Yokosuka was a comprehensive factory that built not only components but also complete ships, with necessary products produced simultaneously on location.

When Oguri wrote the proposal for the shipyard, it was opposed by some people who claimed that there were not enough funds to build it and that it was not yet needed. After the shipyard was completed, Oguri responded to his earlier critics by saying,

Even though the destiny of the Shogunate is limited, the destiny of Japan is not. Now, can it not be said that this project is a tribute to the Tokugawa Shogunate and a benefit to the country? Isn't it better to have a house with a storehouse rather than a house without one?

は限りがない。幕府のしたことが長く日本の為となって、徳川のした仕事が成功したのだ、とのちに言われれば徳川家の名誉ではないか。国の利益ではないか。同じ売家にしても土蔵付き売家のほうがよい」と語っている。明治45年（1912）夏、東郷平八郎は小栗の遺族に「日本海海戦でロシアのバルチック艦隊に勝つことができたのは、小栗さんが横須賀造船所を作っておいてくれたお

Admiral Marquis Tōgō Heihachirō was an admiral of the fleet in the Imperial Japanese Navy and one of Japan's greatest naval heroes. In fact, he was called "the Nelson of the East" (after Lord Horatio Nelson, the British admiral who defeated the French and Spanish

かげ…」と礼を述べ、書額を贈った。まさに日本の運命は売家（政権）に付けた土蔵（造船所）に支えられていたのだ。

村上泰賢

参考文献：
司馬遼太郎『三浦半島記』（朝日新聞社、2005）
佐藤雅美『覚悟の人 —小栗上野介忠順伝—』（岩波書店、2007）
村上泰賢編『小栗忠順のすべて』（新人物往来社、2008）

at the Battle of Trafalgar). In the summer of 1912, he wrote a thank you letter stating that he "was able to win the Battle of Tsushima against the Russian Baltic Fleet thanks to Oguri's building of the Yokosuka Shipyard." The fate of Japan's "house" (government) had thus been supported by its "storehouse" (the Yokosuka Shipyard).

Later, the writer Shiba Ryōtarō (1923–1996) mentioned three people in the Japanese diplomatic mission who had especially contributed to the modernization of Japan — Oguri, Fukuzawa Yukichi of the *Kanrin Maru*, and Katsu Kaishū. He specifically praised Oguri by calling him "The Father of Meiji."

By Taiken Murakami
Translated by Mark Bookman and Masako Hamada

Selected Reference: Michael Wert, *Meiji Restoration Losers: Memory and Tokugawa Supporters in Modern Japan* (Cambridge, MA: Harvard University Asia Center, 2013).

If you go: The second Philadelphia Mint building was located at 1331–37 Chestnut Street, at Juniper Street. The Mint operated there from 1833 until 1902, when the building was razed.

1.6 Japan's Early Ambassadors to the United States: The Iwakura Mission

岩倉使節団：明治政府が派遣した外交団

1872年6月22日から25日まで、岩倉具視（1825‐1883）が率いる日本の使節団100余名がフィラデルフィアに滞在した。彼らは日本の新しい政府である明治政府が欧米に送った、最初の使節団であった。彼らにはどのような目的があったのであろうか。また彼らは、今からが約140年前のフィラデルフィアに対して、どのような印象を持ったのであろうか。

1867年に成立したばかりの明治政府は、近代化された欧米の国力の強さを十分に理解していた。日本が近代国家となるためには、欧米に学ばなければならない。そのためにはまず実際に使節団を送って欧米各国を視察して、そのなかで日本が取るべき方向を選択するのがよいと判断した。

この使節団は総勢107名という大集団であった。構成は、明治政府の右大臣という要職にあった岩倉具視を特命全権大使とし、のちに日本の指導者になった木戸孝允、大久保利道、伊藤博文らを副使とし、その他書記官などの外交団が46名、その随行員（多くは政府のそれぞれの専門官）が18名、欧米各国への留学生が43名であった。留学生の中には津田梅子をはじめとする日本最初の女子留学生5名が含まれている。外交団の年齢は若く、大使の岩倉具視の47歳が最年長で、平均年齢はなんと32歳であった。これは当時の日本の活力を表しているだろう。

使節団は1871年12月（日本の暦では

The Japanese diplomatic mission led by Iwakura Tomomi (1825–1883), with over one hundred members, stayed in Philadelphia June 22–25, 1872. The Iwakura Mission was sent to the West by the new Meiji government of Japan and was the first such diplomatic mission. What was the purpose of their visit? What were their impressions of Philadelphia over 140 years ago?

The Meiji government, established in 1867, fully understood the national power of the newly industrializing United States and Europe. In order to modernize itself, Japan needed to learn from the West. To accomplish this goal, the Japanese government decided to send a diplomatic mission to Western countries such as the United States and various countries in Europe to observe and select methods appropriate for Japan.

The Iwakura Mission had as many as 107 members. The mission was organized with the Minister of the Right in the Meiji cabinet, Iwakura Tomomi, appointed as Envoy Extraordinary Ambassador Plenipotentiary. The mission also included: as vice-ambassadors, future leaders of Japan, such as Kido Takayoshi, Ōkubo Toshimichi, and Itō Hirobumi; forty-six other members who acted as secretaries and the like; another eighteen members from various government offices; and forty-three students sent to study in Western countries. Among these students were five young women, including

Iwakura Tomomi on the 500 yen note, issued 1969–1994. Wikimedia Commons

11月)に日本の横浜を出発し、翌年1月にサンフランシスコに到着した。その後は鉄道でネバダ州・ユタ州などを経てシカゴに到着、さらにワシントンへ行ってグラント大統領に謁見し、次にフィラデルフィアに移動したのである。

使節団の任務は江戸時代末期に条約を結んだ各国へ日本の国書を奉呈することと、その条約改正の予備交渉にあった。しかし実際は欧米の近代国家の制度や社会の調査をすることに、最も重点が置かれた。この目的のもとに、随行員の1人であった歴史学者の久米邦武（1839‐1931）は帰国後に全行程を日記体の報告書として出版した。それが『米欧回覧実記』である。なお久米邦武はのちに東京大学教授となった。

『米欧回覧実記』によると「フィラデルフィアは人口ではアメリカ第二の都市であるが、街が清潔で美しいことは一番であり、製造業・貿易業、その他万般にわたって繁栄している」とあり、また「《フィラデルフィア》とは友愛という意味である。

Tsuda Umeko. The average age of the mission members was quite young, about thirty-two years, with Iwakura the senior member at age forty-seven. The youth of the mission members was a sign of the vitality of the new Japanese government.

The Iwakura Mission left Japan from Yokohama in December 1871 and arrived in San Francisco the following month, January 1872. From there the group traveled by railroad through Nevada, Utah, and on to Chicago and Washington, DC for an audience with President Grant, before going to Philadelphia. The official diplomatic task of the Iwakura Mission was to renegotiate the treaties that the previous Edo shogunal government had signed with the Western nations. But in fact the greater emphasis was placed on the group's fact finding concerning the society and modernization of the Western countries it visited. To memorialize their findings one of the mission's members, the historian Kume Kunitake (1839–1931) published a report of the trip in five volumes

アメリカの国民は人との交際は和やかで、特にフィラデルフィアの人は温和であり、また活気もある。アメリカ人が友愛の気性に満ちているのは、フィラデルフィアの考え方に基づいているのであろう」という。もちろん使節団は独立戦争時の最初の議事堂も見学して、「ここに愛国者達が集まり、苦労して独立の権利を得たのだ。その時のありさまはいかがであったかと想像する」と当時を思いやり、議事堂の中に保存されていた自由の鐘も見ている。さらに、「フェアモント公園はスクイケル河を抱き両岸が丘になっていて、山水の景観を備えたすばらしい公園である」と感動している。

4日間のフィラデルフィア滞在を終えた岩倉使節団は、マーケット駅から列車でニューヨークに向かった。彼らは、その後、イギリス・フランス・ベルギー・オランダ・ドイツ・ロシア・デンマーク・スウェーデン・イタリア・オーストリア・スイスを巡って、1873年9月に日本に帰国している。

今井雅晴

after his return to Japan. It was entitled *True Account of a Tour of America and Europe (Beiō kairan jikki)*. Kume subsequently became a professor at Tokyo University.

According to the *True Account*, "Philadelphia is the second largest city in the United States by population, but it is the first in cleanliness and beauty, flourishing in manufacturing, trade and other aspects." He further notes, "'Philadelphia' means 'friendship.' The American people are peaceful in their dealings with others, and Philadelphians are especially cordial, friendly and energetic. The fact that Americans are filled with friendship is probably based on the way of thinking in Philadelphia." Of course, the Iwakura Mission also visited the first Congress Hall, now known as Independence Hall, dating from the Revolutionary War. "This is where patriots gathered and struggled for the right to independence. I can imagine how it must have been then" Kume noted as he looked at the Liberty Bell, which was housed in Independence Hall. He also wrote, "Fairmount Park borders both sides of the Schuylkill River, where the land slopes uphill. It is a magnificent park in terms of its landscape."

When the four-day stay in Philadelphia was completed, the Iwakura Mission took the train from Market Street Station to New York. Subsequently they went to England, France, Belgium, the Netherlands, Germany, Denmark, Sweden, Italy, Austria, and Switzerland before returning to Japan in September 1873.

By Masaharu Imai
Translated by Felice Fischer

Selected References: Donald Keene, *Modern Japanese Diaries* (New York: Henry Holt, 1995; reprint New York: Columbia University Press, 1998), pp. 90–118; Alistair Swale, "America, 15 January–6 August 1872: The First Stage in the Quest for Enlightenment," in *The Iwakura Mission in America and Europe: A New Assessment,* ed. Ian Nish (Richmond, Surrey: Japan Library, 1998), pp. 11–35.

If you go: Independence Hall and the Liberty Bell Center are part of Independence National Historical Park and are located at 520 Chestnut Street and 525 Market Street, Philadelphia, PA 19106.

Fairmount Park encompasses approximately 9200 acres on the east and west sides of the Schuylkill River in Philadelphia and is one of the largest urban green spaces in America.

Learning from Each Other:
Commerce and Art
モノや文化の交流

2 Philadelphia Expo and Museum
万国博覧会＆商業博物館

2.1 Japan and the Philadelphia Centennial Exposition: Art, Industry, and Impact

独立100周年記念万国博覧会：明治政府が紹介した日本

アメリカの独立100周年を記念して、1876年にフィラデルフィアで開催された万国博覧会は、同地の人々の日本に対する関心を大いに刺激した。明治新政府がアメリカの万国博覧会に公式参加したのは、これが初めてのことであり、日本は万博参加38カ国の1つとなったのである。

万国博覧会日本委員会の委員長は西郷従道中将（1843‐1902）で、西郷は1870年にアメリカに来たことがあった。日本は1875年に博覧会の準備室をフィラデルフィアのペン・スクエア4番地に開いた。特使のセキザワ・アケオが、東京の西郷中将と万国博覧会アメリカ総事務局長のアルフレッド・ゴショーンとの連絡役を務めた。日本では活発な準備活動が始まった。政府は日本中の職工たちに最高の陶磁器、七宝細工、ブロンズ鋳物を作るように指示し、職工たちに図案を提供することもあった。

1875年10月10日の締め切りには、日本家屋用の木材と屋根瓦が2軒分と約7000箱の品々が、フィラデルフィアへの船積みを待っていた。11月に大工たちと日本家屋の建築資材が横浜を出発し、そして1876年2月22日には西郷中将とその一行も出航した。西郷中将はフェアモント公園の万国博覧会の敷地に建てた「日本家屋」を住居とした。この「日本家屋」は建築中から注目され、万博公式オープンの5月10日以前からすでに人々を引きつけていた。

The single event that most stimulated early Philadelphians' interest in Japan was the Centennial Exposition of 1876, held in Philadelphia to celebrate the one hundredth anniversary of American independence. This marked the first time that the new Meiji government of Japan officially participated in an American world's fair, one of thirty-eight nations to do so.

The head of the Japanese Commission to the Centennial was Lt. General Saigō Tsugumichi (1843–1902), who had been to America once before, in 1870. The Japanese opened a preparatory office for the Centennial in Philadelphia, at Penn Square 4, in April 1875. The special envoy in charge, Sekizawa Akeo, acted as liaison between General Saigō in Tokyo and the American Director-General of the Centennial, Alfred Goshorn. In Japan, feverish activity had begun, as the government directed craftsmen throughout the country to produce their best ceramics, cloisonné, and bronze castings, in some cases even providing the drawings for them.

By the deadline of October 10, 1875, some 7,000 boxes of wares, as well as the lumber and roof tiles for two Japanese houses, were awaiting shipment to Philadelphia. The materials for the houses and the carpenters left Yokohama in November, and on February 22, 1876, General Saigō and his entourage set sail as well. Saigō's residence in Philadelphia was the "Japanese Dwelling"

Shippokuwaisha's (Cloisonné enamel manufactory) exhibit,
Centennial International Exhibition, 1876. Free Library of Philadelphia

フィラデルフィアの人たちは、日本の大
工が見慣れない文字や紋が描かれてい
る濃紺のハッピを着て木の足場に登り、
釘を使わない木組み工法（継手と込栓
でつなぎ合せる工法）で木材を組み立
てていくのを見ていた。このアメリカで
最初の日本家屋は、屋根が緑色の瓦で
覆われていた。博覧会『公式カタログ：
日本部門』によると、住宅を設計したの
は金沢（加賀）のS・コムラで、フィラデル
フィアの万博会場において建築したの
は東京出身のI・マツオであった。マツオ
は博覧会のもう一つの日本家屋である

on the Centennial Exposition grounds in
Fairmount Park. The Japanese Dwelling had
already attracted crowds as it was being built,
even before the Exposition was officially
opened on May 10. Philadelphians watched
the carpenters, wearing dark blue jackets
decorated with strange characters and
logos, as they climbed up wood scaffolding
and fit the wood framework of the house
together with joinery that required no nails.
The roof of this first Japanese building in
America was covered with green tiles. The
Official Catalogue of the Japanese Section

Cabinet, "Plants of Four seasons and Mount Fuji," purchased from the
Japanese Commision of the Centennial Exposition. Philadelphia Museum of Art

「日本の売店」も建てた。そこでは値の
張らない陶磁器や彫り物などの土産物
が売られ、当時の話によれば、女性の買
い物客の間で特に人気があったという。

日本政府の展示は博覧会メイン・ホ
ール内にあり、日本の出品者には1万
7000平方フィート（約1580平方メート
ル）が割り当てられた。博覧会を訪れる
人たちが日本の展示物の中で真っ先に
目にする物は、一対のブロンズの花瓶だ
った。花瓶は精巧な鋳造で、竜、蛇、鳥、
植物などの凝った装飾がほどこされて
いた。大勢の人々がその鋳造技術を賞
賛したが、その中にはアーネスト・フェノ
ロサや、博覧会の会長ジョゼフ・R・ホー
リー将軍も含まれていた。会長自身、頂
上に象がのっている仏塔の形をした大
きなブロンズの香炉を購入した。

ブロンズ製品以外にも、日本の展示品
には、有田・薩摩・京都・横浜など日本各
地の陶磁器、漆の家具・お盆・重箱、七

issued for the Centennial lists "S. Komura,
Kanazawa, province of Kaga" as the designer
of the house, and "I. Matsuo of Tokyo" as
the builder on site. Matsuo is also listed as
the builder of the other Japanese structure at
the Centennial, the Japanese Bazaar, which
sold inexpensive ceramics, carvings, and the
like as souvenirs. This became particularly
popular with women shoppers, according to
contemporary accounts.

The official display sponsored by the Japanese
government was located in the Centennial's
Main Hall, where exhibitors from Japan were
allotted 17,000 square feet. The first sight
that greeted visitors to the Japanese display
was a pair of delicately cast and elaborately
decorated bronze vases that featured dragons,
snakes, birds, and plants. The bronze casting
techniques were admired by all, including
Ernest Fenollosa and General Joseph R.
Hawley, President of the Centennial, who

宝焼き、織物、象牙彫りや木彫り、籠があり、さらにお茶の道具も展示されていた。河鍋暁斎や塩川文鱗といった画家が描いた水彩画や、柴田是真の漆絵集もあった。万国博覧会のカタログは記述が大まかで、具体的にカタログの品と購入された品を一致させるのは難しいが、ウィリアム・T・ウォルターズとヘクター・ティンダル将軍が多くの展示品を購入した。(現在、ウォルターズの購入品はボルチモアのウォルターズ・ギャラリーに納められ、ティンダル将軍の購入品はフィラデルフィア美術館が収蔵している。)ティンダル将軍はフィラデルフィアにある陶器とガラス器の製造会社ティンダル・アンド・ミッチェルの共同経営者であり、博覧会の陶磁器部門審査員の一人だった。また博覧会の終了時には、新設されたペンシルベニア美術館(現在のフィラデルフィア美術館)も日本コレクションを始めるために、直接購入した。

フェリス・フィッシャー
今井元子/戸田徹子 訳

purchased a massive bronze incense burner in the shape of a pagoda mounted atop an elephant for himself.

In addition to the bronzes, the Japanese exhibition included ceramics from all parts of Japan—Arita, Satsuma, Kyoto, Yokohama and elsewhere—lacquer furniture, trays, and lunch boxes; cloisonné; textiles; ivory and wood carvings; baskets; even a display of tea ceremony wares. There were a few "water color pictures," by such artists as Kawanabe Gyōsai and Shiokawa Bunrin, and an album of paintings in lacquer by Shibata Zeshin. Although it is difficult to match up specific objects with the very general descriptions given in the Centennial catalogue, a large number of pieces were purchased by William T. Walters (now in the Walters Art Gallery, Baltimore), and by General Hector Tyndale (now in the Philadelphia Museum of Art). General Tyndale was a partner in the china and glassware manufacturing firm, Tyndale & Mitchell, in Philadelphia, and he was one of the jurors for the Ceramics section at the Centennial. At the close of the Centennial, the newly-established Pennsylvania Museum (now the Philadelphia Museum of Art) also made some direct purchases to start its Japanese collection.

By Felice Fischer

Selected References: Dallas Finn, "Japan at the Centennial," *Nineteenth Century* 2: 3–4 (Autumn 1976), pp. 33–40; Frank H. Norton, ed., *A Facsimile of Frank Leslie's Illustrated Historical Register of the Centennial Exposition, 1876*, intro. Richard Kenin (New York: Paddington Press, 1974).

If you go: Memorial Hall reopened in 2008 as the Please Touch Museum, 4231 Avenue of the Republic, Philadelphia, PA 19131.

Philadelphia Museum of Art, 26th Street and Benjamin Franklin Parkway, Philadelphia, PA 19130.

2.2 Tanaka Fujimaro: Leader of the Japanese Education Delegates to the Centennial
日本の近代教育：海外に初紹介

1876年6月15日、文部大輔田中不二麿（1845‐1909）は、日本国文部省使節団を率いてアメリカ合衆国独立100周年を記念する行事に出席するため、フィラデルフィアに到着した。1876年の独立100周年記念祭の公式開会はユリシーズ・グラント大統領が5月に行ったが、主な行事（万国博覧会）は1776年7月4日の「独立宣言」署名を記念して7月4日にフィラデルフィアで行われる予定であった。この独立100周年記念万国博覧会に日本は2つの展示をすることになっていた。1つは政府による中央展示場での展示、もう1つは教育関連展示と指定された展示場におけるものであった。

1875年にアメリカ政府は6ヶ月間にわたって開催される独立100周年記念万国博覧会への出展を諸外国に呼びかけたのであるが、そのとき田中は文部省に大きな教育展示を出す約束をさせた。彼の意図は、徳川幕府の終焉から5年後の1873年に彼の責任で始まった日本の近代教育制度の進展を、明示することであった。彼はこの教育展示を、「近代教育の展示室」と称した。西欧の国々の展示と並んで日本の展示を出すことは、日本がすでに近代に入っていること、そしてこの地位に到達していたのはアジアでは日本のみであることを示すのであった。

100周年記念万国博覧会に参加すると田中が決意したことで、彼と彼の率いる使節団は、博覧会で展示されていた西欧の近代的学校制度について学ぶ機

On June 15, 1876, Vice Minister of Education Tanaka Fujimaro (1845–1909), leading a delegation of officials from the Ministry of Education, arrived in Philadelphia to attend the one hundredth anniversary of American independence. Although the 1876 Centennial Exhibition was officially opened in May by President Ulysses S. Grant, major festivities were scheduled for July 4 to commemorate the signing of the Declaration of Independence on July 4, 1776, in Philadelphia. The Japanese entered two exhibits in the Centennial, one by the government in the main exhibition area and the other by the Ministry of Education in an area set aside for educational exhibits.

In 1875 when the American government invited foreign nations to enter exhibits in the six-month long Centennial, Tanaka committed the Ministry to enter a major educational exhibit. His intention was to illustrate the progress of the modern Japanese school system that originated in 1873 under his responsibility, five years after the end of the feudal Tokugawa government. He dubbed the educational exhibition the "showroom of modern education." Entering the Japanese exhibit alongside those from the West demonstrated that Japan had advanced into the modern era, the only Asian nation to have achieved that status.

Tanaka's commitment to participate in the Centennial also provided him and his

Tanaka Fujimaro. Morikawa Terumichi,
Kyōiku chokugo e no michi
(Sangensha, 1990): p. 17
田中不二麿. 森川輝紀 著
「教育勅語への道」三元社 , p. 17, 1990

delegation with the opportunity to learn about modern school systems in the West as exhibited at the Centennial. In 1872 he had represented the Ministry of Education in the Iwakura Mission of senior government officials who spent two years in the United States and Europe observing the most advanced Western societies in preparation for the introduction of modern education in Japan. Tanaka was scheduled to spend seven months in America this time, spending a good portion of it in Philadelphia for school visits during and after the Centennial. Philadelphia had also been on his itinerary in 1872.

Among the members of Tanaka's delegation, the most distinguished was the president of Kaisei Gakkō, Hatakeyama Yoshinari. The Ministry had already decided that this preeminent national institution would be reorganized into the University of Tokyo in 1877. Hatakeyama had previously studied for three years at Rutgers College in New Jersey as the modern era in Japan began. At Rutgers he was befriended by a professor of mathematics, Dr. David Murray, and his wife. The Murray home became a social center for samurai youth studying at Rutgers College.

Dr. Murray was waiting at the 1876 Philadelphia Centennial to welcome Tanaka, Hatakeyama, and the Japanese delegation. Murray was then a senior official of the Ministry of Education hired by the Japanese Government in 1873 as Superintendent of Education and Tanaka's senior advisor. Tanaka had sent him and his wife to America six months before the Centennial was to open in May 1876. Murray's assignment

会をも得た。田中は1872年には文部省を代表する文部理事官として岩倉使節団に加わっていたが、この使節団は日本に近代教育を導入する準備として、アメリカとヨーロッパで2年間にわたり、もっとも進歩した西欧社会を観察していた。1876年には、田中は、万国博覧会の前後に学校訪問をすることも含め、フィラデルフィアを中心に7ヶ月アメリカに滞在することになっていた。フィラデルフィアは田中が1872年に訪問した地でもあった。

田中の率いる使節団の中でもっとも高

名な人物は、開成学校校長の畠山義成であった。卓越した国立学校である開成学校を1877年には東京大学に再編成することを、文部省はすでに決定していた。畠山はこれに先立ち、日本の近代が始まった頃、ニュージャージー州のラトガーズ大学で3年間学んでいた。彼が数学の教授デイビッド・マレー（日本では「ダビッド・モルレー」が一般的な表記）夫妻の世話になったのは、夫妻の家がラトガーズ大学で学ぶ若い侍たちが集う場となっていた、この頃のことである。

きわめて珍しい状況のもと、1876年のフィラデルフィア万国博覧会では、モルレー博士が田中、畠山、そして日本の使節団を歓迎しようと待ち受けていた。モルレーはすでに1873年に文部省学監および田中の上級顧問として日本政府に雇用されており、田中はモルレー夫妻を1876年5月の独立100周年記念行事開会6ヶ月前にアメリカに送っていたのである。モルレーの任務は、彼が編集して万国博覧会の展示のために出版する、近代日本の教育に関する最初の歴史書を発行する出版社を見つけること、5月に開始される日本の展示を監督すること、そして万国博覧会の展示などから教育関連の資料を集めることであった。日本では教育博物館の設立が提案されていたが、日本政府はそのための資料収集に使うようモルレーに2万ドルを託しており、開成学校も、書物を中心とする教育関連資料購入のために5000ドルを彼に託していた。

アメリカで学んでいた日本人数人も、日本展示の準備を手助けするため1876年にフィラデルフィアに召集されていた。とくに興味深いのは、ニューヨークのオスウェゴ師範学校でペスタロッチ教

was to locate a publisher for the first history of modern Japanese education under his editorship for exhibition at the Centennial, to oversee the Japanese exhibit from the opening in May, and to begin collecting educational materials from the Centennial exhibits and other sources. He had been entrusted with $20,000 for materials for a proposed educational museum and $5,000 by Kaisei Gakkō to purchase educational materials, primarily books.

Several Japanese already studying in America were also called to Philadelphia in 1876 to assist in the preparation of the Japanese exhibit. Of particular interest were Takamine Hideo, studying Pestalozzian theories of education at the Oswego Normal School in New York, and Isawa Shūji, enrolled at Bridgewater Normal School in Massachusetts. Tanaka planned to appoint these two to head the prestigious Tokyo Teacher Training School upon completion of their two-year study assignment in America. Takamine would later gain fame as the Japanese who introduced progressive education to Japan. All in all it was an outstanding team that represented the Japanese Ministry of Education at the 1876 Philadelphia Centennial.

The Japanese educational exhibit was impressive as the third largest, only behind those of the United States and Sweden, each of which displayed an actual school building. The Japanese allocated a significant amount of money for their exhibit, second only to America. The Ministry of Education shipped a total of 7,000 packages of materials for display. The exhibit consisted of fifteen different sections on school regulations,

育理論を研究していた高嶺秀夫と、マサチューセッツ州のブリッジウォーター師範学校に在籍していた伊沢修二が、フィラデルフィアに召集されていたことである。田中はこの2人を、アメリカでの2年にわたる研修終了後、威信ある東京師範学校の長に任命するつもりであった。高嶺は後に、進歩的な教育を日本に導入した日本人として有名になる。総合してみると、1876年のフィラデルフィア万国博覧会に集まっていたのは、日本の文部省を代表する卓越した人々だったのである。

日本の教育展示は、アメリカと実際の学校の建物を展示したスウェーデンに次ぎ、3番目に大きく、強い印象を与えるものだった。しかし財政的にみると、日本の展示に注ぎ込まれた額はアメリカに次ぎ2番目に大きかった。文部省は展示のために合計7000箱の資料を送った。展示そのものは、学則、教科書、図書館や博物館、日本の学校の模型など、15の部分から構成されていた。

万国博覧会の間にモルレーと田中が参加した最も重要な活動の中には、教育に関する国際会議「万国教育会議」があった。それは、世界中の教育者を集め、各国の教育制度について説明し意見交換するものであり、壮大なペンシルベニア教育館で開催された。田中とモルレーが近代日本の教育状況について講演をしたのは、この国際会議であった。結果的に、フィラデルフィア万国博覧会は、日本からの使節に西欧の教育の進展状況を学ぶ機会を与えただけでなく、1868年の徳川幕府終焉以後の近代日本における教育の進展ぶりを日本人が報告する、最初の機会でもあったのだ。日本使節団は、7ヶ月のアメリカ滞在の後、12月

textbooks, libraries and museums, and models of Japanese schools, among other topics.

Among the most important activities in which both Murray and Tanaka took part during the Centennial were the international conferences bringing together educators from throughout the world for the mutual interchange of views and the explanation of national systems of instruction, held in the magnificent Pennsylvania Educational Hall. At these international conferences Tanaka and Murray gave lectures on the state of modern Japanese education. The Philadelphia Centennial consequently provided the Japanese delegation not only with the opportunity to learn about the progress of education in the West, but it was also the first opportunity since the end of the feudal Tokugawa government in 1868 for the Japanese to showcase the progress of modern Japanese education.

After seven months in America, including a last-minute visit by Tanaka and his wife to the White House to meet President Grant, the Japanese delegation departed from Philadelphia on December 1. Not only was the Vice Minister pleased with the Japanese participation in the one hundredth anniversary of American independence, but also he was invigorated with proposals and educational materials from the 1876 Philadelphia Centennial for improving the new school system in Japan.

By Benjamin Duke

Selected Reference: Benjamin Duke, *The History of Modern Japanese Education:*

1日に日本に向けて出発した。出発間際に田中夫妻はホワイトハウスにグラント大統領を訪問するという記念すべき経験をしている。田中は文部大輔として、日本がアメリカ独立100周年記念行事に参加したことを喜ぶと同時に、1876年のフィラデルフィア万国博覧会で日本の新しい学校制度を改善するための提案や教材を得て、勇気づけられたのであった。

ベンジャミン・デューク
飯野正子 訳

Constructing the National School System, 1872–1890 (New Brunswick, NJ: Rutgers University Press, 2009).

2.3 Philadelphia Naval Shipyard: American Technology to the Pacific
世界に誇るフィラデルフィア海軍造船所

アメリカ海軍の誕生の地、フィラデルフィア海軍造船所は、19世紀初頭から1996年に閉鎖されるまで、造船と軍用技術に関しては世界の中心であった。1797年にフリゲート艦「合衆国（United States）」が進水した時から、軍艦主要生産都市でもあった。さらに1830年代のフィラデルフィアは、ボールドウィン機関車会社とノリス機関車会社があったため、国内の蒸気機関車生産第1位を誇ってもいた。

フィラデルフィアはおよそ200年にわたり、新技術の発展を牽引していた。19世紀初頭に蒸気戦列艦を、そして1851年には世界初の浮きドックを生み出した。20世紀初頭は海軍唯一のプロペラ生産施設を擁し、それから1940年代の最初の原子力爆弾のための核燃料生産もフィラデルフィアで行われた。

19世紀から海軍の重要性が増し、アメリカの国際力が上昇するにつれ、フィラデルフィアの造船所は、重要な役割を果すようになっていく。74砲「フランクリン」と名付けられた最初の戦列艦が、1920年代のアメリカで登場したばかりの太平洋船隊を導いたし、遡ること1853年のペリー提督の黒船での遠征では、外輪蒸気船「ミシシッピ」も使われている。ペリー提督率いる蒸気船を見た日本人が、アメリカの恐ろしいほどまでの技術開発に度肝を抜かれたことは、よく知られている。

そのような技術力により、フィラデルフ

Often touted as the birthplace of the American Navy, the Philadelphia Naval Shipyard is most appropriately described as a global center for manufacturing and military technology from the nineteenth century until its closing in 1996. Long before Baldwin Locomotive and Richard Norris and Company made Philadelphia one of America's premier producers of steam locomotives (1830s), the city was a key manufacturer of warships, beginning with the 1797 launch of the frigate *United States*.

During nearly two centuries of operation, the Naval Shipyard led the development of new technologies, producing steam-powered ships-of-the-line in the early nineteenth century, the world's first floating dry dock in 1851, housing the Navy's only propeller manufacturing facility from the early twentieth century, and producing nuclear fuel for the first atomic bombs in the 1940s. Given the growing importance of naval power from the nineteenth century, the Yard played a critical role in the rise of American global power. Its first ship-of-the-line, the seventy-four-gun *Franklin*, led America's fledgling Pacific Squadron in the 1820s. And as Commodore Matthew C. Perry's flagship on his 1853 expedition, the side-wheel steamer *Mississippi* gave Japan a formidable glimpse of American technological prowess.

Such technological achievement guaranteed the Naval Shipyard a privileged place in

ィア海軍造船所は世界で成長しつつある造船業界において特権的立場を得ていた。当時は日本もロシアも、近代的総軍艦を造るに当たりフィラデルフィアを頼りにしたのである。クランプ造船所で、日本の巡洋艦「笠置」とロシアの巡洋艦「ワリャーグ」と、ロシアの戦艦「レトウィザン」が建造されるが、これらの艦船は、アジアの海に配備され日露戦争（1904‐1905）の発端ともなった。駐米日本公使であり、後に外務大臣となる小村寿太郎の勧めもあって、桝本卯平は、クランプ造船所の技術をつぶさに観察するためにフィラデルフィアに旅した。それは、桝本が三菱重工長崎造船所のチーフ・エンジニアになる前のことである。

太平洋での緊張が高まるにつれて、アメリカ海軍は言うまでもなく、日本との関係に著しく大きな別の役割を担っていく。1907年10月に乾ドック第2号 が、太平洋アメリカ海軍ツアーのために戦艦「ジョージア」を配備するのに使われたが、これは、ルーズベルト大統領の指揮の下、日本にアメリカの威厳を誇示する意図でなされた。日本の真珠湾攻撃は、フィラデルフィアで建造された2隻の駆逐艦（「カシン」と「ショー」）と近代化された一隻の戦艦（「ペンシルベニア」）にダメージを与えた。真珠湾攻撃により、近代化を誇っていたアメリカ海軍戦艦2隻（「オクラホマ」と「ユタ」）が破壊された。

太平洋戦争中、フィラデルフィアは戦争の富の流通点となる。真珠湾攻撃（1941）と対日戦勝日（1945）の間に、海軍造船所は48隻もの新しい戦艦を建造した。その中の多くの戦艦は、その後太平洋で活躍し、朝鮮、ベトナム戦争にも登場する。1939年から1946年まで、

the burgeoning international shipbuilding industry. Both Japan and Russia turned to Philadelphia in their attempts to build modern navies. Shipbuilder William Cramp and Sons built the Japanese cruiser *Kasagi* (1898) and the Russian cruisers *Varyag* (1899) and *Retvizan* (1900), all of which deployed to Asian waters and saw action at the outset of the Russo-Japanese War (1904–1905), at the Navy Yard. In the meantime, at the urging of Japan's ambassador to Washington and future Japanese Foreign Minister Komura Jutarō, Masumoto Uhei travelled to Philadelphia to observe Cramp's techniques before becoming chief engineer at Mitsubishi Heavy Industry's Nagasaki Shipyard.

As tensions rose across the Pacific, the Navy Yard, of course, played a strikingly different role in relations with Japan. In October 1907, Dry Dock no. 2 was used to ready the pre-dreadnought *Georgia* for the Great White Fleet tour of the Pacific, intended by President Theodore Roosevelt to be a show of force against Japan. Japan's raid on Pearl Harbor damaged two destroyers built in Philadelphia (the *Cassin* and *Shaw*) and one battleship modernized there (the *Pennsylvania*), and destroyed two battleships modernized at the Navy Yard (the *Oklahoma* and *Utah*). The Pacific War also transformed Philadelphia into a focal point for American total war mobilization. Between Pearl Harbor and V-J Day, forty-eight new warships were built there, many of which would see action in the Pacific and, subsequently, in the Korean and Vietnam Wars. From 1939 to 1946, 70,000 military and civilian personnel passed through the Philadelphia Yard every day. Peace would, of course, renew U.S.-Japan friendship and restore the Naval Shipyard as

軍関係者と一般市民合わせて7万人が、毎日フィラデルフィア造船所で働いていたことが記録されている。戦後は外国将校がよく訪れる地として復活した。日本海上自衛隊員も定期的に訪問している。

フレデリック・R・ディッキンソン
小林美奈子 訳

a frequent destination for foreign officers, including periodic visits by members of the new Japanese Maritime Self-Defense Force.

By Frederik R. Dickinson

Selected References: Joseph-James Ahern, *Philadelphia Naval Shipyard* (Dover, NH: Arcadia Publishing, 1997); Jeffrey M. Dorwart, *The Philadelphia Navy Yard: From the Birth of the U.S. Navy to the Nuclear Age* (Philadelphia: University of Pennsylvania Press, 2001).

If you go: Site of the first Philadelphia Navy Yard (1801–1876) near Front Street and Federal Street.

2.4   Japan at the Philadelphia Sesqui-Centennial: The Gift of Trees
2回目のフィラデルフィア万国博覧会：独立150周年記念

フィラデルフィアのフェアモント公園にある桜の木立に花が咲く様子は、今では見慣れた光景であるが、その起源は日本政府からフィラデルフィアに桜の木が贈られた1926年にさかのぼる。その年、アメリカ独立150周年を祝い、フィラデルフィアで万国博覧会が開催された。この万博は、50年前の1876年にウエスト・フェアモント公園で開催されたアメリカ独立100周年を祝う万博と同様に、大がかりな国際的行事になるはずだった。1926年の万博会場は、フィラデルフィアの南端にある沼地を新たに埋め立てた土地に設けられ、パッカー通りとフィラデルフィア海軍造船所の間にあった。その新しい公園は、マサチューセッツ州ブルックラインのオルムステッド兄弟が設計したもので、リーグ・アイランド公園と名付けられ、後にフランクリン・D・ルーズベルト公園と改名された。日本は10余りの参加国の1つで、国のパビリオンを建設し、1年におよぶ博覧会で展示を行なった。

万博に参加するにあたり、日本政府は花の咲く観賞用樹木をフィラデルフィアに1600本寄贈した。それは、各国原産の木や花を「常設展示」してほしいという、全参加国政府への要望に応えたものだった。日本が送ったのは桜、桃、梅、野生リンゴなど、いずれも花の咲く樹木で、1926年5月初旬にフェアモント公園内の数ヶ所に植樹された。イースト・リバー通り（現ケリー通り）沿いでは、ポプラ通りにあるリンカーン・メモリアルに近い場所と、グラント・メモリアルとコロ

The groves of Japanese flowering cherry trees that are now a familiar sight in Philadelphia's Fairmount Park have their origins in the gift of trees to the city in 1926 from the Imperial Japanese Government. In 1926 the Sesqui-Centennial International Exposition was staged in Philadelphia to celebrate the 150th anniversary of the American nation. It was intended to be an international extravaganza reminiscent of the Centennial Exhibition held in West Fairmount Park in 1876. The 1926 fair was located on newly reclaimed marshland at the south end of the city, between Packer Avenue and the Philadelphia Navy Yard. The new park, named League Island Park and later renamed Franklin D. Roosevelt Park, was designed by the Olmsted Brothers of Brookline, Massachusetts. Japan was one of a dozen or so nations that built a national pavilion and showed exhibits for the year-long fair.

At the commencement of its participation in the exposition, the Japanese government donated 1600 flowering ornamental trees to the City of Philadelphia in response to a request sent to all the participating governments for permanent displays of trees and flowers native to their country. The trees given by Japan were planted in Fairmount Park around the first week of May 1926. The donated trees included flowering cherry, peach, plum, and crab apple, and were planted in several locations. Along East

View of the Japanese Pavilion on Edgewater Lake. Free Library of Philadelphia

ンビア橋の間に植えられた。ウエスト・リバー通りでは、モンゴメリー通りの基点にあるベルモント・ポンプ場の近くに植えられた。さらにベルモント通りとジョージ・ヒル頂上の間の、丘のふもとにも植樹された。この桜並木は、カトリック・サークルから始まりホーティカルチャー・センターで終わる主要な道路を今も彩っている。木が成長し花をつければ、その光景はフェアモント公園の最も美しい名所の１つとなるばかりでなく、アメリカの最も美しい光景の１つにもなるだろうと期待された。

植樹の数週間後、カトリック・サークルの泉の前で200人を超す観衆が見守る中、贈呈式が催された。5月21日の式典には、松平恒雄駐米日本大使と日本政

River (now Kelly) Drive trees were planted near the Lincoln Memorial at Poplar Drive, and on the stretch of Drive between the Grant Memorial and the Columbia Bridge. Another group was planted on West River Drive near the Belmont Pumping Station at the foot of Montgomery Avenue. The final site was at the base of George's Hill, between Belmont Avenue and the crest of the hill. This allée of cherry trees still ornaments the formal axis that radiates from the circle of the Catholic Total Abstinence Union Fountain and terminates at the Horticultural Center. When full-grown and in blossom, the display was expected to be one of the finest in the United States, as well as becoming "one of the most beautiful features of Fairmount Park."

府を代表する人々が参列した。ケンドリック市長、E・T・ストーツベリー・フェアモント公園委員会会長、ローランド・S・モリス元駐日アメリカ大使など、フィラデルフィアの著名人も列席した。松平大使は贈呈式での挨拶で、「今までにたくさんの日本人がフィラデルフィアから日本に帰国し、フィラデルフィアの皆様のご親切や温かいもてなしについて、素晴らしい話を聞かせてくれました。フィラデルフィアは私たちにとりまして、その名前が意味するとおりの《同胞愛》そのものでした」と語った。

贈呈式の2日前に、日本政府は万博会場の日本パビリオンの鍬入れ式を行った。当時の世界経済の状況や、1923年の関東大震災の復興にかかる継続的な費用もあり、アメリカ独立150周年万国博覧会への日本の参加は限定的なものとなった。とはいえ参加国数がわずか10ヶ国あまりだったため、日本は非常に目立つ存在となった。建物は伝統的な和風建築で、事務室のある2階建てと、茶室とレストランに使われた大きな開放構造の平屋で成り立っていた。日本パビリオンは主会場の中にあり、現存する古典様式の展望台に隣接し、湖を見晴らすことができた。一風変わった様式と美しい眺望のため、日本パビリオンはコーヒーや紅茶を飲むのに人気のある場所となった。(1926年にはまだ禁酒法が有効で、ビールや酒を出すことは禁止されていた。)日本の万国博覧会委員会は、日本の美術品や産物の展示を後援し、農作物から鉱物まで様々なものが紹介された。美術部門では七宝焼きや篭細工品、織物に加え、川合玉堂や竹内栖鳳といった日本画家の作品も展示されていた。

The trees were dedicated several weeks after the planting in a ceremony held in front of the Total Abstinence Fountain before a crowd of over 200 spectators. Participating in the May 21 ceremony were Matsudaira Tsuneo, Japanese Ambassador to the United States, and a delegation of Japanese officials. A host of Philadelphia notables were there as well, including Mayor Kendrick of Philadelphia, E. T. Stotesbury, president of the Fairmount Park Commission, and the former American Ambassador to Japan, Roland S. Morris. During the dedication, Ambassador Matsudaira remarked, "Many of my countrymen have returned from your city and have related wondrous tales of the kindness and hospitality of your people. To us your city has been what its name signifies, 'brotherly love.'"

Two days before the tree dedication, the Japanese government held the official groundbreaking for its Pavilion on the fairgrounds. Japan's participation in the Sesqui-Centennial was limited, owing to world economic conditions and the continuing costs of recovery from the 1923 Great Kantō Earthquake. Nevertheless, their presence was highly visible, since only about a dozen foreign countries had joined the Exposition. The Japanese building was in the traditional style, with a second story that housed offices as well as a large, one-story open structure that was used as a tearoom and restaurant. The Japanese Pavilion was located on a prime site adjacent to an existing classical cast-stone gazebo and overlooking a lake. Because of its unusual style and beautiful vista, the Japanese Pavilion became a popular spot for taking tea and coffee. (It should be noted that the prohibition of

Official group at tree presentation, Fairmount Park, May 21, 1926. Free Library of Philadelphia

松平大使は、10月5日、万博の「日本デー」のためにフィラデルフィアを再訪した。日本の職人たちが「日本デー」の準備のために数日を費やし、提灯や旗、横断幕、模造の桜の花などを連ねて万博会場や観客席を飾り、「日本的雰囲気」をかもしだした。日本デーそのものは、軍隊の儀式と大使の海軍基地見学で始まり、日本の有名な俳優、舞踏家、歌手などによるショーで締めくくられた。このような大掛かりな事業が、日系アメリカ人社会の援助を得て実施されたのは、フィラデルフィアでは初めてのことであり、日本とフィラデルフィアの66年にわたる

alcoholic beverages was still in effect in 1926, and the serving of beer and sake was not allowed.) The Japanese Sesqui-Centennial Exposition Commission also sponsored exhibits of Japanese arts and industries, with diverse contents ranging from agricultural products to mining. The Fine Arts section included works by Japanese painters such as Kawai Gyokudō and Takeuchi Seihō, as well as examples of cloisonné, basketry, and textiles.

Ambassador Matsudaira returned to Philadelphia for "Japan Day" at the

交流に、敬意が払われたのであった。

この1926年の祝賀の後も、人々はフィラデルフィアを美しく彩る日本の桜を楽しみ、植樹を継続した。1933年4月には、ジョージ・ワシントン生誕200周年記念・女性委員会が日本の桜の木637本を寄贈・植樹した。さらに1998年4月には、フィラデルフィア日米協会が、フェアモント公園内に毎年100本の桜を10年にわたって植樹するという長期事業に着手した。手始めとして、メモリアル・ホール裏のランズダウン通り沿いに、100本が植樹された。1926年5月の『フィラデルフィア・インクワイアラー』紙の社説が指摘したように、「アメリカ独立150周年記念万博の鋼鉄と漆喰でできた宮殿」が無くなってしまっても、「日本からの心のこもった贈り物である木々は、ずっと成長し続けることであろう」。

チャールズ・A・エバーズ
今井元子/戸田徹子 訳

exposition, on October 5. In preparation, Japanese workmen had spent several days decorating the fair grounds and auditorium with strings of lanterns, flags, banners and artificial cherry blossoms to lend a "Japanese atmosphere." The Japan Day events began with military ceremonies and tours of the Navy Yard for the ambassador, and ended with a program of entertainments by famous Japanese actors, dancers, and singers. It was the first time in Philadelphia that so large an undertaking was presented with the assistance of the Japanese American community, to honor sixty-six years of friendship between Philadelphia and Japan.

After the 1926 celebrations, Philadelphians continued to enjoy and celebrate the Japanese cherry tree plantings that grace the city. In April of 1933, the Women's Washington Bicentennial Committee contributed and helped plant 637 Japanese flowering cherry trees. Finally, in April 1998, the Japan America Society of Greater Philadelphia undertook a ten-year effort to replenish and expand the original plantings, beginning with a grove of one hundred cherry trees on Lansdowne Drive, behind Memorial Hall, ultimately planting 1,000 additional trees in Fairmount Park. As was pointed out in an editorial in the *Philadelphia Inquirer* in May 1926, after the "palaces of steel and stucco at the Sesqui-Centennial" are long gone "the thoughtful gift of trees by Japan will be flourishing still."

By Charles A. Evers

Selected References: John D. Cardinell, *A Pictorial Record of the Sesqui-Centennial International Exposition* (Philadelphia, PA: Privately published, 1926); Lancaster,

Clay, *The Japanese Influence in America* (New York: Walton H. Rawls, 1963); Steven Conn, *Museums and American Intellectual Life, 1876–1926* (Chicago and London: The University of Chicago Press, 1998), pp. 233–62.

If you go: Catholic Total Abstinence Union Fountain, North Concourse Drive at Avenue of the Republic and States Street, Fairmount Park, Philadelphia, PA 19131.

2.5 Nishikawa Silk: Beauty, Grace, Durability on the Silk Road to Philadelphia
西川製糸：シルクが結ぶ日本とフィラデルフィア

1926年、アメリカ独立150周年記念フィラデルフィア万国博覧会で、西川製糸の創業者西川伊左衛門は、出品した生糸の高品質が認められグランプリを受賞した。日本の蚕糸協会を代表したその表彰状には、受賞の理由に、生糸の「美しさ」「優雅さ」、そして「強靭さ」の3点において優れていると書かれてある。

西川家は17世紀から21世紀まで、武蔵国と呼ばれた現在の東京、昭島市に10数代続く家系である。マシュー・ペリー提督が開国を求めて来日した頃の、安政5年(1857)に生まれた伊左衛門は、鎖国から開国の変革の時代に育ち、若い頃から日本の近代化を目指し、太平洋を越えたアメリカに目を向けていた。

輸出生糸(raw silk)は、明治、大正、昭和の第2次世界大戦が始まるまで、日本経済を支えた花形産業であった。「西川のシルクで、総てのアメリカ婦人に美しいストッキングを」が伊左衛門の夢であり、その製品の100％はアメリカに輸出された。美しさだけでは十分でなく、「強靭さ」が欠かせず、西川製糸の生糸が、アメリカで評価され、歓迎されたのはそこにある。

高品質の生糸を生産するために、努力と研究を欠かさなかった。繭を農家から買い取るだけでなく、繭となる蚕の種を作る蚕種部を新設した。厳しい管理のもと、優れた種だけを選別して、農家に分け与え、心を込めて蚕を育てるように指導、質の良い繭を高価で買い取るとい

In 1926 Nishikawa Izaemon (1857–1936), the founder of Nishikawa Silk, received the Grand Prix Award for the high quality of the raw silk he exhibited at the Philadelphia International Exposition held in commemoration of the 150th anniversary of the founding of the United States of America. The award Nishikawa received on behalf of the Japan Silk Industry Association took note of the "beauty, grace and durability" of the raw silk.

The Nishikawa family has a proud history of more than ten generations from the seventeenth to the twenty-first century as landowners in Musashi County, the present-day Akishima City in the Greater Tokyo Metropolitan Area.

Izaemon was born in 1857, the fifth year of the Ansei era, about the time of the first visit to Japan of Commodore Matthew Perry, and lived through the period of Japan's modernization and the end of its "closed-door" policy. Blessed with foresight, his eyes were focused from his youth on the distant shores of America across the Pacific Ocean.

Export of raw silk was an important industry that supported Japan's economy through the Meiji and Taishō eras and the Shōwa era until the start of World War II. Izaemon's dream was to clad the legs of American women with beautiful stockings made of Nishikawa silk. Indeed, one hundred percent of his

Grand Prix Certificate Award for Nishikawa Silk, 1926. Courtesy of the author

う一貫生産に成功した。このようにして
日本屈指の製糸会社としての地位を確
固たるものにした。「あなたも私も共によ
く」という経営哲学は、現在にも通じる
偉大な教訓として高く評価されている。
アメリカ文化、習慣、知識などを取り入
れるのにも積極的で、横浜の商館のアメ
リカ人バイヤー接待のために、純日本
式の別荘を建て、もてなしをした。この
別荘は文化財建造物として、現在、江戸
東京たてもの園に移築され、高橋是清
元首相邸と並んで保存されている。

2014年にユネスコの世界遺産に登録
が決まった富岡製糸の生糸はフランス

products were exported to the United States. But beauty was not enough; Nishikawa saw that durability was also essential for raw silk products to be loved and welcomed in the United States.

Research and tireless effort were the keys to producing high quality raw silk yarns. Izaemon was therefore not content to purchase cocoons from the farmers. He established a department of silk seeds within his firm, raised the seeds under strict control, and shared the best of them with farmers, telling them to rear them with utmost care. In this way he succeeded in creating an

に輸出されていたが、西川製糸の販売
先はアメリカであった。「西の片倉、東
の西川」と言われ、最盛期には全国5位
であった。戦時中は、軍需工場に転換、
海軍の上陸用舟艇のエンジンや、パラ
シュートも作っていたが、軍需工場ゆえ
に、1945年4月4日にB29 による空襲で
全焼した。

1936年に、「製糸王、蚕糸業界の大恩
人　西川翁逝く」と報じられ、その死を
惜しまれて世を去った西川伊左衛門に
は、心残りだったことが1つあった。フィ
ラデルフィア万国博覧会でグランプリを

Nishikawa Izaemon.
Courtesy of the author

integrated supply chain for the high quality
cocoons he purchased at high cost in order
to produce high quality silk products. His
philosophy of management by mutual
advantage (a win-win style) is as relevant
today as it was then.

Moreover, Izaemon was also keen to adopt
American culture, customs, and knowledge
and went so far as to build an authentic
Japanese villa where he entertained American
buyers from the Yokohama Commercial
Pavilion. He also introduced *ayu* (a sweet
fish) for fishing in the Tama River. His villa,
completed in 1922, is preserved today as a
cultural asset along with the residence of
Takahashi Korekiyo, a respected Minister
of Finance, in the Edo-Tokyo Open Air
Architectural Museum.

When Izaemon left us in 1936, newspapers
mourned "the death of the king of silk
yarns, the great benefactor of the raw silk
industry."   There was just one thing
that Nishikawa Izaemon regretted, and
that was not being able to receive the
Grand Prix in person due to a leg injury.
Eighty years later, the Philadelphia city
government learned of this omission and
invited Izaemon's great-grandson Norihiro
and great-granddaughter Chieko (myself)
to a special commemorative event in 2006
at the Fairmount Park Horticultural Center.
The event was taken up by the media and
was broadcast not only in Philadelphia and
New York but also to the world via NHK
broadcasting satellite.

Every spring Fairmount Park comes
alive with the panorama of blossoming
cherry trees that were sent by the

Sesqui-Centennial International Exposition. Exhibit by the Raw Silk Association of Japan, 1926.
Courtesy of the author

受賞しながら、足の怪我のため式典に出席できなかったことである。80年経た2006年に、それを知ったフィラデルフィア市は、曾孫の昌宏と知恵子をフィラデルフィアに招待し、市長主催記念式典をフェアモント公園内にあるホーティカルチャー・センターで開催した。このニュースは、フィラデルフィア、ニューヨークだけでなくNHK衛星放送で全世界に放映された。

フェアモント公園には、西川伊左衛門が出席できなかった1926年万博の際に日本政府から贈られた桜の木が、現在も残っている。またフィラデルフィア日米協会が毎年4月に主催する「スバル桜祭り」には、曾孫である西川知恵子が「チエコ・ニシカワ・コレクション」と呼ばれる貢献活動を10年に及んで続けている。 また本人の著書『フィラデルフィアへのシルクロード』は、時空を越えた日本とフィラデルフィアを結ぶドキュメンタ

Japanese government on the occasion of the Philadelphia International Exposition in 1926 at which my great-grandfather Izaemon was honored with the Grand Prix. The Philadelphia Japan-America Society takes good care of the cherry blossom trees and organizes the Subaru Cherry Blossom Festival every April for the enjoyment of its citizens. Ever since I learned about this I have contributed to the event through what I call the Chieko Nishikawa Collection. In this way, cherry blossom trees and silk still tell the story of Japan-America friendship that began in the nineteenth century and continues to this day.

An Historic Guide to Philadelphia and Japan begins with the story of John Manjirō. As luck has it, Kazuko Nakahama, a great-granddaughter of John Manjirō and I, Izaemon's great-granddaughter, have been friends ever since we were classmates

リーでもある。

『日本とフィラデルフィアを結ぶ歴史的絆』はジョン・万次郎氏の話から始まっているが、ジョン・万次郎の曾孫である中浜和子と、西川知恵子は学習院では同級生であり、しかも今上天皇の家庭教師であったフィラデルフィア出身のエリザベス・バイニングから一緒に英語を学んでいた。

さらに本文の英文翻訳は、知恵子の親しい友人、原不二子によって可能となった。原の祖父は、国会議員として議席にあること63年、世界議会史上の記録を打ち立て、「憲政の父」と称えられる尾崎行雄（咢堂翁）である。1911年に氏が東京市長の時、ワシントンDCへ3000本の桜の苗木を贈ったことは広く知られている。　以来、毎春ポトマック河畔で「全米桜まつり」が行われているが、こうして日米を結ぶ友好のシンボル、桜を通した絆は現在でも絶えることなく継続している。

西川知恵子

参考文献：
西川千恵子『フィラデルフィアへのシルクロード』（けやき出版、2010）

【参考情報】
江戸東京たてもの園
〒184-0005　東京都小金井市桜町
3-7-1
（都立小金井公園内）
電話: 042-388-3300（代表）
www.tatemonoen.jp

at Gakushūin, the Peers' School (where members of the Imperial Family study.) We were also taught English together by Elizabeth Gray Vining, a Philadelphian, who was the private tutor of the present Emperor when he was Crown Prince.

In my book *A Silk Road to Philadelphia* I relate in Japanese the fascinating story of how Japan and Philadelphia were enduringly bound across time and space by an unbreakable silk thread. A dear friend of mine, Fujiko Hara, has kindly translated these words. She happens to be a granddaughter of Yukio Ozaki (Gakudō, 1858–1954) who served his people in parliament for a world record of sixty-three years and is known as the father of Japanese constitutional democracy. In 1911 as mayor of Tokyo he sent 3,000 cherry blossom trees as a signal of friendship to Washington DC. Planted round the Potomac Basin, the trees are the highlight every spring of the National Cherry Blossom Festival. I am grateful that Fujiko undertook the translation of my message and I sincerely pray that the strong Japan-America bond forged by the cherry blossom trees will last forever.

By Chieko Nishikawa
Translated by Fujiko Hara

2.6 Eitokusai III Yamakawa Yasujirō: Japanese Doll Master Who Worked at the Commercial Museum of Philadelphia
山川保次郎：フィラデルフィアで活躍した名人形師

山川保次郎(1865‐1941)は3代永徳斎として戦前の東京で名を馳せた名人形師である。初代永徳斎で御用人形司を勤める父親のもとで幼少の頃より技を磨き、昭和3年に兄の2代永徳斎から格式高い家業を引継いで、日本橋に構えていた名店の繁栄に尽した。永徳斎の人形は美術工芸品として東京の富裕層にもてはやされる高級品であった。

驚くべきことに、保次郎は3代永徳斎襲名前にフィラデルフィアに20余年住んでいた。しかし、高度の伝統工芸職人が海外渡航、在留する経緯をはじめ、真相は不明だった。1953年に御用人形

Yamakawa Yasujirō (second from left) photographed with his sister, Saitō Sen, and Sen's family, at the Saitō's villa, Tokyo, c. 1938. Courtesy of Saito Toshiaki, Sen's great grandson
山川保次郎(左から2番目)と
齋藤せんの家族　齋藤利明所蔵

Yamakawa Yasujirō (1865–1941) was an acclaimed doll master of pre-World War II Tokyo. Better known by his professional name, Eitokusai III, he was trained since childhood by Eitokusai I, his craftsman father and the purveyor of dolls and miniatures to the Imperial household. In 1928 Eitokusai III inherited his family's distinguished doll making tradition from Eitokusai II, his brother, and continued to uphold the fame and honor of their family store in Nihonbashi, Tokyo. The creations of Eitokusai doll masters were works of art in their own right and were coveted by wealthy families in Tokyo's fashionable circles.

Before succeeding to the Eitokusai title, Yamakawa lived in Philadelphia for twenty years. But no one knew exactly what had induced a traditional craftsman like him to travel around the globe to the U.S. East Coast. He himself never explained it. In 1953, the Eitokusai store went out of business, and much of its outstanding history as well as the surprising story of Yamakawa's long sojourn abroad were forgotten.

I began the quest to unravel Yamakawa's mystery in 2003. Through an extensive search in both Japanese and American sources, I confirmed that he had been employed by the Commercial Museum of Philadelphia from 1907 to 1927 to make life-size, life-like models of diverse people, which were a vital part of the museum's exhibits.

Women picking tea leaves in "the preparation of tea for shipping" Commercial Museum Exhibit, 1910. Anthropology Laboratory and Museum, Temple University, Philadelphia

司永徳斎は閉店し、名店の歴史も保次郎の長期海外生活の謎も忘れ去られた。2003年、私はその謎に挑み、日米双方で調査を重ね、山川保次郎はフィラデルフィア市の商業博物館で、展示用の等身大人物像、いわゆる生き人形を制作していたと突き止めた。

商業博物館は、ペンシルベニア大学生物学科のW・P・ウィルソン博士が1893年のシカゴ万博を見学中に、当時頻繁に開催された万博の展示品を終了後貰い受け、通常展示としてアメリカ人の啓蒙に役立てる構想を得たことに始まる。ウィルソンは翌年創設された博物館の館長に任命され、世界各地の原材料見本、道具、布や衣料、日常生活用品などを精力的に蒐集した。厖大な蒐集資料を研究員が分類し解説をつけたが、展示構成では大部分は見映えしない物品をどう見せるかが問題であった。

The Commercial Museum was the brainchild of Dr. William P. Wilson, Professor in the School of Biology, University of Pennsylvania. While visiting the World's Columbian Exposition in Chicago in 1893, he conceived the idea of a museum to collect artifacts from various world's fairs and exhibit them to teach Americans about the countries that could be potential markets for their products. The museum came into being the next year, and Wilson, as director, assiduously gathered artifacts, including samples of raw materials, tools, textiles, costumes, and everyday commodities from all over the world.

The task of organizing the voluminous quantity of artifacts for display posed a great challenge to the museum staff. While researchers classified and labeled the items so that visitors could learn from them, the installation staff struggled with how to

Exhibits at the Commercial Museum.
Philadelphia City Archivesフィラデルフィア市
古文書館 所蔵

ウィルソンは、1904年セントルイス万博
で日本茶の展示からよいヒントを得たと
思われる。それは日本庭園を描いた幕
を背景に実寸の和室を作り、中には茶
道を楽しむ女性の等身大人形が2体、そ
の両側に茶の見本を並べてあり、まさに
ウィルソンが求めていた外国の人間と
産品を生き生きと見せる展示であった。
人形作者で現場の展示責任者でもあっ
た保次郎とその場で会い、商業博物館
への招聘を決めたと思われる。東京の
外交史料館に、この推測を裏付ける保
次郎の旅券発給記録がある。また、フィ
ラデルフィアの市立図書館や市立古文
書館の収蔵資料には多数の等身大人
物像の写真があり、"E. Yamakawa"作と
の記録もある。"E."は永徳斎の頭文字で
ある。

provide focal points that would capture
visitors' immediate attention and attractively
display the otherwise drab objects.

At the 1904 Louisiana Purchase Centennial
Exhibition in St. Louis, in the Japanese
tea exhibit, Wilson found the solution to
this challenge. He was captivated by life-
size models of two women performing the
tea ceremony, surrounded by rows of tea
products, all arranged in a full size Japanese
room against the backdrop of a landscape
garden. The manner of display perfectly met
Wilson's determination that the Commercial
Museum exhibits should vividly portray
the people and products of foreign lands.
Introduced to Yamakawa, the dolls' creator
assigned to St. Louis, Missouri, Wilson must
have invited the Japanese master to come to
Philadelphia to work for him. Records in
the Foreign Ministry Archives in Tokyo,
showing Yamakawa's passport issuance
records, support this conjecture. The Annual
Reports of the Commercial Museum in the
collection of the Free Library of Philadelphia
and old photographs in the Philadelphia City
Archives provide further testament to scores
of life-size human models created by "E.
Yamakawa", the "E" standing for "Eitokusai."

The photographed models show compelling
and beautiful craftsmanship, conveying
Yamakawa 's empathy for people regardless
of race or their respective circumstances.
The details of the carved heads and limbs,
particularly the application of gofun for
surface coating, reveal the techniques of
traditional doll making in Japan. Gofun
is a paste of powdered shell and nikawa
(gelatin extracted from animal and fish skins,
tendons and bones) and is viscous when

古写真からみる人物モデルは視線を惹く美しさがあり、保次郎のすべての人間への共感が伝わる。頭や手足の細部から日本の伝統的人形制作技法、特に胡粉の技が見てとれる。胡粉とは貝の粉末とニカワを練り合わせたもので、粘液状態のうちに瞼、唇、皺などの細部仕上げに用い、彩色もでき、乾くと陶器のように固まる。高度の伝統技法ではあるが、保次郎は彼の優れた造形技をも発揮して多種多様な大型像をかなりの速さで制作したと思われる。

商業博物館の転変の過程で、大型作品は滅失した。1994年、当時はシビック・センター・ミュージアムとなっていた商業博物館は閉鎖、残存収蔵品は倉庫保管となった。2004年に市が保管物を市内の博物館等に払い下げた際、私はテンプル大学取得品中から小型日本人形4体を、偶然に発見した。「中国」と分類されていたが、本来は「日本：茶の生産と出荷」と題した1910年の商業博物館展示物であった。

2010年に、100年を経た製茶人形を修復すべく、NPO「文京歴史的建物の保存を考える会」の協力で東京へ持ち帰った。専門家による適切な修復と紛失した附属品の補充をした後、保次郎の帰国後の作品と共に、文京区の旧安田楠雄邸で開催した3代永徳斎没後70年記念展で公開披露して反響を呼んだ。製茶人形は、現在はテンプル大学人類学部博物館に収蔵されている。

山川保次郎とフィラデルフィアの縁は解明したが、まだ謎は残る。フィラデルフィアでは妻「たか」と息子「治道」（別名ハリー）と暮らしていたが、1927年帰国の際、アメリカ残留を望んだハリーの消息

warm. The paste in its viscous state can be used to craft details such as eyelids, lips, or wrinkles. Pigments can also be mixed with the paste for realistic coloring. Once dried, the coating hardens like porcelain. With complete mastery of this delicate method, combined with his ingenious sculpting skills, Yamakawa produced numerous large figures, apparently at great speed.

None of the life-size figures has survived the vicissitudes of the Commercial Museum. In 1994, the museum, which had been renamed the Civic Center Museum, was closed, and the about 25,000 items of its collection were put in storage. In 2004 the City decided to disperse them to other museums and institutions, one of which was Temple University. Guided by serendipity, I found four miniature Japanese models created by Yamakawa among the Temple University acquisitions, contained in boxes labeled "China." They were originally made for a 1910 exhibit entitled "Japan: preparing tea for shipping."

The four tea models are now in the collection of the Anthropology Laboratory and Museum at Temple University. In 2010, I arranged for their restoration and conservation in Tokyo with support from the Bunkyo Link for Architectural Preservation, a nonprofit organization of which I am a board member. With minimal mending and cleaning done to conserve their historical quality and re-equipped with replacements of missing accouterments, the four tea models joined later works by Yamakawa in a nine-day exhibition to commemorate the seventieth anniversary of his death in 1941, held at the former Kusuo Yasuda Residence, Tokyo. Afterwards, the models were returned

は未だ歴史の闇に埋もれたままで、今後の解明が待たれる。

圓佛須美子

参考文献:
圓佛須美子『三代永徳斎　米国さんと呼ばれた男』(私家版、2011)

to Philadelphia.

Although Yamakawa's connection with Philadelphia has thus been clarified, mysteries still remain. He lived in Philadelphia with his wife, Taka, and son, Harumichi, alias Harry. In 1927 when Yasujirō and Taka returned to Japan, "Harry" chose to stay on. Perhaps history will yet reveal Harry's story and shed further light on Yamakawa's enigmatic life and creations.

By Sumiko Enbutsu

Selected References: Ruth H. Hunter, *The Trade and Convention Center of Philadelphia: Its Birth and Renascence* (City of Philadelphia, 1962); Steven Conn, *Museums and American Intellectual Life*, 1876–1926 (Chicago: The University of Chicago Press, 1998); Sumiko Enbutsu, *Yamakawa Yasujirō: Japanese Doll Master Who Lived in Philadelphia 1907–1927* (Tokyo: Privately published, 2011).

If you go: Temple University Anthropology Laboratory and Museum, Department of Anthropology, Gladfelter Hall, second floor, 1115 West Berks Street, Philadelphia, PA 19122.

2.7　Where, Oh Where Has Miss Saga Gone? A Little Mystery
人形大使「ミス佐賀」：子供たちへの贈り物

「ミス佐賀」について、或る事実は明らかである。ミス佐賀はフィラデルフィアの子供たちへの贈り物だった。それはアメリカからの「青い目の人形大使」への返礼として、日本から送られた友好関係を示す精巧な人形の1つであった。ミス佐賀は、フィラデルフィアの商業博物館に収められた。

ミス佐賀の歴史の始まりは「青い目の人形大使」である。それは1920年代に、「隣人のような世界関係」を築くというシドニー・L・ギューリック博士の夢に基づく企画だった。博士は日本で宣教師をしていたが、アメリカに帰国した後、人形交換を通して日本とアメリカの子供たちの間に永遠の友情の架け橋を築きたいと願った。まず、アメリカから数多くの「青い目の人形大使」が日本に届けられた。日本からは、1927年11月に58体の人形が送られた。これらの人形の1つがミス佐賀で、フィラデルフィアの商業博物館が住み家となった。

しかしながら、その後の行方がはっきりしない。

Some facts about Miss Saga are clear. She was a gift to the children of Philadelphia, one of the elaborate Friendship Dolls sent from Japan in response to an American gesture. She was sent to the Commercial Museum of Philadelphia.

Ms. Saga's journey to Philadelphia started with Dr. Sidney L. Gulick's (1860–1945) vision of building a "world neighborhood" in the 1920s. He was a missionary in Japan, and after his return to America he hoped to build a bridge to lasting friendship between the children of Japan and America through the exchange of Friendship Dolls. After a large group of American dolls, known as the "Blue-eyed Messengers," was sent to Japan, a group of fifty-eight dolls came in return from Japan in November 1927. Among those dolls was "Miss Saga," a gift to the children of Philadelphia, whose home was in Philadelphia's Commercial Museum.

The subsequent history of Miss Saga, however, is not so clear.

Miss Saga.
Courtesy of Felice Fischer

というのもフィラデルフィア商業博物館は長続きせず、ミス佐賀にとって恒久的な住み家とはなりえなかったからである。1995年にロバート・W・ライデルはフィラデルフィア商業博物館に関する報告書の中で次のように述べている。

「商業博物館はアメリカ史上特異な機関であった。アメリカ合衆国に商務省が設けられる以前、アメリカ実業界に外国の情報を提供する情報センターとしての役割を果たしていた。同博物館は19世紀末から20世紀初頭にかけて頻繁に開催された万国博覧会から数多くの品々を集め、外国文化について豊富な知識を蓄積していた。そして、W・P・ウィルソンの指導の下、アメリカ人が外国市場に進出できるように、アメリカ実業界に対して情報提供に努めていた」。

「ウィルソンは有能な行政官であったが、商業博物館を私物化してしまった。1927年のウィルソンの死後、商業博物館の予算は、フィラデルフィアの政治的不祥事と汚職の犠牲となっていった。1950年に、市は商業博物館をフィラデルフィア・シビック・センター博物館として再組織したが、その間に、博物館の収蔵物のほとんどが消息不明となり、公文書記録の大部分も捨てられてしまった」。

ミス佐賀の物語の結末は、いまだに分からない。第2次世界大戦中の日本に対する反発の中で、彼女は死んでしまったのであろうか。誰かしら個人のコレクションに収まっているのだろうか。それとも、行方不明になって忘れ去られてしまい、救出されるのを待ちながら、どこかに横たわっているのであろうか。

In 1995, Robert W. Rydell wrote a report on Philadelphia's Commercial Museum, in which he stated:

> *The Commercial Museum was a unique institution in American history. In an era before the Department of Commerce was established, it served as a clearinghouse of information about foreign countries for American business interests. With its large stock of artifacts gathered from dozens of world's fairs held at the turn of the century, the museum comprised a wealth of knowledge about cultural conditions of foreign countries and, under W. P. Wilson's direction, endeavored to provide American interests with information that would enable Americans to penetrate foreign markets.*

> *Wilson was an able administrator, but had made the museum his personal fiefdom. After his death in 1927, the museum's budget fell victim to Philadelphia's political scandals and corruption; the displays fell into disrepair; and it increasingly became a source of public embarrassment. In 1950, the city reorganized the Commercial Museum as the Philadelphia Civic Center Museum. During the course of its reorganization, the contents of the Commercial Museum were all but obliterated. Most of the archival records were jettisoned.*

The ending of Miss Saga's story is still unknown. Did she perish during World War II in the reaction against anything Japanese? Did she end up in a private collection? Is she lying somewhere lost and forgotten, waiting

人形を贈るというような親善活動の素
晴らしさは、長期にわたり記憶に残り、
その効果が85年後の今でも感じられる
ことにある。ミス佐賀のような人形大使
たちの話がそれぞれ語られるたびに、
人形たちが生み出した友好的な気持ち
が、読者の心の中によみがえるのであ
る。子供たちに友好を広めようとした時、
ギューリック博士はなんと純真で壮大な
夢を抱いたのであろうか。ミス佐賀がフ
ィラデルフィアに戻って来ることがあれ
ば、親善大使としての役割を再開するこ
とになろう。もしミス佐賀が早すぎる死
を迎えていたとしたら、彼女に代わって
彼女の使命を果たすのは私たちの責務
である。大人による政治や外交工作が
失敗するような場合であっても、子供同
士の親善活動は成功するし、成功しうる
のである。

註:
フィラデルフィアで「ミス佐賀」と呼ばれ
ていた人形は、実際には「ミス東京府」
であった。本来の「ミス佐賀」は1953年
以来、ニューメキシコ州サンタフェの国
際フォーク・アート博物館で「ミス山口」
として収蔵されている。移動展示中に人
形本体と台座の取り違えが生じ、混乱が
多い状態にある。

ウィリアム・ヒギンズ
今井澄子/戸田徹子 訳

参考文献:
高岡美知子『人形大使:もうひとつの日
米現代史』(日経BP社、2004)
是澤博昭『青い目の人形と近代日本』
(世織書房、2010)

to be rescued?

The beauty of goodwill gestures such as the exchange of friendship dolls is that their long-term effect is still making itself felt over eighty years later. Each time the story of one of these miniature ambassadors like Miss Saga is told, the goodwill it engenders is renewed in the reader's heart. What a grand and simple vision Dr. Gulick had when he thought to spread goodwill through children. Should Miss Saga ever reappear she will resume her duties as goodwill ambassador. If she has met an untimely end, then it is up to us to continue her mission for her. Friendship gestures between children can and will succeed where politics and diplomatic maneuvers by adults may fail.

By William Higgins

Note: The original Miss Saga has resided since 1953 in the Museum of International Folk Art in Santa Fe, where she is known as Miss Yamaguchi. The doll known in Philadelphia as Miss Saga was actually Miss Tokyo-fu, thanks to mix-ups as the dolls traveled.

Selected References: Steven Conn, *Museums and American Intellectual Life*, 1876–1926 (Chicago and London: The University of Chicago Press, 1998), pp. 115–50; Alan Pate, *Art as Ambassador: The Japanese Friendship Dolls of 1927*, forthcoming 2015.

If you go: The Newark Museum, 49 Washington Street, Newark, NJ 07102 still has in its collection "Miss Osaka," and "Miss Nagano" is in the Delaware History Museum at the Historical Society of Delaware, 504 North Market Street, Wilmington, DE 19801.

3

Exchanges in Arts and Literature
芸術と文学の交流

3.1 Professor Risley, the Imperial Japanese Troupe, and Philadelphia: A Mania for Acrobats

海を渡った幕末の曲芸団：リズリー先生とフィラデルフィア

プロフェッサー・リズリー（以下、リズリー先生）とは19世紀のアクロバット芸人ならびに興行主で、世界で日本芸人ブームを惹き起こした人物の芸名である。このリズリー先生はフィラデルフィア出身を自称していた。リチャード・リズリー・カーライルは1814年生まれで、ニュージャージー州バス・リバーで育った。だが、その地に長くはいなかった。実際のところ、彼は生涯、同じ場所に長く留まることをしなかった。21歳までにフィラデルフィアのレベッカ・C・ウィリッツと結婚して子供をもうけ、インディアナ州に移り住み、ニュー・カーライルという町をつくっている。リズリーは賞金稼ぎや商人、政治家として成功を収めたが、1840年代の初めにサーカスに転じ、小さな息子ジョンと「リズリー・アクト」と呼ばれ、世界的に有名になった（そして今でも有名な）技を披露し始めた。それは主に両足を使ってジョンを（後にはヘンリーを）ジャグリングするという足技だった。

1842年の芝居のビラによれば、リズリーはフィラデルフィアのチェスナット通りと9番通りの角で、ルファス・ウェルチ「将軍」のニュー・オリンピック・サーカスに出演している。だが間もなくリズリーはありきたりのサーカスの殻を破り、1840年代半ばにはヨーロッパに移り、そこで体操とバレエを一緒にした演技で観客を沸かせた。多くの庶民や貴人を喜ばせ、リズリーの名前はアメリカとヨーロッパの両大陸で有名になった。リズリーは金持ちになり、フィラデルフィア郊外のリドリーに敷地144エーカーの

"Professor" Risley—the stage name of the nineteeth century acrobat and impresario who created a global boom in Japanese performers—called Philadelphia home. Born Richard Risley Carlisle in 1814, and raised in Bass River, New Jersey, Risley did not linger there long; in fact, throughout his life he rarely stayed anywhere very long. By the age of twenty-one he had married Rebecca C. Willits of Philadelphia, had children, moved to Indiana, and formed the town of New Carlisle. After a checkered early career as a bounty hunter, merchant, and politician, by the beginning of the 1840s Risley had turned to performing in circuses with his little son John, popularizing what became internationally known (and is still known) as the "Risley Act." It consisted of juggling John (and later Henry, too) largely with his feet.

Playbills from 1842 show Risley in Philadelphia with "General" Rufus Welch's New Olympic Circus, at the corner of Chestnut and Ninth. Yet Risley soon outgrew the ordinary circus and in the mid-1840s moved to Europe, where he created a sensation with his act, which straddled gymnastics and ballet. He thrilled crowds of thousands, commoners and aristocrats, becoming a household word on two continents. He became wealthy enough to purchase a mansion on 144 acres in Ridley Township outside Philadelphia, but he soon had to sell it, for he was also prone to losing vast amounts of money.

屋敷を購入した。しかし、すぐ売却する羽目になる。リズリーは大金を失ってしまう性質だった。

息子たちが成長してジャグリングができなくなると、リズリーはフィラデルフィアにいる彼らの母親—すなわち終生ほとんど別居していた妻—に預けた。1855年にリズリーは芸人兼興行主として素晴らしい冒険旅行に旅立った。カリフォルニア州北部とオレゴン州のゴールド・ラッシュが過ぎ去った町々を巡回し、それから1857年から58年にかけて、ニュージーランドと

From left to right: Denkichi, with the brothers Sentarō
and Yonekichi and their father,
Rinzō, of the Hamaikari family.
The Library Company of Philadelphia
浜碇一家、左から右へ：
伝吉、千太郎、米吉、父親の林蔵

オーストラリアを訪ねた。1860年には、サーカス全部を引き連れてカルカッタ、シンガポール、バタヴィア（現在のジャカルタ）、マニラ、香港、そして上海を回った。

1864年に日本の横浜に上陸し、西洋式サーカスとアイスクリームを紹介した。座員たちはリズリーを残して横浜を去ったが、リズリーは男女18名の日本の曲芸師をアメリカとヨーロッパに連れて行

When Risley's sons became too big to juggle, he deposited them in Philadelphia to live with their mother, from whom he lived apart most of his life. In 1855, Risley embarked on an extraordinary odyssey as both performer and impresario, touring the post-gold rush towns of Northern California and Oregon, then moving to New Zealand and Australia in 1857–58. In 1860, he took a full circus to Calcutta, then Singapore, Batavia (today's Jakarta), Manila, Hong Kong, and Shanghai. In 1864 he landed in Yokohama, Japan, where he introduced both Western-style circus and ice cream. His performers deserted him in Yokohama, but he hit upon the idea of taking eighteen male and female Japanese acrobats to America and to Europe. At the end of 1866, Risley's "Imperial Japanese Troupe" received the first civilian passports from Japan's still-feudal government, and sailed to San Francisco, where they created a sensation. One boy

くことを思いついた。1866年の終わりに、リズリーの「帝国日本芸人一座」は、まだ封建制度の下にあった徳川幕府から最初の一般人用パスポートを発行してもらい、サンフランシスコに向けて出帆した。そこで一座は大評判となった。すぐに浜碇梅吉という1人の少年曲芸師がスターとなり、その品格と貫録から、「小さなオーライ(オール・ライト)」というあだ名がついた。かつてリズリーがそうであったように、小さなオーライはアメリカとヨーロッパでよく知られる名前となった。そして似たような名前を名乗る模倣者が数えきれないほど現れた。

1867年2月初旬にニューヨークに到着すると、リズリーが予約していた劇場は火事で焼け落ちていた。そこでリズリーはフィラデルフィアから東海岸ツアーを始めることにした。プロの興行主なのでリズリーは抜かりなく、『ノース・アメリカン・アンド・ユナイテッド・ステイツ・ガゼット』などの地元新聞で、帝国日本芸人一座の新奇さや技、素晴らしさを前もって宣伝した。そして日本とアメリカの国旗を派手になびかせた汽車でフィラデルフィアまで移動した。ブロード通りとローカスト通りの角にある豪華なアメリカン・アカデミー・オブ・ミュージックにおいて、帝国日本芸人一座は3月5日に初日を迎えた。大雪だったにもかかわらず、ショーは大成功で「立見席のみ」の掲示が出された。

フィラデルフィアの人たちは7年前に、侍の日本使節団の公式訪問を見たことがあった。とはいえ日本は開国したばかりの、いまだにエキゾチックで神秘な国で、誰一人として普通の日本人を見たことはなく、なにかしら帝国日本芸人一座に似たものを見た者もいなかった。観客

acrobat, Hamaikari Umekichi, quickly became a star, and was given the nickname of "Little All Right" for his panache and grace. Like Risley in former years, he, too, became a household word in America and Europe. He would also spawn countless similarly-named imitators.

On arrival in New York in early February 1867, Risley found that the theater he had booked had burned down, so he decided to start the troupe's East Coast tour in Philadelphia. A true professional, he carefully publicized the troupe's novelty, skill, and superiority, taking out advance advertisements in local papers such as the *North American and United States Gazette*, and traveling to Philadelphia in a train gaily flying Japanese and American flags. The troupe's show opened on March 5 at the opulent American Academy of Music on the corner of Broad and Locust Streets. Despite a huge snowfall, the show was a huge success, with "standing room only" signs posted.

Philadelphians had already seen an official mission of Japanese samurai diplomats seven years earlier. But Japan was still an exotic and mysterious, newly-opened nation, and no one had ever seen ordinary Japanese, or anything remotely resembling the Imperial Japanese Troupe. Audiences went wild over the performers, with their unique top-spinning acts and "butterfly tricks" (using fans to levitate origami butterflies). On March 15, the *Philadelphia Inquirer* declared that "everybody should see the 'Japs.' It is the popular and fashionable idea just now."

Americans in general fawned over the

たちは芸人の独特な
こま回しや（扇子であ
おいで折り紙の蝶々
を浮揚させる）「蝶々
の技」に熱狂した。3
月15日付の『フィラデ
ルフィア・インクワイ
アラー』紙は、「みん
なジャップたちを見
るべし。ちょうど今、人
気ではやりだ」と断言
した。

総じてアメリカ人は日
本人をちやほやした。
地元新聞の記事や一
座のマネージャーで
ある高野広八の日記
からは、フィラデルフ
ィアにおいてお偉方
が一座を大いにもて
なし、造幣局などの市
内見物に連れ出して
いたことが分かる。日
本人たちは、馬が引く
消防トラックの蒸気ポ
ンプや8階建てビルなどを見て、西洋の
科学技術に魅了された。男たちは、とり
わけ広八は、アメリカ女性に夢中で、3月
11日には親切にも誰かが一座の男たち
をフィラデルフィアの売春街に連れて行
った。

新聞の切り抜きや芝居のビラ以外に、リ
ズリー先生の私生活に関する情報は少
ない。しかしながら1867年には、すでに
お祖父さんになっていた。というのもリ
ズリーの息子のジョンに2人の子供が
いたからである。ジョン（とヘンリー）は
フィラデルフィアの有名なコンチネンタ
ル・ホテルで働いていた。そこでジョン

Sumidagawa Koman with book in hand.
The Library Company of Philadelphia

Japanese. From local newspaper articles and the diary of Takano Hirohachi, the troupe's manager, we know that in Philadelphia they were wined and dined by the city's high and mighty, and given tours of the city, including the local mint. They were fascinated by Western technology, such as steam pumps used by the local horse-drawn fire trucks, and eight-story buildings. The men, especially Hirohachi, were also fascinated by American women, and on March 11, someone kindly took them to the local red light district. Information on Risley's private life is scarce, other than from press clippings and playbills. In 1867, however, he was already a grandfather, for his son John had two children. John (and Henry) worked at Philadelphia's famous Continental Hotel, John as the proprietor of a newsstand and ticket vendor for events. It is no coincidence that the Continental Hotel was one of the first places the Japanese visited in the city.

After Philadelphia Risley and the Imperial Japanese Troupe performed throughout the

は新聞や催し物チケットの売場を開いていた。コンチネンタル・ホテルは日本人たちがフィラデルフィアで最初に訪れた場所の1つだったが、これは偶然ではない。

リズリーたちと帝国日本芸人一座はフィラデルフィアを離れ、北東部地方を回り、ワシントンD.C.ではホワイトハウスを見学し、アンドリュー・ジョンソン大統領に会った。5月のニューヨーク公演の頃には、芸人一座の人気は全国的なものになっていた。それから一座はパリ万国博覧会で公演するためにヨーロッパに渡り、ついにはロンドンやアムステルダム、マドリード、リスボンなどの首都で芸を披露した。一座は無数の群集の前に立ち、初期のジャポニズム人気を煽った。1868年にリズリーとの契約が終了すると、一座の半数は日本に戻った。他の日本人は西洋に残り、リズリーのところや他の一座に移ってしばらく演技を続け、それから歴史の中に消えていった。

1869年の初め、再びヨーロッパに行く前に、リズリーは帝国日本芸人一座の縮小版をフィラデルフィア公演で試してみた。しかしリズリーの幸運はすでに尽きかけていた。リズリーは1873年末にはフィラデルフィアにいて、驚くべきことに、日本に戻る計画があると公言していた。しかし彼の体調は思わしくなく、息子のジョンも同年初めに亡くなっていた。リズリーのスターである「小さなオーライ」はフィラデルフィア地域にいたのかもしれない。一説によると、彼は地元のディオン・ブラザーズの玉突き場でバーテンダーをしていたとのことである。

1874年の春、存命の息子ヘンリーが父

Northeast. In Washington, DC they toured the White House and met President Andrew Johnson. By the time the troupe opened in New York in May, it was a national phenomenon. The troupe then traveled to Europe for the Exposition Universelle in Paris, eventually performing in capitals such as London, Amsterdam, Madrid, and Lisbon. They appeared before crowds of thousands and helped fan the flames of nascent Japonisme.

When their contract with Risley expired at the end of 1868, half of the Japanese in the troupe returned to Japan. Others remained in the West, some performing a while longer with Risley or in other troupes and then vanishing into history.

Risley brought a stripped-down version of the troupe back to Philadelphia in early 1869, before touring Europe with them again, but his luck had started to run out. At the end of 1873 he was back in Philadelphia, and announcing, remarkably, that he planned to go back to Japan. But Risley was in poor health. His son John had died earlier in the year. His star, "Little All Right," may have still been in the area, but according to one report, he was working as a bartender in the local Dion Brothers' billiard room.

In the spring of 1874, Risley's surviving son, Henry, committed him to the lunatic asylum of the Blockley Almshouse, where he passed away on May 25. In the words of one contemporary writer, Risley was "broken down in constitution, and reduced from affluence to positive penury." He is buried in the now-closed Mt. Moriah cemetery and is today part of a nearly-lost history.

親をブロックリー養老院の精神病院に入れた。そしてリズリーは5月25日に亡くなった。当時の記者の1人によれば、リズリーは「体を壊し、金持ちだったのに、ひどい赤貧状態に転落していた」という。リズリーの亡骸は現在では閉鎖されているマウント・モライア墓地に葬られ、ほとんど失われた歴史の一部になった。リズリーが生み出した日本の曲芸に対する熱狂は第1次世界大戦まで続いたが、それから忘れ去られてしまったのである。

フレデリック・L・ショット
戸田徹子 訳

参考文献：
宮永孝『海を渡った幕末の曲芸団』(中公新書、1999)

The mania he created for Japanese acrobats would last until the First World War, and then be forgotten.

By Frederik L. Schodt

Selected Reference: Frederik L. Schodt, *Professor Risley and the Imperial Japanese Troupe: How an American Acrobat Introduced Circus to Japan—And Japan to the West* (Berkeley: Stone Bridge Press, 2012).

3.2 Ernest Fenollosa and Philadelphia: Treasures of Japanese Art
アーネスト・フェノロサ：日本美術の父

アーネスト・フェノロサ（1853－1908）は今から100年以上も前に、日本の伝統的な美術品の素晴らしさをアメリカおよび世界に知らせた「日本美術の父」といわれている人物である。フィラデルフィア美術館には彼が大切にした日本美術品百数十点が所蔵されている。いったいどのような事情によって、これらの貴重な美術品がフィラデルフィア美術館にもたらされたのであろうか。

Ernest Fenollosa (1853–1908) introduced the wonders of Japanese traditional art to America and the world more than one hundred years ago, and is known as "the father of Japanese art." Over one hundred works of Japanese art that he treasured are in the collection of the Philadelphia Museum of Art.

In 1876, when Fenollosa was twenty-three years old, he came to see the International Centennial Exhibition, held in Philadelphia to commemorate America's independence. There were many Japanese works of art displayed, and it was Fenollosa's first contact with the marvels of Japanese culture. This experience in Philadelphia was the starting point of Fenollosa's study of Japanese art. Two years later Fenollosa went to Japan with his wife Lizzie. As one of the so-called *o-yatoi*, or foreigners invited to work in Japan by the Japanese government, Fenollosa was responsible for teaching philosophy at Tokyo University. While in Japan he became captivated by the beauty of Japanese art, which had been neglected after the Meiji Restoration in Japan. Together with Okakura Kakuzō (a.k.a.

Ernest Fenollosa, c. 1890. Wikimedia Commons

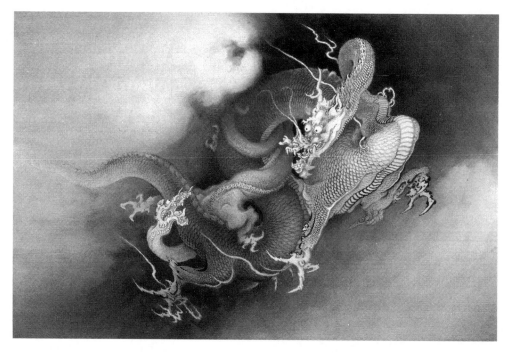

Two Dragons in Clouds by Kanō Hōgai, c. 1885. Philadelphia Museum of Art

フェノロサは23歳の時、フィラデルフィアで開かれた独立100周年記念万国博覧会を見学している。ここには日本から多くの美術品も展示されており、フェノロサはこの時初めて日本文化の素晴らしさに接したのである。1876年のことであった。つまり、フィラデルフィアはフェノロサの日本美術研究の原点だったことになる。2年後、フェノロサは日本政府に招かれて妻リジーとともに日本へ渡った。彼はいわゆるお雇い外国人の1人として東京大学教授となり哲学を担当した。この間、彼は日本では明治維新後、見捨てられていた日本美術のすばらしさに注目し、岡倉天心らの協力者とともに、日本美術の復興と啓蒙に努めた。フェノロサは日本の伝統的な美術の再発見者だといえる。岡倉天心はフェノロ

Tenshin), Fenollosa strove to bring about a renaissance and enrichment of Japanese art. One could say that Fenollosa rediscovered traditional Japanese art. Okakura, a student of Fenollosa's at Tokyo University, became the leader of the movement to create a new Japanese painting style (*Nihonga*), which was rooted in tradition.

Fenollosa also collected many works of Japanese art and sent them to America. When Fenollosa returned to America, he was appointed the first head of the Asian art section at the Museum of Fine Arts, Boston, and continued to collect and study Japanese art. In 1908, while traveling through Europe, Fenollosa died suddenly in England. In accordance with his wishes, part of his ashes

サの教えを受けて、伝統を基礎にした新しい日本画を生み出す運動の指導者となった人物である。

またフェノロサは日本美術品を多数収集し、アメリカに送った。やがてアメリカに帰ったフェノロサは、ボストン美術館の初代東洋部長に任命され、さらに多くの日本美術品の収集と研究に当たっている。1908年、彼はヨーロッパ旅行に出掛け、その途中のイギリスで亡くなった。遺骨の一部は生前の希望によって、日本の三井寺にも埋葬された。

フェノロサの2人の子供であるカノーとブレンダは日本で生まれた。長男カノーは7歳で亡くなったが、長女ブレンダは成人してブリンマー大学に入学した。後にボストンのマサチューセッツ工科大学でも学んでいる。その後フィラデルフィアに来て、実業家モンキュアー・ビドルと結婚した。ビドル家はフィラデルフィアではよく知られた実業家一族である。

ブレンダは父の芸術的素養を受け継いでか、造園設計に関心を示し、それを仕事にした。そして彼女は1941年と1957年の2度に渡り、「父アーネスト・フェノロサの記念のために」日本美術品を100点あまりフィラデルフィア美術館に寄贈した。フェノロサが育てた有名な画家狩野芳崖の「雪柳雉子図」「飛竜児戯図」、同じく橋本雅邦の「毘沙門天図」「観音調停図」などの傑作がこの中に含まれている。その他、火鉢や袈裟など、フェノロサが日本で使用した日常生活品なども入っている。(フェノロサは出家していたので、僧の衣服である袈裟も持っていた。)

ブレンダは1959年に亡くなりフィラデ

was brought to Japan and buried at Miidera Temple.

Fenollosa's two children, Kano and Brenda, were born in Japan. His son Kano died at age seven, but his daughter Brenda grew to adulthood and enrolled at Bryn Mawr College. Later she also studied at the Massachusetts Institute of Technology. She subsequently married the Philadelphia businessman Moncure Biddle, and they settled in Philadelphia. The Biddles were a well-known family in Philadelphia.

Brenda followed in her father's artistic footsteps, and she developed an interest in the field of landscape architecture, which she pursued professionally for a time. In 1941 and again in 1957, Brenda Fenollosa Biddle donated some one hundred Japanese works of art in memory of her father, Ernest Fenollosa, to the Philadelphia Museum of Art. Included among these donated works are such masterpieces as *Pheasant on a Snowy Branch* and *Two Dragons in Clouds* by the famous artist Kanō Hōgai, whom Fenollosa had supported, as well as two paintings by Hashimoto Gahō, *Bishamonten Pursuing an Oni* and *The Intercession of Kannon*. Also included were personal items that Fenollosa used in his daily life in Japan, such as a hibachi, and costumes. Fenollosa had become a Buddhist, so there are also Buddhist vestments.

Brenda Fenollosa Biddle died in 1959 and is buried at St. Thomas' Episcopal Church in Fort Washington, a suburb of Philadelphia. In 1978 her eldest son Owen Biddle also donated about forty pieces from the collection of his grandmother Lizzie Fenollosa to the

ルフィア郊外のフォート・ワシンントン
の聖トマス教会に埋葬された。そして
1978年、ブレンダの長男のオーエン・ビ
ドルは祖母のフェノロサ夫人（リジー）
のコレクションから、フェノロサの遺品
40点余りをフィラデルフィア美術館に寄
附した。こうして、合わせて百数十点の
日本美術品がフィラデルフィア美術館に
所蔵されるに至ったのである。これらの
美術品は、この美術館が所蔵する数多
い日本美術品のうちでも、重要な一部分
をなしている。

1997年秋、日本に茨城県立岡倉天心記
念美術館が開館するにあたっては、フィ
ラデルフィア美術館も大いに協力した。
天心の師匠であるフェノロサが結ぶ縁
である。開館特別展には、狩野芳崖と橋
本雅邦の上記4点の絵が送られて展示
されたのである。

今井雅晴

Philadelphia Museum of Art. Thus, there are over one hundred forty works of Japanese art from Fenollosa in the Philadelphia Museum of Art, forming an important part of the museum's Japanese holdings.

In the fall of 1997, the Philadelphia Museum of Art participated in the opening exhibition of the new museum dedicated to Fenollosa's student and colleague, the Okakura Tenshin Memorial Museum, in Ibaraki Prefecture. The four paintings by Kanō Hōgai and Hashimoto Gahō formerly in Fenollosa's possession were sent to Japan for the opening exhibition.

By Masaharu Imai
Translated by Felice Fischer

Selected References: Felice Fischer, "Meiji Painting from the Fenollosa Collection" *Philadelphia Museum of Art Bulletin* 88: 375 (Fall 1992): 1–24; Christopher Benfey, *The Great Wave: Gilded Age Misfits, Japanese Eccentrics, and the Opening of Old Japan* (New York: Random House, 2004); Karatani Kōjin, "Japan as Art Museum: Okakura Tenshin and Fenollosa," in *A History of Modern Japanese Aesthetics*, ed. and trans. Michael F. Marra (Honolulu: University of Hawaii Press, 2001), pp. 43–52.

If you go: The Philadelphia Museum of Art, 26th Street and Benjamin Franklin Parkway, Philadelphia, PA 19130.

3.3 John Luther Long:
The Metamorphosis of Madame Butterfly
ジョン・ルーサー・ロング：フィラデルフィアで構想された『蝶々夫人』

『蝶々夫人（マダム・バタフライ）』の物語とテーマは1世紀にわたって、日本女性だけでなく、東アジア女性やアジア系アメリカ女性に対する人々の見方をかたち作ってきたが、この蝶々夫人の話を初めて世に出した人物はジョン・ルーサー・ロング（1861 - 1927）であり、もともとフィラデルフィアで構想されたものであった。

ロングは弁護士で、1861年にペンシルベニア州ハノーバーで生まれ、ラファイエット大学で教育を受けた。ロングの蝶々夫人物語は非常に好評だったので、すぐに劇やオペラの登場人物となった。ヒロインにはよくあるように、自分を犠牲し、最後は自殺するという姿をとるようになっていく。しかし、ロングの蝶々夫人は決して死にはしなかった。その後、年月を経て、ニューヨークのブロードウェイで、デイビッド・ヘンリー・ホワング作成の『M・バタフライ』（1989）で皮肉られた現代版ができた今日でさえ、蝶々夫人は我々を魅了し悩ませ続けている。

1853年にマシュー・C・ペリー提督が黒船で日本に来て以来、西洋はこの遠い国日本をもっとよく知りたいと願っていた。その後の数十年のうちで素晴らしい成功を収めたものの１つに『お菊さん』（1888）がある。それは長崎という港町への旅に基づく、ピエール・ロティ（本名ジュリアン・マリー・ビオー、1850 - 1923）の小説である。ロティは日本の遊女を現地妻とする「仮の結婚」をした経験があり、それが西洋の男

Madame Butterfly, a story and a motif that have shaped the way we view women of Japan and indeed of all East Asia and Asian America for a century, was imagined in Philadelphia. The author responsible for first presenting this tale to the world was John Luther Long (1861–1927), a lawyer born in Hanover, Pennsylvania, and educated at Lafayette College. Of such appeal was the narrative that soon Butterfly transformed into a theater and opera character, sacrificing herself, as such heroines often did, in an act of suicide. Long's Butterfly, however, did not in any sense die. She continues to charm and trouble us, even when transplanted to the ironies of David Henry Hwang's *M. Butterfly* (1989).

From the time that Commodore Perry's ships approached Japan's shore in 1853 the West desired to know more of that far-off country. One of the sensational successes of the ensuing decades was *Madame Chrysanthème* (1888), a novel based on the journey to the port city of Nagasaki by one Pierre Loti (born Julien Marie Viaud in 1850). Loti had participated in a "temporary marriage" to a Japanese courtesan, a type of arrangement that had piqued the curiosity of Western men. John Luther Long fed the public's preoccupation via his novella *Miss Cherry-Blossom of Tokyo*, issued in 1895 by the Philadelphia publisher Lippincott. The character B.F. Pinkerton appears here briefly, suggesting that Long already knew the story

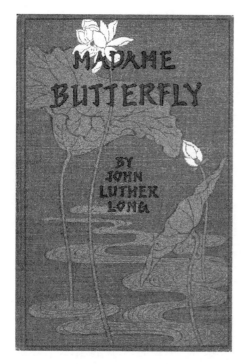

Cover of Long's book, *Madame Butterfly*. The Franklin Inn Club

性たちの好奇心をそそった。その後、ロングが1895年にフィラデルフィアの出版社リッピンコットから『東京の桜嬢』という短編小説を出版し、人々の好奇心をさらに満たしていった。この小説には、すでにB・F・ピンカートンという人物がわずかながら登場していることから、ロングは後に自分を有名してくれるお蝶さんの構想を、すでに心の中に描いていたに違いない。

ロング自身は日本へ旅行したことはなかったが、姉のサラ・ジェイン（ジェニー）・コレルから日本の話を聞いていた。ジェニーはメソジスト監督教会の宣教師で、1873年に横浜に到着し、1892年に夫のアービン・ヘンリー・コレル博士

that would become his claim to fame.

Long himself never traveled to Japan, but he learned of it from his elder sister Sarah Jane (Jennie) Correll, a Methodist Episcopal missionary who arrived in Yokohama in 1873 and was transferred to Nagasaki in 1892 with her husband, Dr. Irvin Henry Correll. Dr. Correll was ordered to take a medical leave back in Philadelphia in 1897, and it is at this point that Jennie Correll recalled filling in the details of the tragic story of one Cho-san for her brother. The plight of Cho-san and her baby, deserted by her lover, provoked the sympathy of the Christian woman who lived on the opposite hill. As John Luther Long penned the story, Jennie Correll corrected the particulars for accuracy. Madame Butterfly, published in *The Century Magazine* of January 1898, hit a chord with the American audience, and was included in a book of Long's Japanophile stories that sold well. Long quit the law when his writing became profitable. His literary ambitions are evidenced by his role as one of the founding members of The Franklin Inn Club, a private club that has operated since 1902. It is located on Camac Street, near Locust Street, and holds copies of Long's works.

Woven into the story of Madame Butterfly are all the things that were known or believed about Japan at the time from travel books and essays, learned and otherwise: filial piety toward ancestors, reincarnation, the Japanese house as a paper-walled place of no privacy, and Japanese women, all helpless, hapless, and adorable. The story depicts Cho-Cho-San as a laughing, silly girl, who shakes her child violently and speaks "Southern" pidgin.

と共に長崎に転勤した。コレル博士
は1897年に、フィラデルフィアに戻
り療養休暇をとるように命じられて
いる。ジェニーの記憶では、お蝶さん
という女性の悲劇的な物語を弟に詳
しく語ったのは、この時のことであっ
た。愛人に捨てられたお蝶さんとその
子供の苦境は、海の向こうに住むキ
リスト教徒の女性たちの同情心をか
き立てた。ロングが物語を書き、ジェ
ニーが正確さを期して細部を修正し
た。1898年1月の『センチュリー・マガ
ジン』に発表された「蝶々夫人」はアメ
リカ人の心を打ち、ロングの親日的な
物語を集めた本に収められた。本はよ
く売れた。著作が売れるようになると、
ロングは弁護士を辞めた。ロングの
文学的野心は、1902年から活動を続
けている私的なクラブ「フランクリン・イ
ン」の創立者の1人となったことからも
分かる。フランクリン・インはローカスト
通りに近いカマック通りにあり、ロングの
著作を所蔵している。

蝶々夫人の物語には、旅行案内書や随
筆、学問的なもの、学問的でないものな
どを基にして、その当時、日本について
知られていたことや信じられていたこと
など、ありとあらゆることが織り込まれて
いた。すなわち、孝行、輪廻、紙で仕切ら
れたプライバシーのない日本の家、まっ
たく無力で不運、でも愛らしい日本女性
といったものなどである。蝶々さんは自
分の子供を乱暴に揺さぶり、「南部なま
り」の変な言葉をしゃべる、嘲笑すべき
愚かな女として描かれている。蝶々さん
は西洋と日本の結合の象徴でもあり、ピ
ンカートンから論理的に考えることや個
人としてくつろぐことを教えられ、またア
メリカでは離婚ができないと信じ込まさ
れたのであった。ピンカートンは、まった

John Luther Long. The Franklin inn Club

Cho-Cho-San is also a symbol of the union of the West and Japan, having been taught by Pinkerton to reason, to relax in private, and to believe in an America with no divorce. Pinkerton is an utterly heartless cad.

On March 5, 1900, David Belasco (1853–1931) staged *Madame Butterfly, A Tragedy of Japan*, at the Herald Square Theater in New York. The production of Belasco's play in London the next month helped bring the story to the attention of Giacomo Puccini, whose opera version, *Madama Butterfly*, debuted in Milan in 1904. Belasco had preserved many elements of Long's tale, but the ending was changed. Long's Butterfly had, after becoming aware that Pinkerton was back with his wife and planning to take her young son to the States, attempted suicide, but was rescued by the maid and left town with the boy. The successful suicide became a key element of the opera, however. The Philadelphia premiere of *Madama Butterfly* took place in 1907 at the Academy of Music,

く冷酷で卑劣な男である。

1900年3月5日、デイビッド・ベラスコ（1853 - 1931）がニューヨークのヘラルド・スクエア劇場で『蝶々夫人―日本の悲劇』を上演した。翌月、ベラスコの劇がロンドンで上演された時、ジャコモ・プッチーニがその物語に注目した。そして1904年に、プッチーニのオペラ『蝶々夫人』がミラノで初演されたのである。ベラスコはロングの書いた話の内容をかなり残してはいたが、結末部分は変更した。ロングの蝶々夫人は、ピンカートンが妻と一緒に来て、蝶々夫人の幼い息子をアメリカへ連れて行こうとしていることに気付き、自殺を試みるが、女中に助けられ、子供を連れて町を去る。一方、オペラの『蝶々夫人』では、自殺が重要な構成要素となった。1907年のフィラデルフィアでの『蝶々夫人』初演では、ミュージック・アカデミーにおいてエンリコ・カルーソがピンカートンを演じた。

ロング自身は、この物語が自分の代表作だとは思っていなかった。1927年に亡くなるまで、ロングはフィラデルフィアのエルキンズ・パークに住んでいたが、ピンカートンや蝶々夫人のモデルについて、決して明かすことはなかった。コーネル大学のアーサー・グルース教授の研究では、モデルはウィリアム・B・フランクリン（1868 - 1942）という名の海軍の軍人と、長崎の無名の芸者であるとしている。また野田和子氏は、スコットランドの商人トーマス・グラバー（1838 - 1911）と日本人妻、山村ツル（1848 - 1899）のひ孫であるが、野田氏はツルがグラバーの妻となる前にした結婚の話に、変更や脚色が加えられたものであると信じている。蝶々夫人にモデル争いがあるということは、その話

with Enrico Caruso as Pinkerton.

Long himself did not consider the Madame Butterfly story his best work. He resided in Elkins Park until his death in 1927, never having disclosed the models for Pinkerton or Butterfly. Research by Cornell University's Arthur Groos points to a Navy man by the name of William B. Franklin (1868–1942) and a nameless courtesan of Nagasaki. Kazuko Noda, the great-great-granddaughter of Tsuru Yamamura (1848–1899), wife of the Scottish merchant Thomas Glover (1838–1911), believes that it was her ancestor's story of a previous marriage, with changes and elaboration. That there would be rival claims to the identity of the model for Madame Butterfly speaks to the power of the story and its history—the history of the West's thoughts on Japan and its precious, loyal women.

By Linda H. Chance

Selected References: Arthur Groos, "Madame Butterfly: The story," *Cambridge Opera Journal* 3:2 (Jul. 1991): 125–58; Cecilia Segawa Seigle, "A Samurai's Daughter," *Opera News* 58:8 (Jan. 1994); Yoko Kawaguchi, *Butterfly's Sisters: The Geisha in Western Culture* (New Haven and London: Yale University Press, 2010).

If you go: The Franklin Inn Club, 205 South Camac Street, Philadelphia, PA 19107.

Suburban home of John Luther Long, 1250 Ashbourne Road, Elkins Park, PA 19027.

やその背景にある歴史―西洋が日本な
らびに可愛らしくて忠実な日本女性を
どのように捉えてきたかの歴史―が重
視されていることを示している。

リンダ・チャンス
今井元子/戸田徹子 訳

3.4   Niō-mon: The Japanese Temple Gate in Fairmount Park

仁王門：フェアモント公園にあった山門

フェアモント公園にある松風荘の敷地には、以前、「日本のパゴダ（仏塔）」として人気のあった建築物が、約50年間（1905‐1955）存在していた。そのパゴダが1955年に火事で焼失した時には、「フィラデルフィアで最もよく知られ、最も愛された歴史的建造物の1つ」と新聞に書かれた（『フィラデルフィア・インクワイアラー』紙、1955年5月7日）。この「パゴダ」は、実際には寺の山門で、高さが45フィート（13.7メートル）あり、屋根が外側に曲線を帯びて広がっていたので、パゴダのように見えたのだった。この山門は紆余曲折を経てフィラデルフィアに到着したのだが、その歴史的背景の全容が解明されることはないかもしれない。

山門は1903年から1904年にかけて日本からアメリカに運ばれた。1904年にミズーリ州セントルイスで開催されたルイジアナ購入記念万国博覧会（セントルイス万国博覧会）で、日本政府の展示物の一部として建てられたものであった。K・サノという人物が所有しており、山門を日本美術の小さなギャラリーにしていたようである。万国博覧会で配布されたサノ氏執筆のパンフレットには、「仁王門」は常陸国フルマチ村の清音寺という古いお寺の山門として建てられたと記されている。筑波大学の今井雅晴教授の最近の研究により、清音寺は茨城県水戸市の近くにある下古内（しもふるうち）と現在呼ばれている地にまだ存在していることが判明した。

The present site of the Japanese House and Garden in Fairmount Park was occupied for about fifty years (1905–55) by a popular structure known as the "Japanese Pagoda." At the time of its destruction by fire, newspapers referred to it as "one of Philadelphia's best known and best loved landmarks." (*Philadelphia Inquirer*, May 7, 1955). This "pagoda" was in fact a temple gate. Its height of forty-five feet and its splayed, curved roof gave it the appearance of a pagoda. It arrived in Philadelphia via a roundabout route, the entire story of which may never be known.

The gate was exported from Japan to the United States in 1903–04 and erected in St. Louis, Missouri as part of the Official Japanese Empire Exhibit at the Louisiana Purchase Exposition of 1904. It was apparently owned by a Mr. K. Sano and operated by him as a small gallery of Japanese art. According to the pamphlet Sano wrote and distributed at the Exposition, the "Nio-Mon" was built as the main entrance to the ancient temple of Seionji in the village of Furumachi, Hitachi Province. Research by Professor Masaharu Imai, emeritus of Tsukuba University, has revealed that the Seionji temple is still in existence in present-day Shimo-Furuuchi, near Mito, Ibaraki Prefecture. The temple gate was originally commissioned in 1344 by Satake Yoshiatsu (1311–1362), a feudal lord, in memory of his father, and it was restored around 1600. According to Sano, Lord Satake

Niō-mon Temple Gate in Fairmount Park. Photo by Bruce Murray, Sr. (1893-1969)
Copyright: Shawn M. Murray www.brucemurray.com

山門はもともと1344年に佐竹一族の第10代当主佐竹義篤（1311‐1362）が、亡き父親の記念碑として造らせたもので、1600年頃に再建された。サノ氏によると、佐竹公は山門を建立し装飾するために、著名な建築家、画家、彫刻家を雇ったということである。セントルイス万国博覧会で撮影された写真には、山門の2階のギャラリーに、清音寺から運ばれてきた美術品が展示されているのが写っている。そのうち幾つかの仏像は、14世紀の狛犬一対や仏陀座像と共に、今でもフェアモント公園委員会の所蔵品として、フィラデルフィア美術館に収められている。この山門の名前の由来となった仁王（仏陀を守る役割をする門番）の像

employed well-known architects, painters, and sculptors to construct and decorate the gate. A photograph taken at the St. Louis Exposition shows some of the art works from Seionji temple installed in the gallery of the upper story of the gate. Several of the Buddhist sculptures, including a pair of fourteenth century guardian lions and a seated Buddha, are still in the collection of the Fairmount Park Commission and housed at the Philadelphia Museum of Art. The Niō, or Two Benevolent Guardians, after which the gate (mon) was named, were destroyed by fire.

は、2体とも火事で焼失してしまった。

セントルイス万国博覧会が終わると、山門は解体され売りに出された。そこでフェアモント公園芸術協会が公園への寄贈品として受け取るという条件で、フィラデルフィアに住むジョン・H・コンバース氏とサミュエル・M・ボークレーン氏の2人が購入した。両氏はセントルイス万国博覧会に出品したボールドウィン機関車会社の共同経営者で、フェアモント公園芸術協会のメンバーだった。山門を寄付した2人は、できるだけ早くフィラデルフィアの地に山門を移築してもらいたいと熱望した。しかし予想されたことではあったが、適切な敷地の選択や、再建・維持・治安にかかる費用の交渉が手間取り、さらには他の理事や市の役人の干渉もあって、建造は遅れ、最終的に建物と周りの庭園が完成したのは1908年になってからのことだった。

At the close of the Louisiana Purchase Exposition, the temple gate was dismantled and offered for sale. It was purchased by two Philadelphians, John H. Converse and Samuel M. Vauclain, with the understanding that the Fairmount Park Art Association would accept it as a gift to donate to the Park. Converse and Vauclain were partners in the Baldwin Locomotive Works, which had also exhibited at the St. Louis Exposition, and both were members of the Fairmount Park Art Association. The donors were eager to have the temple gate reassembled as quickly as possible in Philadelphia, but as might be expected, the selection of an appropriate site, negotiations over the cost of re-erection, maintenance and security, as well as the meddling of other board members and city officials, resulted in delaying the final completion of the installation of both the building and the surrounding gardens until 1908.

Pair of guardian lions from Niō-mon Temple Gate.
Philadelphia Museum of Art

Mr. Sano was contracted to assist in the reassembly of the structure. Professor Ernest Fenollosa, Curator of the Japanese Collections at the Museum of Fine Arts, Boston from 1890 to 1897, was asked to come and make recommendations on the selection of a site. On November 10, 1905, the site at the intersection of South Horticultural Drive and Lansdowne Drive was chosen, near an existing lotus pond. Mr. Vauclain defrayed the cost of the reconstruction, around

サノ氏は建物の再組み立ての契約をしていた。アーネスト・フェノロサ教授は1890年から1897年までボストン美術館の日本美術の学芸員だったが、フィラデルフィアで、敷地を選んでくれるように頼まれた。1905年11月10日に、南ホーティカルチャー通りとランズダウン通りが交差する地点が選定されたが、この場所は現存する蓮池の近くになる。ボークレーン氏は1905年に約3000ドルの再建費用を負担している。建物には、黒い下地の上に赤い色が塗られた12本の丸木の柱が使われた。この柱が、回縁のついた2階と瓦葺きの入母屋造りの屋根を支えていた。山門の移築は1905年から1906年にかけての冬に完了した。

山門の周囲は、Y・ムトウという人物の設計で日本風に造園された。費用はジョン・T・モリス氏が提供した。かつてモリスは自分の土地に日本風の庭園を造ったことがあり、その土地はいまモリス森林公園となっている。山門の造園計画には蓮池が含まれていた。モリス氏はその場所を、1876年の万国博覧会の時に日本村があった場所だと誤解していたが、実際には博覧会の救護所が置かれた場所だった。造園では設計上「山」が不可欠で、山を造成するために数トンの石と敷石と表土が使われた。できあがった庭園は1909年2月にオープンした。今日でも、蓮池を作るために設けた堰の輪郭が分かる。

山門の移築が完了するとすぐに、山門を破壊行為から守ることが大きな課題となった。1909年に、2体の仁王の玉眼が剥ぎ取られてしまった。このような治安上の問題から、付属の美術品はフィラデルフィア美術館に納められた。山門は公

$3,000 in 1905. The structure consisted of twelve round wooden columns, painted red with black bases. These supported an upper story with a circumferential balcony, and a tiled *irimoya* roof. The reconstruction of the temple gate was completed during the winter of 1905–06.

The landscaping around the gate was done in Japanese fashion, according to the designs of one Y. Muto. The funding was provided by John T. Morris, who had installed Japanese garden features at his own estate, now the Morris Arboretum. The landscaping at the temple gate incorporated the lotus pond, which Morris mistakenly believed was the site of the Japanese Village during the 1876 Centennial Exposition but was in fact the First Aid Station locale. The landscaping required several tons of stone, flagging, and topsoil to form a "mountain" as one element of the design. The resulting garden was dedicated in February 1909. The outlines of the dam that enclosed the lotus pond can still be seen today.

Apparently vandalism and security became a problem almost immediately upon completion of the gate installation. The glass eyes of the two guardians were broken away in 1909. Because of these security problems, the accompanying collection of artifacts was placed at the Philadelphia Museum of Art. The gate underwent complete rehabilitation in 1936, using craftsmen employed by the Works Projects Administration (WPA). But the structure suffered continuous neglect and vandalism over the next two decades. The final event in the Niō-mon gate's history was its complete destruction by fire on the evening of May 6, 1955. Ironically, scaffolding

共事業促進局（WPA）が雇った職人によって、1936年に完全修復されたが、その後の20年間は全く手入れがなされず破壊行為にさらされていた。1955年5月6日の夜、仁王門は火事で全焼し、その歴史に幕が引かれることとなった。皮肉なことに、本格的な修理の準備で、建物の周囲に足場が組まれていたため、その足場を使って破壊者たちが建物に接近できたのであった。

しかしながら、山門が1955年までフェアモント公園に存在していたという歴史的事実は重要だった。その事実があったゆえに、後に、ニューヨーク近代美術館で展示された日本家屋と庭園（後の松風荘）を、フィラデルフィアに移築しようという案が1956年に生まれたからである。

チャールズ・A・エバーズ
今井元子/戸田徹子 訳

had been erected around the entire structure in preparation for a complete renovation, but that provided the access for the vandals.

The fact that the temple gate stood in Fairmount Park until 1955 proved to be of great importance, however. It became the inspiration for the relocation to Philadelphia in 1956 of the Japanese House and Garden, Shōfūsō, after its exhibition at the Museum of Modern Art in New York.

By Charles A. Evers

Selected Reference: Clay Lancaster, *The Japanese Influence in America* (New York: Walton H. Rawls, 1963; reprint, New York: Abbeville Press, 1983).

If you go: Lansdowne Drive, West Fairmount Park, near the site of the Japanese House and Garden, Philadelphia, PA.

3.5 Sunkaraku-an: A Teahouse for Philadelphia
寸暇楽庵：フィラデルフィア美術館にある茶室

アメリカ人が初めて日本の茶道に直に触れたのは、1876年にフィラデルフィアで開催された独立100周年記念万国博覧会の時であった。そこでは茶会の道具のみが展示された。その後の1893年のシカゴ万国博覧会では、日本の展示の一部として実物の茶室が設けられた。バジル・チェンバレンは『日本の事物』（1890）において、茶会を「ティ・セレモニー」と名付け、英語で茶会について説明した最初の人となった。しかし、アメリカ人の茶会に対する関心を最も高めたのは、当時ボストン美術館東洋部長であった岡倉覚三（岡倉天心、1862 - 1913）が著した『茶の本』（1906）であった。

フランク・ロイド・ライトの著書と建築物によって、アメリカ人の日本建築に対する認識は大いに高まっていた。それゆえ、フィラデルフィア美術館の館長で建築史家でもあったフィスク・キンバル氏が本物の日本の茶室を手に入れ、アメリカの美術館で最初の常設展示にしたいと思ったことは、驚くにあたらない。

東京の『国民新聞』に掲載された記事（1928年9月）には、フィラデルフィアのために茶室を手に入れようとしている状況が、次のように書かれている。「アメリカのペンシルベニア州フィラデルフィアの大富豪であるH・F・ジェイン氏は、最近、茶室を入手した。その茶室とは仰木敬一郎（別名、魯堂）氏の邸宅の敷地内に建つ《寸暇楽》で、ジェイン氏の丁重な依頼に仰木氏が応えたものである。この美しい建物は、ペンシルベニア博物

Americans first came into direct contact with the Japanese art of tea here in Philadelphia at the 1876 Centennial Exposition, where utensils for the tea ceremony were exhibited. The 1893 Chicago World's Columbian Exposition included an actual teahouse as part of the Japanese display. The first English-speaking author to describe tea gatherings and to name the occasion "tea ceremony" was Basil Chamberlain in his 1890 work, *Things Japanese*. But the prime stimulus to American interest in tea ceremony was the publication in 1906 of *The Book of Tea* by the then Curator of Oriental Art at the Museum of Fine Arts, Boston, Okakura Kakuzō (1862–1913, also known as Tenshin).

The work of Frank Lloyd Wright, both as an author and as an architect, did much to heighten American awareness of Japanese architecture. So it is not surprising that Fiske Kimball, director of the Philadelphia Museum of Art, and an architectural historian, would want to obtain the first authentic Japanese teahouse for permanent exhibition in any American museum.

The circumstances of the acquisition of a teahouse for Philadelphia were described in an article published in *Kokumin Shinbun*, Tokyo, in September 1928: "A short time ago, Mr. H. F. Jayne, a millionaire of Philadelphia, PA., U.S.A., acquired, in response to his courteous request, from Mr. Keiichirō Ōgi,

Teahouse Sunkaraku (Evanescent Joys), designed by Ōgi Rodō. Philadelphia Museum of Art

館の中に移築される予定で、移転の準備は9月15日から始まる」。

アメリカの「大富豪」ホレイス・ジェインは、フィラデルフィア美術館の前身であるペンシルベニア博物館の東洋美術部門の部長でもあった。館長に命じられて、ジェインはフィラデルフィアにできた新しい美術館に納める建築物を手に入れるため、1928年夏、日本と中国を旅行した。ジェインは茶室ばかりでなく日本の寺も見つけだし、この時に手に入れた茶室と寺は、今もフィラデルフィア美術館に設置されている。

「寸暇楽」(「つかの間の喜び」)という名の茶室は、仰木敬一郎(1863‐1941)茶道名の魯堂でよく知られている)が所有していた。仰木は茶室や田舎の別荘を専門とする建築家であったが、魯堂を名乗る茶道の師匠であり、茶道具の収集家でもあった。魯堂は、蜂須賀家が

alias Rodō, the Sunkaraku Tea Room which stands on the premises of his mansion. This esthetic structure is going to be re-erected in the Pennsylvania Museum, and preparations for its removal shall be commenced from the 15th of September next."

The American "millionaire" Horace Jayne was in fact the Curator of Oriental Art at the Pennsylvania Museum, as the Philadelphia Museum of Art was then called. Jayne had been sent by the museum's director on a trip to Japan and China in the summer of 1928 to acquire architectural units for the new museum building in Philadelphia. Jayne found not only the teahouse, but also a Japanese temple building, both of which are installed in the museum today.

The teahouse, named Sunkaraku ("Evanescent Joys" or "Momentary Leisure"), belonged to Ōgi Keiichirō (1863–1941,

所有していた古い茶室の木材を使用して、1917年に東京の自宅の敷地内に「寸暇楽庵」を建てた。軒下に掛けられている扁額の「寸暇楽」という3文字の漢字は、出雲の大名で茶道に造詣が深いことで有名な松平不昧（1751‐1818）の書であると言われている。

主人がすべての準備を終えるまで、客は「寄り付き」と呼ばれる小部屋で待つ。そこから「つくばい」を通って、茶室へと石の小道が続いている。茶室の裏には小さな準備室がある。そして茶室自体は2枚の畳と1枚の台目で構成されている。台目とは、主人がお茶をたてるために座る、4分の3の大きさの畳である。主人の席にある曲線を帯びた中央の柱は、樹皮を付けたままの南天である。床柱はこれも、樹皮が付いたままの赤松で

better known by his tea name, Rodō), an architect specializing in country villas and teahouses. Rodō was also a tea master and collector. He had erected the Sunkaraku-an teahouse for himself in 1917 on the grounds of his residence in Tokyo, using elements from an older teahouse that had belonged to the Hachisuka family. The three-character inscription "Sunkaraku" on the signboard under the eaves is said to be by Matsudaira Fumai (1751–1818), daimyo of Izumo Province and renowned tea connoisseur.

There is a small *yoritsuki* waiting room for the guests to gather until the host has completed all the preparations. A stone path leads from there past a *tsukubai*, or stone wash basin, to the teahouse itself. The teahouse has a small preparation room at the back, and the

ある。

東京における最期の茶会は1928年9月13日に催された。魯堂が主人で、客には当時の三井財閥の長である団琢磨男爵夫妻、茶道に造詣が深く歴史家でもある高橋義雄（茶道名、箒庵）が含まれていた。その後、茶室は解体され、5つの箱に梱包されて、船でフィラデルフィアに送られることになる。1929年の株暴落に始まる大恐慌と、大戦中の日本に対する敵意のため、日本の茶室を建てるというフィスク・キンバル氏の計画が最終的に実現したのは、1957年になってからのことだった。

フェリス・フィッシャー
今井元子/戸田徹子 訳

tearoom itself is two tatami mats and one *daime*, or three-quarter size mat, for the host to sit while making the tea. The curved central post at the host's seat is a section of nandina, bark still intact. The main post of the tokonoma alcove is red pine, also with its bark intact.

A final tea ceremony took place in Tokyo on September 13, 1928, with Rodō as host, and the guests including the then head of the Mitsui conglomerate, Baron Dan Takuma and his wife, as well as the tea connoisseur and historian, Takahashi Yoshio (tea name, "Sōan"). The teahouse was disassembled and shipped to Philadelphia in five crates. Because of the financial Depression caused by the 1929 stock market crash and the hostilities during the war, Fiske Kimball's plan for the Japanese teahouse was not completed until 1957.

By Felice Fischer

Selected References: Christine M.E. Guth, *Art, Tea, and Industry: Masuda Takashi and the Mitsui Circle* (Princeton, NJ: Princeton University Press, 1993); Jean Gordon Lee, "SUN KA RAKU," *Philadelphia Museum of Art Bulletin* 53:256 (Winter, 1958): 39–42.

If you go: Philadelphia Museum of Art, 26th Street and Benjamin Franklin Parkway, Philadelphia, PA 19130.

Learning From Each Other:
People-to-People
人の交流

4

Japanese in Philadelphia
フィラデルフィアに来た日本人

4.1 Haraguchi Kaname: "Master Engineer" in the U.S., Japan, and China
原口要：アメリカ、日本、中国で活躍したエンジニア

原口要（はらぐちかなめ、1851 - 1927）はアメリカで土木工学を学んだ鉄道技術者、都市計画家である。大学卒業後、実地を踏むため、しばらくアメリカに留まり、橋梁会社や鉄道会社で働き、ペンシルベニア鉄道会社の技師として、フィラデルフィア‐ウェスト・チェスター間の鉄道敷設に従事した。

原口要は1851年、肥前島原藩士進藤伊織の3男として生まれ、1869年に島原藩士原口謙介の養子となった。上京し、安井息軒などの下で漢学を修める。1870年に藩の貢進生となり、大学南校に入学し英語を学び、開成学校に進学した。

原口は1875年に文部省官費留学生として、アメリカに留学。松本荘一郎や平井誠二郎らと共に、ニューヨーク州トロイにあるレンセラー工科大学で土木工学を専攻した。レンセラー大学はハドソン川を望む高台に位置し、1824年創設の英語圏で最も古い工科大学だった。松本荘一郎は1876年に、そして原口と平井晴二郎は1878年に同大学を卒業し、3人とも鉄道技術者ならびに鉄道官僚として、日本の鉄道路線を構想・整備し、鉄道発展に大きな役割を果すことになる。

卒業後、原口はまずトロイの上水改良工事とニューヘブンの下水新設工事に関わった。ニューヨークにある、かの有名なブルックリン吊橋建設にも参加した。ニューヨークのデラウェア橋梁会社

Rensselaer Polytechnic Institute (RPI) alumni Matsumoto Sōichirō, Haraguchi Kaname, and Hirai Seijirō were the fathers of Japan's railroad system. Especially worthy of note is Haraguchi Kaname (1851–1927), who helped complete the Philadelphia–West Chester branch line of the Pennsylvania Railroad. Haraguchi was a railroad technician and urban planner who studied civil engineering in the United States. After his university graduation, he remained in America and worked in bridge construction and at railroad companies to gain practical experience.

Haraguchi Kaname was born in 1851 in Hizen (an old province of Japan in the area of Saga and Nagasaki Prefectures), the third son of Shindō Iori, a member of the Shimabara clan. In 1869 Haraguchi Kensuke, also a member of the Shimabara clan, adopted the young Kaname, who traveled to the capital to study the Chinese classics under scholars such as Yasui Sokken. In 1870, Haraguchi received a scholarship from his clan and entered Nankō University to study English, and then advanced to Kaisei Gakkō, the future University of Tokyo.

In 1875, Haraguchi traveled to study in the United States as one of the first recipients of a Monbushō (Japanese Ministry of Education) scholarship. Together with Matsumoto Sōichirō and Hirai Seijirō, he attended RPI in Troy, New York to study civil engineering.

Rensselaer Polytechnic Institute (RPI). Oku no Hosomichi Musubi no Chi Kinenkan Museum
奥の細道むすびの地記念館 所蔵

に就職して、各種橋梁の設計を担当し、その数は30にも達したという。またピッツバーグの製鉄所に出張し、数ヶ所の鉄橋の設計と工事監督を担当した。その後、ペンシルベニア鉄道会社に職を得た。ここでは主任となり、ウェスト・チェスター線の企画と敷設に従事し、この工事を1年ほどで完成させた。そして、ヨーロッパへと旅立った。

ウェスト・チェスターの地元紙は、工事主任である原口が30才未満と歳若で、ペリー提督が日本に開国を求めた頃に生まれたことを紹介した。そして日本人がアメリカ人のために鉄道を敷設するなど、ペリーは想像だにしなかったであろうと、日本の進歩を驚異の念をもって、次のように報じた。

「昨年来日本人原口氏当地鉄道建築ノ主任トナリ今ヤ全ク其ノ工ヲ竣ヘ無事ニ汽車ヲ通ズルニ至レリ其ノ人ヲ見ルニ年齢三十未満ニシテ回顧スレハ借日水師提督ペルリー氏初テ日本ニ航シ浦賀

Founded in 1824 and situated on high ground overlooking the Hudson River, RPI is the oldest school of civil engineering in the English-speaking world. Matsumoto Sōichirō graduated in 1876, and Haraguchi Kaname and Hirai Seijirō graduated in 1878. All three would go on to play major roles in the planning and development of Japan's railways as railroad technicians and officials.

After graduating, Haraguchi first worked on the improvement of the water supply in Troy, New York, a new drainage system in New Haven, Connecticut, and even the building of the famous Brooklyn Bridge in New York City. While employed by New York's Delaware Bridge Company he was in charge of designing as many as thirty bridges. He also traveled to an ironworks in Pittsburgh where he supervised the design and construction of several railroad bridges.

Haraguchi next became a senior railroad official with the Pennsylvania Railroad and

ノ戸チ叩キテ日本人ノ眠ヲ覚シタルハ
定メテ此人ノ出生セシ頃ナルベシ然ニ
ペルリー氏如何ニ開国ニ望ヲ属セシモ
其時ノ赤児今日我輩米国人ノ為メニ鉄
道ヲ造リ興フベシトハ想像ノ及バザリシ
所ナルベク日本ノ進歩驚クニ甚タリ云
々」。(『日本博士伝』、268頁)

原口はイギリスやフランス、オランダな
どヨーロッパ諸国を回り、1880年10月
に日本に戻った。

東京府御用掛けとなり、原口は都市計
画や上水道・下水道の工事、品川湾改
修などに関わった。吾妻橋や鎧橋、高
橋、浅草橋など多くの鉄橋を架設した
が、なかでも吾妻橋は日本で最初の鉄
橋だった。その後、工部省と逓信省にお
いて、主として東京とその近郊の鉄道建
設に従事した。1894年に逓信省の初代
鉄道技監に任じられ、奥羽、中央、山陰、
九州などの鉄道整備に寄与した。

日本に博士学位制度が導入されること
になり、1888年に25名の者が日本最初
の博士に選ばれたが、原口はその1人と
なった。退職後、一時台湾鉄道の顧問を
務めたこともあった。また清国政府の鉄
道顧問となり、中国の鉄道の計画や運
営に関与したばかりでなく、中国の若者
たちを鉄道マンとして養成し、鉄道事業
を通して日中の交流や親善にも尽くし
た。

なおペンシルベニア鉄道のウェスト・チ
ェスター線は後に、セプタ(SEPTA)の
R3(ウェスト・チェスター線)の一部とな
った。しかしながら乗客数減少と線路の
劣化により、1986年に運行が停止され
た。10年間ほど放置されていたが、熱烈
な鉄道ファンの要望に応えて、現在では

engaged in the planning and construction of the West Chester branch line, which was completed within a year. Before he left Philadelphia for Europe, a local West Chester newspaper profiled the young railroad supervisor, not yet even thirty years old, who had been born around the time of Commodore Perry's 1853 trip to Japan to demand its opening to the outside world. The paper admired Japan's progress with a sense of amazement and pondered whether Perry could ever have imagined that a Japanese man would soon be building railroads for America.

Haraguchi traveled to England, France, the Netherlands, and various other countries across Europe before returning to Japan in October 1880, where he joined the Tokyo municipal government to do municipal planning, construction on the city's waterworks and sewer system, and projects such as the improvement of Shinagawa Harbor. He built the Kabuto Bridge, Takahashi Bridge, and Asakusa Bridge, among many others, including the Azuma Bridge, Japan's first iron railway bridge. At the Ministry of Industry and the Ministry of Communications he continued to build railways mainly within Tokyo and across its suburbs. In 1894 he was appointed the Ministry of Communications and Transportation's first "chief engineer" and contributed to the development of the Ōu, Chūō, San'in, Kyūshū, and other railways.

When the doctoral degree was introduced to the Japanese educational system in 1888, Haraguchi was among the twenty-five candidates honored to become the country's first recipients. After retiring, he worked

グレン・ミルズとウェスト・チェスター間の7.7マイル（12.4キロメートル）が観光用に復興されている。

レンセラー工科大学同窓生の松本荘一郎と原口要、平井晴二郎は黎明期の日本鉄道事業の立役者たちだった。なかでも原口要はペンシルベニア鉄道会社のウェスト・チェスター線竣工に関わり、フィラデルフィアにゆかりの人となったのである。

戸田徹子
参考文献

「工学博士原口要君」、花房吉太郎・山本源太編『日本博士全伝』（博文館、1892）、267‐269頁

原口要「清国の交通」『早稲田講演：支那革命号』（1911年1月10日発行）、94‐126頁

briefly as a railroad advisor to the Taiwan Railway Company. He also served as an advisor to the Qing Chinese government, not only participating in the planning and administration of Chinese railways, but also training young Chinese rail workers, thereby strengthening Sino-Japanese relations.

The Pennsylvania Railroad's West Chester branch line eventually became part of SEPTA's R3 (West Chester) line, but was taken out of service in 1986 as ridership dwindled and the track deteriorated. Nearly a decade later, in response to the requests of passionate railroad enthusiasts, it was restored to its current service as a 7.7-mile (12.4 km) scenic sightseeing route from Glen Mills to West Chester.

By Tetsuko Toda
Translated by Paul Schuble

Selected Reference: Dan Free, *Early Japanese Railways, 1853–1914: Engineering Triumphs That Transformed Meiji-era Japan* (Rutland, VT: Tuttle, 2008).

If you go: The Market Street Station boarding location of the West Chester Railroad is 230 E. Market Street, West Chester, PA 19382.

4.2 Shiba Shirō: A Literary Bridge Between Philadelphia and Japan
柴四朗: ペンシルベニア大学で学んだ政治小説家

東海散士こと柴四朗（1852 - 1922）は、小説家、ジャーナリスト、そして政治家。1880年代前半にペンシルベニア大学で学び、帰国後、『佳人之奇遇』を著わした。

柴四朗は会津藩士の家に生まれた。会津藩は戊辰戦争で徳川側について敗北を帰し、さらに薩長連合の容赦ない攻撃によって、会津の地は廃墟となった。会津藩士は捕われ、北の地に送られた。会津藩士の若者の多くは学問を修める機会を失い、さらに薩摩、長州、そして土佐などの雄藩出身者が明治政府の中枢を占める時代となり、立身出世の途が閉ざされた。だが、一方で、敗北をばねに洋学に活路を求め、海外に飛び出した会津人も少なくなかった。柴もその1人で、アメリカに留学した。

柴は岩崎家（三菱）から資金援助を得て、1879年1月に渡米した。27歳の時である。その渡航目的は「財政・金融・経済」の勉強だった。柴はまずサンフランシスコにある商業専門学校パシフィック・ビジネス・カレッジで学び、1880年12月にディプロマを取得した。次に東海岸に移り、ハーバード大学に入学し政治学を専攻したが、ここにいたのはごく短期間で、フィラデルフィアに転居し、1882年9月にペンシルベニア大学のウォートン・スクールに入学した。ウォートン・スクールはアメリカで最初の大学レベルのビジネス・スクールだった。ウォートン・スクールの創設者であるジェームズ・ウォートンは保護関税の主唱

Shiba Shirō (1852–1922), better known by his pen name, "Tōkai Sanshi," was a novelist, journalist, and politician who forged lasting connections between the people of Japan and Philadelphia. He studied in Philadelphia in the early 1880s, and wrote a famous political novel, *Strange Encounters with Beautiful Women (Kajin no kigū)*, which popularized Philadelphia in Japan, after returning to his native land.

Shiba Shirō was born into an Aizu samurai family. The Aizu domain (Fukushima Prefecture) fought against the Imperial Army during the Meiji Restoration resulting in the total devastation of the Aizu area. The Aizu samurai were captured and sent to the far north in Japan, where life was harsh for them. The youth were especially unfortunate, for they had few chances to be educated. Since the Meiji Government was totally controlled by those who had led the Imperial Army—those who came from Satsuma, Chōshū, and Tosa—the defeated side had no opportunities to get positions in the new government. As a result, some Aizu youth ventured abroad for advanced education rather than remaining feckless at home. Shiba Shirō was one of them.

With financial help from the Iwasaki family (founders of the Mitsubishi Corporation), Shiba came to the United States in 1879 when he was twenty-seven with the aim of studying "financial administration, money and

Shiba Shirō. Aizu Buke Yashiki Museum, Fukushima, Japan
会津武家屋敷所蔵

banking, and economics." He received a diploma in December 1880 from the Pacific Business School in San Francisco and briefly studied politics at Harvard before moving to Philadelphia. From September 1882 to December 1884, he studied at the Wharton School of Finance and Economy at the University of Pennsylvania, which was the first university business school in the United States, and which graduated him as part of its first class. The Wharton School was founded by a strong advocate for protective trade duties and tariffs, James Wharton. Embracing his ideas, Shiba often wrote articles on that subject for Japanese magazines. His academic achievements probably encouraged Iwasaki Hisaya (who would become the third Mitsubishi president) and other Mitsubishi people to study at the University of Pennsylvania, especially at the Wharton School.

During his stay in Philadelphia, Shiba became acquainted with Mary Morris, even before Nitobe Inazō and Uchimura Kanzō came to the United States. Mary was a Quaker who organized the Women's Foreign Missionary Association of Friends of Philadelphia in 1882 and launched Quaker missions in Japan

者であり、柴はその影響を受け、在米中、しばしば日本の雑誌に保護関税支持の記事を書き送っている。1884年12月に、柴はウォートン・スクールの第1期生として卒業した。その後、柴に続き、岩崎久彌(三菱財閥第3代目)や三菱の将来を担う人材がペンシルベニア大学、特にウォートン・スクールに留学するようになった。

さらに柴はフィラデルフィア滞在中にメアリ・モリスと出会い、旧知の間柄となる。新渡戸稲造や内村鑑三が渡米する

以前のことである。メアリはクエーカー
で、1882年にフィラデルフィア・フレン
ズ婦人外国伝道協会を組織し、1885年
には日本伝道を開始した。またメアリは
日本人との交際を広げ、フィラデルフィ
ア郊外のオーバーブルックにある自宅
で月に一度、日本人学生のためにバイ
ブル・クラスを開くようになっていた。

柴は1885年1月に横浜に到着した。だ
が、すぐには職に就かず、まず東海散士
のペンネームで1885年10月に『佳人之
奇遇』を出版し、大人気を博した。これは
主人公である東海散士が世界を駆け巡
る政治小説で、物語はフィラデルフィア
の「独立閣」すなわちインディペンデン
ス・ホールで2人の美女と出会う場面か
ら始まる。明治初期、この印象深いシー
ンで、フィラデルフィア（「費府」）の地名
は日本中に知られるところとなった。こ
の小説はその後もシリーズものとして書
き続けられ、1897年までにその数は全
16巻（8巻16編）に及んだ。

1885年12月、谷千城が第1次伊藤内
閣において農商務大臣に任命され、柴
は大臣秘書官となった。そして1886年
3月から1887年6月までの1年3ヶ月の
間、農商工業の調査を目的とするヨーロ
ッパ視察に随行した。この時の見聞はの
ちに『佳人之奇遇』に生かされることに
なる。谷が帰国して間もなく大臣を辞任
すると、柴も辞職。その後は執筆活動に
従事し、ジャーナリストとして活躍した。
日本で国会が開設されたのは1890年
であるが、柴は1892年の第2回衆議院
議員選挙に福島第4区から立候補し初
当選を果たし、その後8回にわたって再
選を重ねて衆議院議員を務めた。大隈
重信内閣では、農商務次官、外務参政
官の役職についた。1915年に政界を辞

in 1885. Mary developed relationships with Japanese living in Philadelphia, holding a Bible class for Japanese students at her home in the Overbrook section of Philadelphia.

Despite his academic success in the study of economics and finance, Shiba did not enter the business world. Shortly after returning to Japan, he published *Strange Encounters with Beautiful Women*. The novel begins with a scene in which the main character meets two beautiful women in Independence Hall in Philadelphia. The novel won enormous popularity among Japanese youth and was serialized and published in eight installments between 1885 and 1897, making Philadelphia seem both impressive and familiar to readers throughout Japan.

In December 1885, Tani Tateki, the Minister of Agriculture and Commerce, appointed Shiba as his secretary. Shiba accompanied the Minister on a fact-finding tour to Europe from March 1886 to June 1887. Although Shiba resigned the position very soon after his return to Japan to pursue an active career in journalism, this European tour also provided material for his political novel.

In 1890, the Imperial Diet (Congress) was established. Shiba won a seat in the new Assembly as a representative from the fourth district of Fukushima in 1892, and was reelected eight times. In the Ōkuma Cabinet, Shiba first served as parliamentary vice-minister of Agriculture and Commerce, and later vice minister of Foreign Affairs, from which post he retired out of political life in 1915. He passed away at his residence in Atami in 1922 at the age of sixty-nine.

し、1922年に熱海の別荘でその生涯を
終えた。享年69歳だった。

柴の人生は実に多彩だったが、フィラデ
ルフィアに焦点を絞ると、小説を通して
アメリカ合衆国誕生の地・フィラデルフ
ィアを日本に紹介したばかりでなく、フィ
ラデルフィア・フレンドと日本を結び、さ
らにペンシルベニア大学と日本を結ぶ
役割を果たしたのであった。

戸田徹子
参考文献：

「東海散士」、昭和女子大学近代文
学研究室編『近代文学研究叢書』21巻
（1964）、337‐371頁

柳田泉「『佳人之奇遇』と東海散士」、
『（明治文学研究第8巻）政治小説研究
上巻』（春秋社、1967）、361‐483頁

大沼敏男・中丸宣明校注『（新日本古典
文学大系 明治編17）政治小説 2』（岩波
書店、2006）

Shiba Shirō was influential in connecting Japanese people to Philadelphia in a number of areas. He introduced the City of Brotherly Love through his popular novel; he encouraged members of Philadelphia's Religious Society of Friends to get involved with Japan; and he inspired men from Mitsubishi to major in business, the newest cutting-edge academic field, at Wharton.

By Tetsuko Toda

Selected References: Steven A. Sass, *The Pragmatic Imagination: A History of the Wharton School, 1881–1981* (Philadelphia: University of Pennsylvania Press, 1982); Guozhe Zheng, "The Politics of Canon Formation and Writing Style: A Linguistic Analysis of *Kajin no kigū*," in *The Linguistic Turn in Contemporary Japanese Literary Studies: Politics, Language, Textuality*, ed. Michael K. Bourdaghs (Ann Arbor: Center for Japanese Studies, University of Michigan, 2010), pp. 221–43.

If you go: Independence Hall, 520 Chestnut Street, Philadelphia, PA 19106.

4.3   Ogawa Kazumasa: Photographic Pioneer
小川一真：日本写真界のパイオニア

1860年（万延元年）8月15日、小川一真（1860‐1929）は忍藩主松平下総守忠誠の藩士の次男として武蔵国忍（現埼玉県）に生まれる。幼年時代に藩校「培根堂」で学んだ後に上京し、小川は旧久留米藩主有馬頼咸の学塾であった有馬学校に入学する。有馬学校は英学に重点を置いた洋学塾であった。その当時、英語を学び欧米の学問を身に付けることは、立身出世を慮る上で効力を大いに発揮したのである。

1868年の明治維新は政治面だけではなく社会全般にわたって大変革をもたらした。新政府下においては政治力や財力、教育度の高さが各人の社会的地位を測る1つの基準となった。明治政府は西欧文明を摂取することに全力を注ぎ、若者に勉学に謹むことを奨励したのである。小川は工部大学校に進学し建築と土木工学を修めることを希望していたが、家族の経済的援助を受けることが不可能になり、夢を断念することを余儀なくされた。彼は有馬学校に在学中に、趣味が写真撮影であった英国人教師の1人から初めて写真術の手ほどきを受けたのだが、それが契機となり写真師になることを決意する。幸い故郷近くの熊谷で写真館を営んでいた写真師吉原秀雄に助手として採用され、吉原から学ぶべきすべての知識と技術を吸収した。また最新のコロジオン湿板法を習い覚え、自らも感光材を製造することを試みるが失敗に終わる。小川は日本の写真技術が欧米諸国と比較していかに遅れをとっているかを痛感し、海外で写

Ogawa Kazumasa (a.k.a. Isshin, 1860–1929) was born on August 15, 1860 in the province of Musashi (present-day Saitama Prefecture), the second son of a samurai retainer of the lord of Oshi Castle, Matsudaira Tadazane. After receiving his primary education at the Oshi clan school, Ogawa went to Tokyo for further schooling at the Arima School, which provided a Western-style curriculum. There he studied English, a necessary tool for obtaining the Western knowledge that would help him pursue a useful career at that time. The Meiji Restoration of 1868 brought about a change of government as well as a transformation of the social system. In the new system, political influence, wealth, and education were the measures of prestige. The new government was eager to adopt features of Western civilization, and encouraged young people to pursue education to contribute to the nation's development.

Ogawa originally planned to study architecture and civil engineering in the School of Engineering, but when his family could no longer support him, he decided to become a photographer. Ogawa had his first rudimentary lessons in photography at the Arima School from an English teacher, whose hobby was taking pictures. He returned home and became an assistant to the photographer Yoshiwara Hideo, learning as much as he could. He learned the latest collodion wet-plate negative process. Ogawa experimented

Ikuta Shrine, Kōbe, photographed by Ogawa Kazumasa. Nagasaki University Library
長崎大学附属図書館所 所蔵

真術の修業を行うことを夢見るようにな
る。1881年にまず東京に戻り英語の勉
強を再開し、写真師としての活動も続け
た。

翌年、小川は横浜に移り、居留地の警察
署専属の通訳として働くことになる。諸
々の経緯を経て東洋艦隊の旗艦「スワ
タラ号」の司令官フィリップ・H・クーパー
との知遇を得、ついに水夫として乗船す
ることを許可され、渡米の夢が現実のも
のとなる。

小川の直属の上官はマサチューセッツ
州出身であり、彼はボストンで有名だっ

with making his own collodion emulsion and
photo-printing paper, using Japanese paper,
however his efforts proved unsuccessful.
Realizing that Japan was far behind the West
in photographic technology, Ogawa was
determined to study abroad. He returned
to Tokyo in 1881, to continue his study of
English and to work in a photographic studio.

The following year Ogawa moved to
Yokohama, where he was employed as an
English interpreter for the Yokohama Police
in the foreign settlement. There he was
introduced to Commander Philip H. Cooper,
captain of the frigate *Swatara*. Ogawa signed

たリジィ&ヘイスティング写真館に小川を推薦する。その恩恵を被り、1883年の初頭より小川は同写真館で働くことができた。ボストン滞在中に、小川には岡部長職子爵との運命的な出会いがあった。岡部はすでに外務省の官僚であったが、小川が先端技術を学ぶために様々な局面において支援することを約束する。その結果、小川はカーボン・プリントやコロタイプといった最新の写真技術を習得できたのである。次に小川は高品質な乾板製造法を学ぶことに関心が移り、1885年にボストンを離れフィラデルフィアに向かった。

フィラデルフィアを選んだ理由に、乾板製造の草分けであったジョン・カーバットがいたことが挙げられる。カーバットは同地を拠点に華々しい活動を展開していた。彼は写真製版術の先駆者でもあり、X線写真の研究に貢献し、そしてフラッシュ撮影に必要なマグネシウム・パウダーの供給業者としても名を馳せていた。カーバットは1876年に開催された独立100周年記念フィラデルフィア万国博覧会の写真館の総監督を務めた。1885年1月にウェイン・ジャンクションに新設されたカーバットのキーストーン乾板製造工場で小川は乾板製造法を学んだ。カーバットの許に、およそ半年間滞在したと考えられている。

帰国後、小川は岡部の支援を得て、東京に「玉潤館」という名の写真館を開いた。営業開始早々に帝国陸軍参謀本部陸地測量部写真班の教官に任命される。また、1888年5月5日から9月3日にかけて、政府3省－宮内省、内務省、文部省より組織された畿内宝物取調調査に写真技師として参加することを要請される。これは京都と奈良の古社寺を中

on the ship as a sailor and set sail on August 1, 1882 to seek his fortune in the United States. Ogawa's supervisor on board the ship was a lieutenant from Boston, who recommended Ogawa to the photo studio Rizey & Hastings in Boston where Ogawa began working in 1883. While in Boston, Ogawa met Viscount Okabe Nagamoto, a bureaucrat in the Ministry of Foreign affairs, who supported Ogawa in his quest for the latest knowledge of photographic technique and equipment. Ogawa learned the newest photographic processes, such as carbon printing and collotype. Quick to learn and eager to experiment with high quality dry-plate techniques, Ogawa left Boston for Philadelphia in 1885.

He chose Philadelphia because the first and foremost manufacturer of gelatin dry-plates, John Carbutt, was based in Philadelphia. Carbutt, who established his firm in 1871, also pioneered photomechanical printing processes and went on to develop X-ray film techniques and became a supplier of magnesium powder for flash photography. He had been Superintendent of Photography Hall at the 1876 Philadelphia Centennial Exhibition. Ogawa went to work with Carbutt at his Keystone Dry Plate Factory, which opened in January 1885 at Wayne Junction, where he worked with and learned from Carbutt for about six months.

After his return to Japan, Ogawa opened his own studio, called Gyokujunkan, in Tokyo and was appointed instructor of photography at the Imperial Military Academy. Ogawa was also official photographer for a survey of temple and shrine art treasures under the aegis of the Ministry of Education and

心に美術遺宝の調査・登録を行い、歴史的美術作例を国のために保存することを目的とした政策である。取調掛員として、アーネスト・フェノロサや岡倉天心らが同行していた。1889年に岡倉天心は美術雑誌『国華』を創刊するが、小川はその写真責任者として抜擢されたのである。

1893年に開催されたシカゴ万国展覧会に併せて開催された写真展覧会に招待され、小川は2度目の渡米を果たした。この展覧会に出品した写真作品が評価され、小川は金賞を受賞した。小川の評判は急速に高まり、1895年にはイギリスの王立写真協会の正式会員に推挙される。そして1910年には帝室技芸員に任命されるに至る。

小川が残した最大の功績として、明治天皇の大喪の礼を記録したことが挙げられるだろう。小川は宮内省より御大葬謹写団団長を任命され、写真撮影の全権を委ねられたのである。これが功を奏し、宮内省御用掛に就任し、大正天皇の御真影をも手掛けた。1929年、写真家として確固たる地位を築き上げた小川は70歳の生涯を閉じた。

木下京子

Cultural Affairs from May 5 to September 3, 1888. Among the government-appointed art inspectors were Ernest Fenollosa and Okakura Tenshin. When Okakura started his art journal *Kokka* the next year, Ogawa was named chief photographer.

Ogawa's second visit to the United States in 1893 was in connection with the World's Columbian Exposition in Chicago, where he received a Gold Medal for the art photographs he exhibited there. Ogawa's reputation soon spread. He was named a member of the Royal Photographic Society (London) in 1895 and was also appointed an Imperial Household Arts and Crafts member in 1910. His greatest triumph came two years later when the Imperial Household Agency gave Ogawa the responsibility of recording the Meiji Emperor's funeral. Ogawa was made a member of the Imperial Household photographic staff, and took the official portrait of the Taishō Emperor. Ogawa died in 1929 at the age of seventy, his reputation as a photographic pioneer assured.

By Kyoko Kinoshita

Selected Reference: Terry Bennett, *Early Japanese Images* (Rutland, VT and Tokyo: Charles E. Tuttle, 1996), pp. 52–54.

If you go: The Philadelphia Museum of Art, 26th Street and Benjamin Franklin Parkway, Philadelphia, PA 19130.

4.4 Dr. Okami Keiko: The First Japanese Female To Study Medicine In America
岡見京子：アメリカの医科大学で学んだ最初の日本女性

19世紀後半、徳川幕府の封建的な考え方が根深く残っている日本社会で、女性が高等教育、ましてや医学教育を受けるのは、大変難しい時代であった。そのような社会情勢下で、岡見京子（1859‐1941、戸籍名は「けい」）は日本で最初の女医となり、しかも日本の医科大学ではなくアメリカの医科大学で医師の資格を取っている。

岡見京子は1859年に青森で生まれ、父親の貿易業のため1867年に上京した。京子は1873年に横浜共立女学校に入学し、在学中にキリスト教の洗礼を受けた。そこには、当時、活躍していた福沢諭吉の娘も通学していた。福沢諭吉（1835‐1901）は、幕末から明治中期の日本を代表する啓蒙思想家、教育家、慶応義塾大学の創始者である。

1881年に桜井女学校（現在の女子学院）に英語教師として奉職した。25歳のとき、キリスト教徒である岡見千吉郎とめぐり合い結婚した。千吉郎は工部美術学校画学科（現在の東京芸術大学）で学び、頌栄女学院で絵画を教えていた。2人の結婚は当時では大変に珍しい恋愛結婚で、2人ともキリスト教の信仰を深め、貧民救済の伝道活動をしていた。

1884年、結婚後まもなく夫の千吉郎は新渡戸稲造（1862‐1933）と共に渡米し、ミシガン大学の農学部に入学した。京子も同年に渡米し、1885年にフィラデルフィアにあるペンシルベニア女子

Toward the end of the nineteenth century, when remnants of the feudalistic ideas of the Tokugawa era were still prevalent in society, it was very difficult for women to receive a higher education, let alone a medical education, in Japan. It was in such times that Okami Keiko (maiden name Nishida; 1859–1941), called Kei in her Japanese family register, became Japan's first female medical doctor not by attending a Japanese medical school but an American one.

Nishida was born in Aomori Prefecture in 1859 and moved to Tokyo because of her father's trading business in 1867. She entered the Yokohama Kyōritsu Girls' School in 1873, graduating in 1878. (A daughter of Fukuzawa Yukichi, the writer, teacher, translator, entrepreneur and journalist who founded Keiō-Gijuku University, also attended this institution.) Nishida became a Christian while she was a student at the school. Then she enrolled in Tokyo Girls' School, also known as Takebashi Girls' School.

In 1881 Nishida became an English teacher at Sakurai Girls' School (now Joshi Gakuin). In 1884, at the age of twenty-five, she married an art teacher, Okami Senyoshirō, who taught at Shōei Girls School. Okami Senyoshirō graduated from Kōbu Art School Painting Department (now Tokyo National University of Fine Arts and Music). Their marriage was a "love match" rather than an

At the Woman's Medical College of Pennsylvania, 1885.
Left, Anandibai Joshee of India; center, Keiko Okami;
right, Sabat Islambooly of Syria. Legacy Center Archives,
Drexel University College of Medicine, Philadelphia

arranged marriage, a rare phenomenon in Japan during that era. Okami Keiko and her husband were both Christians and did missionary work with the poor.

After their marriage Okami's husband went to the United States with Nitobe Inazō to study at the Michigan College of Agriculture in 1884. Okami followed her husband to America and in 1885 she entered the Women's Medical College of Pennsylvania (WMCP, now Drexel University's College of Medicine), founded in 1850 as the world's first medical school for women. In addition to Okami, other female international students who attended the college were Dr. Anandibai Joshee from India (class of 1886) and Dr. Sabat Islambooly from Syria (class of 1890).

医科大学（現在、ドレクセル大学・医学部）—1850年に創立された世界で初の女性のための医科大学 — に入学した。留学生の中には、インド出身のアナンバイ・ジョシー（1886年卒業）や、シリア出身のサバット・イスラムビリー（1890年卒業）が在籍していた。

Writing in 1960, Nagatoya emphasizes that Okami Keiko was the first Japanese woman to study medicine in an overseas school and receive the degree of doctor of medicine. During her studies in Philadelphia, Okami lived in the Morris family's residence. Mr.

長門谷洋治(1960)は、当時の社会状況からみて、京子がアメリカの医科大学で学び、医学博士号を授与された最初の日本人女性となったことは画期的であると高く評価している。フィラデルフィアで留学中、京子はモリス家に下宿した。モリス氏はペンシルベニア鉄道会社の重役で、モリス夫妻はクエーカーであった。モリス夫妻は日本人留学生たちをよく自宅に招き、京子も日本人留学生たちと交流した。

京子は1889年に卒業後、夫と共に日本に帰国した。夫は頌栄女学校で教鞭を取り、一方、京子は医籍登録をして医術開業免許を受け、慈恵病院(現在の東京慈恵会医科大学)の院長、高木兼寛医学博士の招きで新設の婦人科主任になった。当時の女性差別のある中、高木が京子を採用したことは、勇気ある行動であった。しかし、京子は3年後にこの病院を辞職し、1893年に自宅で開業したがうまくいかず、桜井女学校で親しかった宣教師のマリア・ツルーと協力してサナトリウム「衛生園」開設の計画を立てる。京子は趣意書を書き、フィラデルフィア・フレンズ婦人外国伝道協会などに資金援助を依頼した。東京都は、日本にはこのような施設の前例がないという理由で不許可にしたが、1897年に赤坂病院の分院として、女性のための「衛生園」を開園することができた。

その間、京子は 1) 結核の予防と快復期療養のケア、2) 看護婦養成学校の設立、3) 派遣看護婦制度の設立 に尽力した。サナトリウムの考えは当時は先駆的発想で、一般の日本人には理解しがたく、また入院費も高額なため、僅かに外国の婦人、宣教師たちが利用するにすぎなかったため、1906年に閉園した。

Morris was an executive of the Pennsylvania Railroad Company in Philadelphia and Mr. and Mrs. Morris were members of the Society of Friends. The Morrises invited Japanese students to their home on a regular basis, and there Okami became acquainted with other Japanese students.

After Okami graduated from the Women's Medical College, she returned to Japan with her husband in 1889. Her husband became a teacher at Shōei Girl's School. Okami obtained a license to practice medicine and was appointed to the respected post of head of the newly founded Department of Gynecology at the Jikei Hospital (now the Jikeikai Medical College) at the invitation of Dr. Takagi Ken, who was a Director of the hospital. Dr. Takagi's employment of Okami was considered courageous in a society that still discriminated against women. She remained in this position for three years until she resigned in 1892.

In 1893, she started to practice medicine at home, and later opened a sanitarium, "Eisei-en" along with a missionary, Mrs. Maria True (1841–1896), who was her colleague at Sakurai Girls' School. She wrote a proposal to the Women's Foreign Missionary Association of Friends of Philadelphia for funding for the sanitarium. However, her proposal was not accepted by the Tokyo Prefectural Government because there was no precedent for anything of this kind in Japan. It was finally approved by the Tokyo Prefectural Government in 1897 as a branch of Akasaka Hospital.

Meanwhile she worked: to prevent tuberculosis and to take care of convalescent

1906年、再び英語教師として女子学院の教壇に立ったが、2年後に乳がんに冒されたため辞任した。癌の治療で大変な時、オペラ歌手の娘のミレー（恩人メアリ・モリスの名を命名）が追い討ちをかけるように1914年に肉腫で亡くなった。大きな痛手を受けた千吉郎と京子はバイブル・クラスを中心に、クリスチャン仲間と交流を深め、農業や園芸の静かな生活に入り、千吉郎は1936年に、京子は1941年に亡くなった。

岡見京子は男尊女卑の日本社会の中で、19世紀後半に日本人女性として初めてアメリカの医科大学で勉強し、医学博士の資格を取得し、女性のためのクリニックを開き、病める人々を救済し、看護婦の教育に力を注ぎ、敬虔なクリスチャンとしての生活を全うしたのである。彼女の業績は今でも多くの女性に引き継がれている。

浜田昌子

参考文献:
松田誠「かつて慈恵に在学した興味ある人物 その4：慈恵病院女医第一号・ドクター岡見京子」(2007)

patients; to establish a school to train nurses; and to introduce a system of dispatching nurses when they were needed. Even though the principle of the sanitarium was innovative, it seemed that Japanese people did not understand the function of such a hospital at that time so the people who used this hospital were primarily foreign women and missionaries. Unfortunately her practice was closed in 1906 due to poor management—the cost of hospitalization was too high for local people.

In 1906 Okami became an English teacher at Tokyo Jogakuin, resigning the position two years later due to her developing breast cancer. During this difficult period of her own illness and treatment, Okami's daughter Milee (named after Mrs. Mary Morris), an opera singer, died from a tumor in 1914. After their daughter's death, Senyoshirō and Keiko devoted their time to running Bible classes and having gatherings to exchange ideas with friends. They embraced a quiet life of farming, gardening and faith. Senyoshirō passed away in 1936 and Keiko died in 1941.

Okami Keiko had to overcome serious social barriers to work as a medical doctor and to open a clinic for women during the male-dominated Meiji era, but she maintained her focus on treating sick people, saving lives, and educating nursing students despite the difficulties. She will always be remembered as the first Japanese woman to study medicine in America and to receive the degree of doctor of medicine.

By Masako Hamada

Selected Reference: Y. Nagatoya, "Dr. Keiko

Okami, Japan's first female medical student who studied abroad," *Journal of the American Medical Women's Association* 15 (Dec. 1960): 1175–77.

4.5 Uchimura Kanzō:
Finding a True Calling in Philadelphia
内村鑑三：フィラデルフィアで人生を見つけたクリスチャン

内村鑑三（1861‐1930）は日本を代表するクリスチャンである。独自な伝道活動を展開したばかりでなく、教師、著述家、ジャーナリストでもあった。内村は大学生のときにキリスト教に入信した。若い鑑三の目に、来日した宣教師たちは西洋文明の優位性に便乗して、キリスト教を伝道しようとしているがゆえ、傲慢になっているように見えた。また教派間の対立にもうんざりしていた。宣教師たちに対する反発とアメリカでの留学経験から、内村はキリスト教の日本への土着化を求めるようになり、『聖書の研究』を発行し、「無教会」というキリスト教グループを発展させた。

徳川幕府がまさに崩壊しつつあった時期に、内村は武士階級に生まれた。日本の近代化と歩調を合わせるかのように、内村は英語を学び、札幌農学校（現北海道大学）に入学する。この学校では教頭ウィリアム・S・クラークの影響を受けて、多くの学生がキリスト教徒になったが、内村と新渡戸稲造もその仲間だった。内村は水産学を専攻し、卒業後は漁業の専門家として開拓使に勤めた。

1884年から1888年にかけて内村はアメリカに留学する。1884年11月に渡米し、まずフィラデルフィアで8ヶ月間を過ごしたのだが、そこで内村はどのような生活を送り、その経験は彼の人生にどのような意味をもったのだろうか。

内村が留学したのは、結婚が破局に終わった罪悪感から逃れるためだった。友

Uchimura Kanzō (1861–1930) was one of the most prominent Japanese Christians. He was an evangelist in his own way, as well as a teacher, journalist, and writer. Converted to Christianity when he was a college student, he considered Western missionaries in Japan arrogant because he felt they imposed their own cultures on the converts in the name of Christianity. He also grew tired of denominational rivalry among missionaries. His observations of the formative years of Protestant missions in Japan and his experience studying in the United States led Uchimura to develop a form of Christianity adapted to the Japanese culture. He started the publication of *Seisho no kenkyū* (Bible Studies) and developed a movement called Mukyōkai (Non-Church).

Uchimura Kanzō was born to a samurai family during the last days of the Tokugawa government. Growing up as the modernization of Japan was taking place, he learned English and entered Sapporo Agricultural College (presently Hokkaido University). Many students there became Christians under the influence of William S. Clark, Uchimura Kanzō and Nitobe Inazō among them. Uchimura majored in fishery and, for some years after graduation, worked as a scientist for the Kaitakushi (Hokkaido Developmental Agency).

Uchimura studied in the States from 1884 to 1888. He left Japan in November 1884,

人であるウィリス・ホイットニーからウィスター・モリス夫妻を紹介してもらい、まずフィラデルフィアを目指したのである。モリス夫妻はクエーカーで親日家だった。なかでも夫人のメアリ・モリスはフィラデルフィア在住の日本人学生たちの間で母のように慕われていた。また夫ウィスターの方も内村にとって忘れがたい人物であり、「ウィスター・モリス氏に関する余の回顧」という記事を残している。

モリス夫人は月に一度、日本人たちを自宅に招きバイブル・クラスを開催していた。内村は新渡戸稲造と共に、その会に出席した。またモリス夫人が結成したフィラデルフィア・フレンズ婦人外国伝道協会の会合にも参加した。この伝道協会に対し、内村は自分がいかにしてキリスト教徒となったかを語り、日本伝道においては教派対立を避けるべきことをアドバイスしている。

フィラデルフィアで内村は2つの問題に悩まされた。1つは結婚で失敗したこと。もう1つは生涯の職業を選ぶということだった。当初、内村はフィラデルフィアで医学校に入学するつもりだった。だが資金不足から、まずは生活費を稼がなければならなかった。内村はフィラデルフィア郊外のエルウィンにある、ペンシルベニア知的障害児訓練学校で看護人として働き始めた。この学校はアメリカで第2番目に古い障害児施設で、学校長のアイザック・ニュートン・カーリンは誠実で献身的な医師であり、カーリン夫妻は内村に親切だった。

内村は生徒に歩行や階段昇降、ダンベル体操の訓練を施し、おむつ交換などの汚れ仕事も担当した。また1日おきに

Uchimura Kanzō. Imai Museum Kyōyūkai
今井館教友会所蔵

with Philadelphia as his first destination, where he lived for about eight months. His Philadelphia experience was to change the course of his life.

Uchimura came to the United States primarily to get over the failure of his first marriage. He chose Philadelphia because his friend, Willis Whitney, had introduced him to a Quaker couple there, Mr. and Mrs. Wistar Morris, who were very kind to Japanese people. Mary Morris was especially regarded as a "mother" for Japanese students who were studying in

夜勤もあった。日本においては高等教育を受けた少数エリートの1人であり、政府の役人だった内村は、看護人の仕事が気に入らず、自分の父親に不平不満を書き送っていた。

しかしながら、エルウィンでの体験を通して、内村は次第に障害者や貧しい者たちに思いやりを持つようになり、また人種間に優劣の差はないことも実感した。そして、医者ではなく牧師になる決心をしたのである。ウィスター・モリスから医学校の学費提供の申し出があったにもかかわらず、内村はフィラデルフィアを離れ、マサチューセッツ州のアマースト大学に向かった。だが内村にとってエルウィンはアメリカにおける故郷ともいうべき場所になっており、休暇の折々にエルウィンを訪問した。福祉施設「エルウィン」には今でも、内村鑑三が道普請した「鑑三ロード」が残されている。

戸田徹子

参考文献：
内村鑑三著、鈴木俊郎訳『余は如何にして基督信徒となりし乎』（岩波書店、1958）
鈴木範久『内村鑑三』（岩波新書、1984）
鈴木範久『内村鑑三の人と思想』（岩波書店、2012）

【参考情報】
内村鑑三記念今井館教友会（今井館聖書講堂）
東京都目黒区中根1-14-9
電話：03-3723-5479
www.imaikankyoyukai.or.jp

Philadelphia. Uchimura was so impressed by Wistar that he later wrote an article on this benevolent man, "My Reflections on Mr. Wistar Morris."

Mary Morris invited Japanese people to her home in Overbrook once a month to read the Bible, and Uchimura Kanzō and Nitobe Inazō often visited the Morrises. They also attended the meetings of the Women's Foreign Missionary Association of Friends of Philadelphia, which Mary Morris had founded. At one meeting, Uchimura related how he had become a Christian and advised the association to avoid denominational rivalry.

In Philadelphia Uchimura had difficulty making progress toward his future vocation because of his limited financial resources. He had planned to enter medical school when he arrived in Philadelphia, but he had to work to support himself. He got a job as a caregiver at the Pennsylvania Training School for Feeble-Minded Children (now known as "Elwyn"), at Elwyn, in suburban Philadelphia. The school was one of the earliest for children with intellectual disabilities in the United States. The school director, Dr. Isaac Newton Kerlin, was dedicated to his work, and his family was kind to Uchimura.

Uchimura was involved in caretaking, helping the students walk or exercise with ladders and dumbbells, and with their personal hygiene, as well as being on night watch every other night. In Japan, Uchimura was one of the highly educated elite and a government official, and his work at Elwyn was not in keeping with his expectations for someone of his background. Uchimura was not very happy with the work and wrote to his father of his dissatisfaction.

However, while doing this humbling work, Uchimura gradually developed empathy for the poor and handicapped. The Elwyn experience helped him recognize the commonality among all human beings. His experience in Elwyn influenced Uchimura's decision to become a preacher instead of a medical doctor. Declining Wistar Morris's generous offer to pay for his expenses to medical school, Uchimura left Philadelphia for Massachusetts to enter Amherst College. He returned on his vacations to Elwyn, which remained his oasis in the United States. The "Kanzō Road," which Uchimura Kanzō cleared and repaired, still exists at Elwyn.

By Tetsuko Toda

Selected References: Kanzō Uchimura, *The Diary of a Japanese Convert* (Fleming H. Revell, 1895); John F. Howes, *Japan's Modern Prophet: Uchimura Kanzō, 1861–1930* (Vancouver and Toronto: UBC Press, 2005).

If you go: Elwyn's Historical Archives and Museum, 111 Elwyn Road, Elwyn, PA 19063.

4.6 Iwasaki Hisaya: A Rich but Humble Student and Philanthropist
岩崎久彌：裕福で謙虚な三菱財閥3代目

岩崎久彌（1865‐1955）は三菱創業者岩崎彌太郎の長男である。ペンシルベニア大学のウォートン・スクールで学び、明治から大正にかけて、日本の産業化がもっともダイナミックに進展する時期に三菱財閥3代目の総師を務めた。

1865年、久彌は土佐藩（高知県）に生まれた。明治維新の3年前である。父親の彌太郎は海運業に着手し、三菱を興した。この会社はその後、鉱山、金融、倉庫、造船など、近代国家が必要とする様々な経済分野に進出していく。久彌は9歳で上京し、慶應義塾に入学した。12歳の時に、父親が開校した三菱商業学校に転学し、英文テキストを使用して教科を学んだ。1886年、20歳で渡米。最初の2年間を大学入学準備に費やし、その後、ペンシルベニア大学に入学し、ウォートン・スクールに進学した。ウォートン・スクールはアメリカで最初の大学レベルのビジネス・スクールだった。久彌は学士（財政学）を取得し、卒業した。

久彌は質素な下宿に住み、ごく普通の学生生活を送った。当時、多くの日本人がフィラデルフィアで学んでいたが、お金に苦しんでいる学生がいると、久彌は匿名で経済的支援を与えたという。さらに姻戚関係があり、慶応義塾と三菱商業学校の恩師でもあった馬場辰猪（28章参照）をペンシルベニア大学病院で看護し、ウッドランド墓地に埋葬したのも久彌だった。

1891年に久彌は帰国。留学生活は5年

Iwasaki Hisaya (1865–1955) was the eldest son of the founder of the Mitsubishi Corporation, Iwasaki Yatarō. He came to the United States in 1886 to study at the Wharton School of the University of Pennsylvania, graduating with a BS in finance. He became the third president of Mitsubishi and ran the corporation for twenty-two years, coinciding with a period when Japanese industry developed dynamically from the late Meiji to Taishō periods.

Iwasaki was born in Tosa domain (Kōchi Prefecture) in 1865, three years before the Meiji Restoration. His father, Yatarō, launched a shipping firm, which he later expanded by founding Mitsubishi to provide the diverse goods and services modernized countries needed, such as mining, finance, warehousing, and shipbuilding.

Iwasaki moved to Tokyo at the age of nine and attended school at Keiō Gijuku. At twelve, he transferred to the Mitsubishi Commercial School, which his father had established, where he learned various subjects using English textbooks.

In 1886, when he was twenty years old, Iwasaki went to the United States. At that time, during the last quarter of the nineteenth century, the United States was experiencing the fastest development of its major industries in its history, and he was there to observe it. He ultimately entered the Wharton School of Finance and Economy, which opened in 1881 as the first university business school in the world.

While he was at the university, Iwasaki rented a simple room at a boarding house and lived quite a normal student life. There were many Japanese students in Philadelphia, with whom he socialized. Iwasaki anonymously gave financial support to those Japanese students who were without means. It was also Iwasaki who nursed Baba Tatsui at the Hospital of the University of Pennsylvania and laid him to rest in the Woodlands Cemetery.

Iwasaki Hisaya. Mitsubishi Archives 三菱史料館所蔵

At the University of Pennsylvania, Iwasaki made friends with Lloyd Carpenter Griscom (1872–1959). Griscom's father was the shipping magnate Clement A. Griscom. The Griscom family lived at the estate called "Dolobran" near Haverford College in the suburbs of Philadelphia. Iwasaki was sometimes invited there for Sunday dinner. When Griscom traveled around Europe as a graduation trip, Iwasaki joined him.

On the voyage across the Atlantic, Griscom traveled first class while Iwasaki booked a third class cabin. Towards the end of the tour,

間に及んだ。アメリカ史において19世紀末の4半世紀はまさに石炭、石油、鉄鋼、鉄道、銀行などの基幹産業が発達し、独占化が進行する時代だったが、久彌はこの変化を目の当たりにしてきたことになる。1893年、久彌は28歳の若さで三菱の社長に就任した。社長職を辞するのは1916年のことであり、久彌の社長任期は日本の近代産業の発展期に重なる。この間、久彌は事業の多角化と分業

化(事業部制)を推進した。他方で、久彌は日清戦争(1894)や日露戦争(1904)、第1次世界大戦(1914)に対処しなければならなかった。

ところで久彌はペンシルベニア大学在学中、ロイド・C・グリスコムと友達になった。グリスコムの父親は大きな船舶会社を経営するクレメント・A・グリスコムで、グリスコム家はフィラデルフィア郊外のハバフォード大学の近くにドロブランと呼ばれる屋敷を所有し、久彌はよく日曜の食事に招かれた。また久彌とグリスコムは卒業旅行として、一緒に欧州に出かけた。グリスコムは上等船室で、久彌は下等船室であった。旅も終わりに近づいたところ、ペテルスブルクでグリスコムが帽子を購入しようと毛皮店に立ち寄ったところ、久彌が店のすべての商品を買い取ると言い出し、グリスコムは仰天する。久彌が日本の富豪の御曹司だとはつゆ知らず、グリスコムは人に尋ねてようやくそれを知ったのだった。

その後、グリスコムは外交官となり、奇しくも第11代駐日アメリカ公使(正確には特命全権公使、1902‐1905)として、1902年12月に日本に赴任した。日本滞在中、グリスコムのもとには久彌邸から毎日しぼりたての牛乳が届けられた。

久彌は、父親が貧しい環境から身を起こしていくのを目にして成長したので、祖母である岩崎美和の残した「富貴になりたりといえども 貧しきときの心を失うべからず」という戒めを守り、若いころから謙虚で、他者への思いやりを忘れない人だったと伝えられている。また社会貢献を心掛け、東洋文庫を設立し、清澄庭園と六義園を東京都に寄付した。なお

they visited a fur shop in St. Petersburg. While Griscom bought a fur hat, Iwasaki proposed to buy all of the fur items in the shop. Griscom was astounded, only later learning that Iwasaki was an heir to the family that owned the Mitsubishi conglomerate. Lloyd Griscom became a diplomat and served as the United States Minister to Japan (1902–05). During his stay in Japan, Griscom received fresh milk from Iwasaki's estate every day.

Iwasaki returned to Japan in 1891 after five years of study. He assumed the presidency of Mitsubishi in 1893 at the age of twenty-eight and served until 1916. His presidency occurred during a critical period in the development of Japan's modern industries. He introduced a corporate organizational system of "diversification and division." Iwasaki also had to guide Mitsubishi though the Sino-Japanese War (1894–95), the Russo-Japanese War (1904–05), and World War I (1914–18).

Perhaps because he had observed his father's interest in moving up the social ladder, Iwasaki remained humble and considerate throughout his life. Even after he became president of the Mitsubishi Corporation, he always remembered his grandmother's precept: "Don't forget what it is like to be poor." Iwasaki was a philanthropist as well. He bought the private library of George E. Morrison and started the Tōyō Bunko, a library and research institute that specialized in Asian studies. He donated two gardens—Kiyosumi Garden and Rikugien Garden—to the Tokyo Metropolitan Government. Iwasaki's eldest daughter, Sawada Miki (1901–1980), founded the Elizabeth Saunders Home, which cared for children

第2次世界大戦後、大磯の旧岩崎家別邸に、混血児のための保護施設「エリザベス・サンダーズ・ホーム」を設けた澤田美喜は、久彌の長女である。

1896年、久彌は東京の茅町にジョサイア・コンドル設計の邸宅を新築したが、この茅町本邸は英国ジャコビアン様式を基調とし、久彌が留学していたペンシルベニアのカントリー・ハウスのイメージを採り入れた木造建築物である。現在、この屋敷は東京都の「旧岩崎邸庭園」として保存、公開されている。

戸田徹子

参考文献:
岩崎家伝記刊行会編『(岩崎家伝記5)岩崎久彌伝』(東京大学出版会、1979)
成田誠一『岩崎久彌物語:雲がゆき、雲がひらけて』(東京都公園協会、2001)

【参考情報】
旧岩崎邸庭園
〒110-0008
東京都台東区池之端1-3-45
電話:03-3823-8340
www.kensetsu.metro.tokyo.jp/kouen/kouenannai/park/kyu_iwasaki.html

of mixed parentage in occupied Japan after World War II. The Home in Ōiso used to be one of the Iwasaki family residences.

In 1896 Iwasaki built a gorgeous western-style mansion in Kaya-chō, Tokyo, which was designed by Josiah Conder (1852–1920). The mansion was basically in the Jacobean style of seventeenth century England. However, Conder incorporated into its design architectural elements from Pennsylvania where Iwasaki had gone to university, such as a second-story colonnade, which is in the Ionian style of a Pennsylvania country house. The Tokyo Metropolitan Government now owns this building, which is open to the public as Kyū-Iwasaki-tei Gardens.

By Tetsuko Toda

Selected Reference: Lloyd C. Griscom, *Diplomatically Speaking* (New York: The Literary Guild of America, 1940).

4.7   Baba Tatsui: Statesman, Political Author
馬場辰猪：フィラデルフィアで生涯を終えた自由民権運動家

馬場辰猪（1850‐1888）という人について知る人は、今やほとんどいないかもしれない。ましてこの人物が1886年の夏に日本からアメリカへ亡命し、時には古色な甲冑を纏いながら、日本について太平洋岸から大西洋岸へ遊説して廻ったなどについては、なおさらのことであろう。なぜこのような時代に遥々渡米してきて、そのようなことをしたのであろうか。誰もが疑問に思うに違いない。

1850年5月15日に土佐藩（高知県）の士族の家に生まれた馬場は、長じて藩留学生として江戸に遊び、福沢諭吉の塾で学んだ。やがて選ばれて、1870年にはさらにイギリスへ留学し英語を習得した後、ミドル・テンプル法学院で法律学を修める。そして1878年に日本に帰国し、当時まさに激しさを増そうとしていた民選議院の設立を求める有力な支持者として、政治結社の同衆や交絢社に参加しながら政治活動に奔走した。とくに板垣退助の率いる自由党の結成には指導者の1人となって協力したが、同党首の外遊問題で意見を異にするや、同党を脱退して新たに独立党を結成するなど、つねにその雄弁家としての弁舌の矛先は、当時の自由民権思想に対して過酷な圧力を加えた薩長の藩閥政府に向かって、執念といえるほどに激しく燃え続けていたのである。

しかし馬場は、イギリス留学の頃から、少しずつ肺を侵されつつあった。それが自由民権運動への熱烈な闘志に沸き立ちながらも、結局は異国の地で夭折し

F ew people today may recognize the name Baba Tatsui (1850–1888). Even fewer would know that in the summer of 1886 he fled Japan and came to the United States, where he toured the country from the Pacific to the Atlantic coast lecturing about Japan, carrying his bundle of antique Japanese swords under his arm. This essay explores the circumstances of Baba's American adventure.

Baba was born on the fifth day of the fifth month of Kaei 3 (1850) to a family in Tosa (present day Kōchi Prefecture), and was sent by the local government to Edo (now Tokyo) as a student to attend Fukuzawa Yukichi's private school, later known as Keiō University. In 1870 he was chosen to continue his studies in England, and received a law degree at the Middle Temple in London. Upon his return to Japan in 1878, Baba embarked on various activities in the political arena, including as a supporter of the Popular Rights Movement, which sought to establish a popularly elected Diet. Baba became a leader in founding Japan's first national political party, the Jiyūtō (Liberal Party), along with Itagaki Taisuke. But Baba had differences of opinion with the party head about foreign travel, and left the Jiyūtō to found a new independent political party. His attacks on the Satsuma-Chōshū ruling circles, bitter opponents of the Popular Rights Movement, grew increasingly fervent.

Unfortunately, Baba had contracted lung disease during his stay in England. In the

ていかなければならなかった致命傷になっていく。そして1885年に図らずも、横浜で爆発物を購入したという嫌疑で当局に逮捕され、数ヶ月も拘置されてしまう。こうなっては、自由民権運動を掛替えのないものと考えていた馬場にとって、生きる道は、国外にしかなかったといってよい。それは藩閥政府からの圧迫と干渉の及ばない海外で、引き続き自由民権の理念を説こうとする亡命の旅に他ならなかった。

Baba Tatsui. Fukuzawa Memorial Center.
Keiō University
慶應義塾福澤研究センター所蔵

馬場は翌1886年6月12日にアメリカに向け出帆した。かつてイギリスで勉学しながら、なぜアメリカを目指したのか判然としないが、多分、馬場にとってアメリカは英語が通じ、何にもまして移民の国であり、亡命も受け入れてくれ易い国に思えたからであろう。時に馬場はまだ若く36歳だった。

ただ注目すべきは、馬場が日本の甲冑や弓矢や刀剣の類を一緒に運び出していることである。現今の、出入国時のセキュリティーの厳しさを知るわれわれには、想像もつかないことである。

かくて、同月26日にサンフランンスコに上陸してアメリカ大陸に一歩を印した馬場は、まずその近郊のオークランドに

end, this became the mortal wound that felled him on foreign soil, even as the combative spirit of the Popular Rights Movement welled within him. In 1885 Baba was unexpectedly arrested in Yokohama on suspicion of a bombing attempt and spent several months in detention. The best solution for Baba was to leave the country and to try to continue his work for the Popular Rights Movement from abroad.

He sailed from Yokohama for the United States on June 12, 1886 at the young age of thirty-six. Baba's English proficiency would have served him well in either England or America. Perhaps he chose America because he would be an exile in a land of fellow immigrants. One notable fact about his departure was that he took with him a collection of Japanese arms and armor, which seems unimaginable in our own security-conscious age.

He landed at San Francisco on June 26, 1886, and his first five months were spent in the nearby city of Oakland. While there, he prepared a manuscript entitled "The Weapons and Armor of Ancient Japan," which would be the basis of his popular lectures to introduce Japan to Americans. He delivered his first talk on November 5 of the same year, showing the actual pieces of armor, swords, bows and arrows to his audience.

居を決めて約5ヶ月を過ごす。その間に同地で講演者としての地位を確立するために、「古代日本の武器と甲冑」と題する講演原稿を用意し、11月5日に初めて英語で日本を紹介する講演を行った。その時に日本から持って来た甲冑や刀剣・弓矢を実際に身に纏って聴衆に見せたり、それらの品を展示したりもしたという。しかしその講演会は、完全に失敗に終わってしまったようである。

そこで馬場は、太平洋岸に見切りをつけてサンフランンスコから東部に向かい、11月21日にニューヨークに到着する。その時、ニューヨークに翌1887年の2月末まで滞在するが、その年の2月24日に同地のアメリカン・インスティチュートで行った同じ演題の講演会は、参集の聴衆も多くて、漸く彼自身も満足させるものになったらしい。しかし馬場はさらに移動して、何故か3月にはフィラデルフィアへ居を変えて行った。おそらく自由民権の理念の闘士として、アメリカ合衆国憲法の発祥の地に強い憧れを抱いたのであろうか。その年にフィラデルフィアでは、憲法100周年を祝する記念行事がいくつか催されていたはずである。

それ以後、馬場はフィラデルフィアを定住地として、同地のフランクリン・インスティチュートやペンシルベニア大学のほか、東はボストン、西はワシントンへも足を運んで、同じ「古代日本の武器と甲冑」という演題のもとに、実際にも持参した日本の武具類を身につけて見せながら、遊説し続けたのである。

ただ、ここで我われが留意しておくべきことは、当時、馬場が行った講演が単に日本事情の紹介のためではなかったと

Baba Tatsui's gravesite.
The Woodlands Cemetery, Philadelphia

However, his debut seems to have been a dismal failure, so Baba left San Francisco and head east, arriving in New York at the end of the month and staying until February 1887. This time his lectures at the American Institute attracted large audiences, and he seemed satisfied with his efforts. Then, for reasons that remain unclear, he moved again in March, this time to Philadelphia. Perhaps as a champion of popular rights, he felt a particular attraction to Philadelphia as the birthplace of the American Constitution. There were also many events taking place there in conjunction with the 100th anniversary of the Constitution.

いうことである。馬場の講演には、必ず日本の自由民権運動についてアメリカ人に訴えるという意図が伴っていたからだ。であればこそ、馬場は講演以外にもアメリカ滞在中に多くの論文や記事を新聞や雑誌に発表して、祖国日本で言論の自由を弾圧する藩閥政府を遥か海外から攻撃し続けたのであった。

それは、文化的には自国を賞賛しながら、政治的には自国政府を弾劾するという奇妙な広報活動であったといってよいだろう。もちろんそのような馬場の言動に当時の日本政府も神経を尖らせないはずがなかった。

それにしても馬場の最期は哀れなものであった。すでに患っていた肺病が悪化し、1888年にフィラデルフィアを終焉の地とたらしめてしまう。享年38歳であった。40点を超える彼の甲冑・刀剣コレクションはフィラデルフィア美術館に購入された。現在美術館には、当時の彼の講演草稿や文書とともに、13点の甲冑類が収蔵されている。馬場は今、ペンシルバニア大学近くにあるウッドランド墓地に眠っている。

松村正義

参考文献：
萩原延壽『馬場辰猪』(朝日新聞社、2007)

In any case, for the remainder of this life he resided in Philadelphia, delivering his lecture about Japanese arms and armor at the Franklin Institute and the University of Pennsylvania, and traveling to lecture in Boston and Washington, DC as well. It should be noted that these lectures were not limited to introducing the audience to Japanese culture. Baba invariably included the subject of Japan's liberal democratic movement. Besides his lectures, Baba wrote numerous newspaper articles and essays during his stay in America, continuing from abroad to pressure the Japanese government leaders who suppressed free speech at home.

He was hospitalized with consumption and died in Philadelphia on November 1, 1888, at the age of thirty-eight. His collection of over forty pieces of Japanese arms and armor were sold to the Philadelphia Museum of Art. The museum collection still includes thirteen of these, as well as a manuscript and some correspondence. Baba Tatsui's grave is at the Woodlands Cemetery in West Philadelphia.

By Masayoshi Matsumura

Selected Reference: Eugene Soviak, "The Case of Baba Tatsui: Western Enlightenment, Social Change and the Early Meiji Intellectual," *Monumenta Nipponica* 18 (1963), pp.191–235.

If you go: The Woodlands Cemetery, 40th and Woodland Avenue, Philadelphia, PA 19104.

4.8   Ichinoi Masatsune: Pioneer of Modern Dentistry
一井正典：近代西洋歯科のパイオニア

一井正典（いちのい　まさつね）は1862年6月8日に熊本県人吉市で生まれ、14歳のとき、最年少で西南ノ役に従軍。1885年に美山寛一牧師の世話で渡米後、1889年から1892年の4年間、フィラデルフィアに在住した人物である。

当時フィラデルフィアが、東海岸の各都市でも科学や文化がより近代的、先進的だったことが、一井をこの街に導いた。一井は近代西洋歯科医学の道をこの先進の地で選んだが、そのきっかけはサンフランシスコで開業していたドクター・ヴァンデンバーグの教えにあった。ヴァンデンバーグは一井が渡米した1885年当時、市内で歯科を開業していた。引退後に一井を農夫として雇い、彼の誠実さと力量を察知して、当時、北10番通り108－110にあったフィラデルフィア・デンタル・カレッジへの進学を勧めたのだった。

一井は受験成績も抜群で、予科を免除され1889年春、2年次に編入学を果たし、ジョン・ゲンフィル氏ら教会関係者の世話で通学した。そして1891年春、一井は136名中トップの成績で卒業、2等金賞を授与されている。この大学は1863年の創立で、43年後の1907年に現在のテンプル大学歯学部に併合されたが、現存する大学ではアメリカで4番目に古い歯科大学である。当時、口腔外科で有名なガレットソンが学長を務めており、アメリカの歯科大学の中でも特に口腔外科や補綴治療に先んじていた。

Ichinoi Masatsune was born on June 8, 1862 in what would become modern-day Hitoyoshi City, Kumamoto Prefecture. When the Satsuma Rebellion broke out, he entered military service at just fourteen years of age, making him the youngest person to enlist. He traveled to America in 1885 through the offices of Methodist minister Kan'ichi Miyama, and lived in Philadelphia from 1889 to 1892.

In those days Philadelphia stood at the forefront of scientific and cultural currents, in particular the field of modern dentistry. Ichinoi came to Philadelphia on the recommendation of one Dr. Vandenburg, a dentist who was practicing in San Francisco when Ichinoi first arrived there in 1885. After Vandenburg retired, he hired Ichinoi as a farmhand. Impressed with Ichinoi's energy and sincerity, Vandenburg encouraged him to study dentistry and directed him to the Philadelphia Dental College, then located at 108–110 North Tenth Street.

Earning exceptional scores on his entrance exam, Ichinoi was allowed to bypass the preparatory courses and enrolled in the two-year dental program in the spring of 1889. He received support from Dr. John Genphill and others affiliated with a church near the dental college. In the spring of 1891, Ichinoi graduated at the top of his class of 136 students and was awarded a gold medal. The Philadelphia Dental College was founded

Ichinoi Masatsune at his graduation, 1891.
Temple University
School of Dentistry

in 1863 (it merged with Temple University School of Dentistry in 1907), making it the fourth oldest dental school in the U.S. During Ichinoi's time there the school dean was Dr. J.E. Garretson, the famed oral surgeon, and the school was known for its advances in oral surgery and prosthetic treatment.

After graduation Ichinoi accepted a position at the dental college as an assistant professor. He also opened his own practice at 1836 Brandywine Street. It was the first dental practice established by a Japanese in America. With both a teaching position and a practice, his reputation grew, and he was well respected amongst his colleagues. The transcriptions of lectures he gave after returning to Japan cover this period in detail.

卒業後は大学から助教師の職を薦められたが、ブランディワイン通り1836番地での開業を決意した。それは日本人としてアメリカでの初めての開業だった。大学助教師を兼ねた開業は評判を呼び、同業者からも嫉まれるほどであった。それらは帰国後の講演録『ドクトル一ノ井正典君演説筆記』に詳しく記されている。

フィラデルフィア時代の友人には、寺島誠一郎（台湾拓殖製茶会長）、松方正雄（福徳生命保険社長）、津田元親（津田仙長男）、林民雄（日本郵船専務）、岩崎久彌（三菱社長）、福沢桃介（大同電力社長）、津田梅子（津田塾大学創始者）らがいた。彼らも帰国後は一流の財界人となった。なかでも一井と岩崎は仲が

Ichinoi's friends during his time in Philadelphia included many Japanese who would go on to prominence after their return to Japan. Among them were Terashima Seiichirō (head of tea production for the Taiwan Development Company), Matsukata Masao (chairman of Fukutoku Seimei Insurance), Tsuda Motochika (eldest son of Tsuda Sen), Hayashi Tamio (Japan Postal Shipping manager), Iwasaki Hisaya (chairman of Mitsubishi), Fukuzawa Tōsuke (chairman of Daidō Electric) and Tsuda Umeko (founder of Tsuda College). Among these, Ichinoi was particularly close with Iwasaki Hisaya, with whom he remained in contact throughout his life. When Ichinoi was teaching at the Takayama Dental School (present-day Tokyo Dental College) in 1900, he helped prepare Noguchi Hideo for a period of study abroad by sharing all manner of information about Philadelphia.

Ichinoi Masatsune at his clinic in Kudan, Tokyo. Courtesy of Ichinoi Kureo
一井呉夫所蔵

良く、帰国後も晩年まで交流が続いた。また高山歯科医学院（後の東京歯科大学）講師時代の1900年、野口英世の渡米留学の際にはフィラデルフィアに関する多くの情報を野口に与えている。

その後1892年には、オレゴン州ポートランド歯科医師会から招かれ、日本への帰国準備もあったので、2年ほど補綴治療の教授を兼ねてポートランド市デークムビルで開業した。1894年には日清戦争が勃発、バンクーバー経由で10年ぶりに帰国した。横浜から郷里人吉の町に帰省し、在米時代に一井を支えた恩人、江島五藤太らにお礼を済ませて上京。1895年3月、神田に西洋歯科医として32歳で開業したのである。帰国前

In 1892 Ichinoi was invited by the Portland Dental Association to work in Portland, Oregon, where he spent the next two years teaching prosthetic treatment and operating a practice in the downtown Dekum Building. The First Sino-Japanese War broke out in 1894, and he traveled via Vancouver to Japan, returning home for the first time in ten years. He went from Yokohama to his hometown of Hitoyoshi where he paid respects to Ejima Gotōta, one of his patrons during the years he spent in America. He then moved to Tokyo, and in March of 1895 at the age of thirty-two he opened a modern American-style dental practice in Kanda. At about the time of Ichinoi's return to Japan both the Tokyo Dental Association and the Japan Dental Association were being established, and he had a hand in their founding, becoming a permanent member of both organizations. Dentistry was developing rapidly in Japan: in 1902 Takayama Kisai, another student of Dr. Vandenburg, was elected the first chairman of the Japan Dental Association; Tokyo Medical College opened a department of dentistry; and in 1906 the Dental Practitioners Law was enacted.

During this time of positive momentum for dentistry, Ichinoi brought his knowledge of modern techniques to bear when he joined the Ministry of Education's Medical Certification Committee in 1900. He also held workshops on gold crown techniques and porcelain work, drawing participants from the whole country. He was at the height of his abilities and taught a great many students. In 1903 he opened a Western-style practice in Kudanshita, Tokyo. Through an introduction from General Nogi, he became the dentist to the imperial household, treating the Meiji,

Ceremony at Ichinoi's 150th Birthday Celebration in Hitoyoshi, June 8, 2012
一井生誕150周年献花式.　人吉市永国寺 所蔵

後には歯科医会（東京都歯科医師会）、そして日本歯科医会（日本歯科医師会）が発足し、正典は常議員として東京及び日本歯科医師会の設立にも寄与した。同じドクター・ヴァデンバーグの兄弟子、高山紀齋が1902年に日本歯科医会の初代会長となり、東京大学医学部にも歯科学教室が創設されるなど、歯科界の全国的な動きが急に加速し、1906年の「歯科医師法の制定」にもつながったのである。

これらの機運の中、近代西洋歯科を身に付けた一井は、1900年には文部省医術開業試験委員に就任。また全国的な金冠術やポーセレン術の講習会開催などで、その医術的手腕を発揮し、多くの弟子たちを育てた。1903年には九段下

Taishō, and Shōwa emperors.

Ichinoi's life began in the Edo period, spanned the Meiji and Taishō eras, and went into the Shōwa years as he pursued the vision of a new Japan. He died in 1929. When we consider what it takes to live with the uncertainties of our contemporary society, Ichinoi's perseverance, in the spirit of John Manjirō and others, provides a model for later generations of Japanese to follow new directions.

The 150th anniversary of Dr. Ichinoi's birth and his significant contributions to dentistry were celebrated in June 2012 with commemorative exhibits and lectures in both his hometown of Hitoyoshi and at the

に洋館の医院を新築。さらに乃木大将らの紹介で明治、大正、昭和の3天皇の侍医を務めた。

新しい日本の「時代の夢」を追い求め、江戸、明治、大正、昭和の4つの時代を生き抜いた一井正典の生き方は、混迷する現代社会を生き抜く上で、先人のジョン万次郎らと同様、次世代の日本人の新たな指針となることだろう。

2012年6月には、一井の生誕150周年を迎え、テンプル大学歯学部や地元人吉市では人物展や講演会等の記念行事が行われた。今後、地元フィラデルフィアの人たちに、彼の「存在」と「志」をどのような形で伝えてゆくかが大切だ。

松本晉一

参考資料:
松本晉一『維新の若きサムライ、一井正典とその時代』(熊本県歯科医師会発行、2012)

Temple University School of Dentistry. His aspirations are an important legacy for his adopted home of Philadelphia.

By Matsumoto Shin'ichi, Pedodontist,
Hitoyoshi City
Translated by Sam Malissa

If you go: Ichinoi's contributions are displayed at the Maurice H. Kornberg School Of Dentistry, Temple University, 3223 North Broad Street, Philadelphia, PA 19140.

4.9 Tsuda Umeko at Bryn Mawr: The Ideal of Women's Education

津田梅子：フィラデルフィアで学んだ女子大学創立者

津田梅子（1864‑1929）は日本で最初に海外留学をした女子学生である。津田の留学先はアメリカであった。しかもその時わずかに7歳だった。いったん日本に帰国した津田が、女子高等教育の理想に燃えて再びアメリカに勉強に来た時、留学先として選んだのはブリンマー大学であった。何故このような人生を選ぶことになったのだろうか。またブリンマーではどのように過ごしたのであろうか。

津田が初めてアメリカに来たのは1872年1月（日本の暦では1871年12月）のことであった。そのころの日本は明治時代に入ったばかりである。日本は二百数十年にわたる鎖国政策をやめて海外と積極的に交流し、特に欧米諸国と肩を並べる国力を養おうと努力し始めた時期であった。その時重要視されたことの1つが若者への教育である。しかも、アメリカでの女性の自立と活躍の様子を見た日本政府は、若い女性5人をアメリカへ送って勉強させることにした。その5人の1人として最年少で選ばれたのが津田で、留学予定期間は10年であった。

津田はワシントンのジョージタウンに住む親日派のチャールズ・ランマン、アデライン・ランマン夫妻に引き取られて、我が子のように可愛がられて育ち、アメリカ風の自由な雰囲気の教育を受けてのびのびと勉強した。この間、フィラデルフィア郊外のブリッジポートのオールド・スウェズ教会でキリスト教の洗礼も受けている。津田は最初の予定よりも1年長

Tsuda Umeko (1864–1929) was one of the first five young Japanese women to study abroad. She came to America as the youngest member of an official delegation. Although Tsuda returned to Japan after eleven years, her passion for women's education brought her back to America to enroll at Bryn Mawr College. Tsuda's experience at Bryn Mawr proved central to her life.

Tsuda first arrived in America in January 1872 as part of the Iwakura Diplomatic Mission. It was soon after the Meiji Restoration, which brought Japan out of over two hundred years of relative isolation from the rest of the world. The new Meiji government opened relations with foreign nations, and was eager to learn from and become the equal of Europe and America. Further, having observed the independence and vivacity of American women, the Japanese government sent five young women to the United States to study. These young women, the youngest of whom was seven-year-old Tsuda Umeko, studied abroad for a period of ten years.

Tsuda was taken into the home of Adeline and Charles Lanman of Georgetown, in Washington, DC, who treated her as if she were their own daughter. Tsuda received her education in the free and liberal atmosphere of the United States. She was also baptized as a Christian at Old Swedes Church in Bridgeport, a suburb of Philadelphia. Tsuda

Tsuda Umeko in her dorm room at Bryn Mawr College. Bryn Mawr Special Collections

くアメリカに滞在し、18歳の時に日本に帰った。

しかし日本には津田に十分な仕事がなかった。またアメリカに比べてあまりにも日本の女性の地位が低いことを見た津田は、次第に女子教育に生涯の目標を定めるようになった。そして1889年、25歳の時に再びアメリカに来て、ブリンマー大学に入学したのである。この大学は1885年に創立されたばかりの、新しい意欲にあふれた女子大学として知られていた。津田はアメリカの知人たちの勧めもあって入学し、生物学を専攻した。津田は文学面にもすぐれていたが、他方、理科的な学科に抜群の能力を持っていたのである。これは父の津田仙が農学者だったことによる影響も考えられよう。津田は生命の神秘を究めてゆく生

stayed one year longer than originally planned and returned to Japan at the age of eighteen.

But finding no employment in Japan and observing the comparatively low position of Japanese women made her determined to devote her life to Japanese women's education. In 1889, at the age of twenty-five, Tsuda came back to America, and enrolled at Bryn Mawr College, a new aspiring college for women founded in 1885. At Bryn Mawr Tsuda excelled in literature and the sciences, especially biology. These talents may reflect the influence of her father, Tsuda Gen, who was a specialist in agricultural sciences. She studied hard, concentrating on biology, and co-authored (as Umè Tsuda) a paper with her advisor, Professor Thomas Hunt Morgan,

物学に興味を引かれて熱心に研究し、指導教授のモーガン教授との共同研究で「蛙の卵の発生に関する研究」という論文をまとめている。この論文は1894年、イギリスの権威ある学術雑誌『季刊マイクロスコピカル・サイエンス』第35号に掲載された。

優秀な成績を収めた津田は研究者として残ることを大学から要請されたほどであった。しかし、日本の女子教育に尽くしたいという彼女の決意は固く、3年後に帰国した。またこの間、教育・教授法の研究のため、オンタリオ湖の湖畔にあるオスウェゴ師範学校で学んでいる。

日本に帰った後、さまざまな努力によって、津田は念願の女性の高等教育を目指す学校を東京に開くことができ、女子英学塾と名付けられた。1900年のことであった。最初の入学生は10人だったが、津田の理想に燃えた教育のもとで、入学者はしだいに増加していく。この学校の運営に当たって、アメリカの友人たちの協力も大きかった。この女子英学塾が、今日の津田塾大学である。

女子教育に一生を捧げた津田は、1929年に66歳で亡くなった。墓地は津田塾大学キャンパス内にある。ブリンマー大学と津田塾大学とは今日に至るまで姉妹校として親しい関係を続けている。

今井雅晴

参考文献:
高橋裕子『津田梅子の社会史』(玉川大学出版部、2002)
亀田帛子『津田梅子:ひとりの名教師の軌跡』(双文社出版、2005)

entitled "The Orientation of Frog's Egg." This paper was published in 1894, in volume 35 of the English journal, the Quarterly Journal of Microscopical Science.

Tsuda was an excellent student and was invited to stay as a researcher at Bryn Mawr. However, she returned to Japan three years later determined to work for women's education, having attended courses in education at Oswego Teacher's College in New York state to prepare for this mission.

In Japan Tsuda devoted her energy to establishing a women's secondary school in Tokyo, which opened its doors in 1900 as the Women's English School (Joshi Eigaku Juku), now called Tsuda College. The first year's enrollment consisted of ten students, but the number grew steadily with her fervent devotion to the ideal of women's education and the management assistance she received from American friends.

After a lifetime devoted to women's education, Tsuda Umeko died in 1929 at the age of sixty-six. Her grave is located on the grounds of Tsuda College. The sister college relationship she established between Bryn Mawr and Tsuda College continues to this day.

By Masaharu Imai
Translated by Felice Fischer

Selected References: Yoshiko Furuki, *The White Plum: A Biography of Ume Tsuda, Pioneer in the Higher Education of Japanese Women* (New York and Tokyo: Weatherhill, 1991); Donald Keene, *Modern Japanese Diaries* (New York: Henry Holt., 1995; reprint New York: Columbia University Press, 1998),

【参考情報】
津田塾大学
〒187-8577　東京都小平市津田町
2-1-1
電話:042-342-5111(代表)
www.tsuda.ac.jp

pp. 304–312; Barbara Rose, *Tsuda Umeko and Women's Education in Japan* (New Haven and London: Yale University Press, 1992).

If you go: Bryn Mawr College, 101 North Merion Ave, Bryn Mawr, PA 19010.

4.10 Kawai Michi: Educator, Christian Activist, and Internationalist
河井道：恵泉女学園創立者

河井道（1877 - 1953）は教育者、キリスト教精神の伝道者、国際平和推進者として、第2次世界大戦の前後を通して欧米社会との絆を築き続けた女性であり、女子教育に情熱を傾け恵泉女学園を創立した。さらに、最初の日本キリスト教女子青年会（YWCA）同盟総幹事として女性の社会的、経済的向上に貢献した。

河井は1877年に三重県伊勢市で生まれた。父は神官であったが、河井が幼少時に失職し、当時、政府が推奨していた北海道移住に応じた。1887年、長老派宣教師のサラ・スミスが新しく開設したスミス女学校（現在の北星女学園）に入学した。授業では札幌農学校（現在の北海道大学）の新渡戸稲造が指導しており、そこで、河井は新渡戸夫妻と知り合い、親交を深めていったのである。学校教育を通して、河井は英語力をつけ、園芸の楽しみを学んだ。

1895年、河井はアメリカから来日したローズ女史が北海道の小樽で女学校を設立するのを手伝い、女子学生を指導したのである。その後、新渡戸夫妻と共に上京。東京で、アメリカから帰国したばかりの津田梅子に紹介された。津田はアメリカでの経験から、後進の日本女性たちがアメリカに留学できるようにメアリ・モリスたちの援助で奨学金制度を設けており、河井はこの奨学金を得て、21歳の時、アメリカに渡った。1898年にペンシルベニア州のアイビーハウスで学

Kawai Michi (1877–1953) was a Japanese educator, Christian activist, and proponent of Japanese-Western ties before, during, and after World War II. She devoted her life to girls' education and founded Keisen Jogakuen, a Christian school for young women in Tokyo. She served as the first National Secretary of the YWCA of Japan in order to improve women's lives through the promotion of social and economic change.

Kawai Michi was born in 1877 in Ise, Mie Prefecture. Her father was a Shinto priest. When Kawai was still a child, her father lost his job and moved his family to Hakodate, in Hokkaido, where the government was encouraging people to settle. There, in 1887, she began attending a newly established boarding school in Sapporo run by a Presbyterian missionary named Sarah C. Smith. Smith Girls' School is now Hokusei Jogakkō. Some classes were taught by professors such as Nitobe Inazō from Sapporo Agricultural College, now Hokkaido University. She became acquainted with Nitobe and his wife and established a friendship with them. Through the schooling there, she improved her English language skills and especially enjoyed learning about gardening.

In 1895, Kawai spent a year helping to start up another girls' school in Otaru, Hokkaido, assisting a Miss Rose from America, and

Kawai Michi, 1904. Keisen University 恵泉女学園所蔵

び、1900年ブリンマー大学に入学した。

留学中に河井は、アメリカで最高の教育を受けたばかりでなく、自主性、独立した考え方を学び尊重するようになっていった。また広い人間関係を築き、交流関係が将来の活動の糧になったのである。

アメリカ滞在中、河井は女性の社会的、経済的向上を目指す活動をしているキリスト教女子青年会（YWCA）に参加する機会に恵まれた。1902年にニューヨークのシルバーベイで開催されたYWCAの会合に参加し、カナダの下院議長を父に持つキャロライン・マクドナルドと出会う。マクドナルドは1905年に万国YWCA連盟の依頼で日本YWCAの設立のため、日本を訪れた。

1904年にブリンマー大学を卒業後、日本に帰国し、津田が創立した女子英学塾（現在の津田塾大学）で教鞭を執り、英

teaching. These experiences would prove useful later in her life. Upon her return to Sapporo, Kawai learned that the Nitobes had moved to Tokyo, and she decided to follow them there. Through the Nitobes, Kawai met Tsuda Umeko, who had recently returned from studying in the United States. As a result of her experiences in the States, Tsuda set up a scholarship fund with the aid of American friends such as Mary Morris to enable Japanese girls to study in America. Kawai was awarded a scholarship from this fund and went to America with the Nitobes at the age of twenty-one, enrolling in Ivy House, an American preparatory school in the Germantown section of Philadelphia. Kawai subsequently entered Bryn Mawr College in Pennsylvania in 1900.

It was a precious time in her life—she was not only studying at some of the best educational institutions in America, but she was also learning to be independent and to understand and appreciate Western ways. She made friendships and contacts that would prove to be of immeasurable service in the future.

While in the United States, Kawai learned of

語、翻訳、歴史などを教えた。河井はま
た、マクドナルドと一緒に日本YWCAの
創立者の1人として、1912年に最初の
日本YWCA同盟総幹事となり活躍した。
任期中、各地方にもYWCAを作り、また
日本YWCAの代表として国際YWCAの
会合にも精力的に出席した。

1923年に河井はクリスチャン仲間と中
国を訪問し、両国間の関係が難しい時
期に、両国の交流と友情の絆を深め、さ
らにYWCA国際会議に出席し活躍した。
同年、関東大震災時には東京YWCA連
合の代表を務め、震災後の救援活動に
大きな貢献をしている。

1929年、河井はキリスト教精神に基づ
いた女子教育のため恵泉女学園を創立
し、学園長となった。この学園には次の
3つの教育理念がある。「聖書―キリス
ト教の教え」「国際理解」「園芸を通して
自然に感謝」。1年次には国語、数学、歴
史、地理、科学、英語、裁縫、聖歌、ゲー
ム、絵画、聖書、道徳、国際関係、園芸の
カリキュラムが組まれている。

河井は日米関係改善に積極的で、1941
年に、北アメリカのキリスト教連盟の会
議に平和使節団のメンバーとして出席
した。また、カリフォルニア州のミルズ大
学から人文学・名誉博士の称号を授与
された。これに関して、河井は、1950年
の著作において、「これを、このゆゆしい
危機の折にあたってアメリカの日本に対
する善意の表われとして、受けるべきで
はないだろうか。自分のためではなく、
自分の国のために。そしてこの困難な時
にあたって、平和と友情のために立とう
と自らに誓う」(11頁)と述べている。

第2次大戦中、軍部の圧力で河井はクリ

the Young Women's Christian Association
(YWCA), which worked to improve
women's lives through social and economic
change. In 1902 she attended a YWCA
conference at Silver Bay, in New York, where
she met Caroline Macdonald, daughter
of the Speaker of the Canadian House of
Commons. MacDonald was sent in 1905 to
Japan by the World Committee of the YWCA
to help establish a Japanese National YWCA
Association.

After graduating from Bryn Mawr in 1904,
Kawai returned to Japan, and became
affiliated with Tsuda Umeko's girls' school,
Joshi Eigaku Juku (now Tsuda Women's
College). Kawai taught English, translation,
and history at the school. Kawai also became
one of the founding members of the Japanese
YWCA, along with Caroline Macdonald,
serving as the first National Secretary of
the Japanese YWCA in 1912. She worked to
expand the Japanese national association and
establish local YWCA branches throughout
Japan. She also traveled to international
meetings of the YWCA where she often
spoke on behalf of the Japanese YWCA.

Kawai and other Japanese Christians visited
China in 1923 to maintain mutual friendship
between China and Japan during a period
of conflict between the two countries.
Following the 1923 Great Kantō earthquake,
Kawai served as the first chairperson of the
Federation of Tokyo Women's Associations,
which played a significant role in organizing
post-earthquake relief efforts.

In 1929, Kawai founded a Christian school
for young women in Tokyo named Keisen
Jogakuen, which means "fountain-of-

Kawai with the students of Keisen University, 1930. Keisen University 恵泉女学園所蔵

スチャンの学校運営に苦労するが、キリスト教精神と教育理念は曲げなかった。また河井は日本に大きな貢献をしている。戦後、連合国最高司令官のダグラス・マッカーサーの副官であったボナ・フェラーズ（1896 - 1973）は河井と一色百合（河井道の教え子で、ボナ・フェラーズとアーラム大学で同級生）に会い、戦争時の天皇の役割について意見を聞いた。フェラーズは河井の考えを取り入れ、覚書を作成し、象徴天皇制へと移行するのを助けた。彼は戦前、日本の社会、歴史、文化に興味を持ち、占領下の日本ではGHQと宮内庁との架け橋となった。

河井はまた、戦後、天皇の子供たちの家

blessings girls' learning-garden. " The school was based on three educational principles: Christianity, internationalism, and respect for nature, especially through gardening. In its first years, the school offered courses in Japanese, mathematics, history, geography, science, English, Japanese sewing, singing and games, drawing, Bible and morals, international studies, and gardening.

Kawai also was active in promoting Japanese-American relations and in 1941, representing Japanese Christian women, she attended a meeting of the Foreign Mission Boards of North America and Canada. While in California, Kawai was awarded an honorary

庭教師としてクエーカー教徒のエリザベス・バイニングを紹介している。1946年、河井は総理大臣の諮問機関として設けられた教育刷新委員会の委員に選ばれ、戦後の日本教育の基本理念について討議した。河井はただ1人の女性委員であった。

河井はクリスチャン活動家として、また国際平和主義者として、女性教育に人生を捧げ、1953年に75歳で亡くなったが、彼女の業績は今でも多くの人に引き継がれている。

浜田昌子

参考文献:
河井道『私のランターン』(恵泉女学園出版、1939)
河井道『スライデング・ドア』(恵泉女学園出版、1950)

【参考情報】
恵泉女学園
〒156−0055
東京都世田谷区船橋5-8-1
電話:03-3303-2115
www.keisen.jp

degree of doctor of humane letters from Mills College. In her 1950 autobiography, Kawai wrote, "'This is a gesture of American goodwill to Japan at this critical moment,' said my soul to me. 'Therefore accept the honor, not for yourself, but for your country, and pledge yourself to stand for the cause of peace and friendship in this hour of tribulation.'" During World War II, she faced difficulties running Christian schools due to pressure from the military authorities, but she never compromised her Christian faith and philosophy of education.

Kawai made another significant contribution to Japan. After the war was over, Kawai and Isshiki Yuri met with General Bonner Fellers (1896–1973), who came from a Quaker family and had attended the Quaker-affiliated Earlham College, where Isshiki was a fellow student. Fellers played a major role in the American occupation in Japan, when he served as liaison between the American headquarters and the Imperial household and was instrumental in the selection of Elizabeth Vining as tutor to the Emperor's children. The purpose of the meeting was to discuss the Emperor's role during the war. Kawai's comments and thoughts about the Emperor's role during World War II influenced Fellers' recommendation in his influential memoranda to General Douglas MacArthur that the Emperor continue to serve as a symbol of the nation of Japan.

In 1946 Kawai was selected and served as a member of a committee (run by the Ministry of Education) to establish a new educational philosophy for Japan. She was the only woman on the committee. Kawai devoted her life to being a girls' educator, Christian activist, and internationalist. She passed away in 1953 at the age of seventy-five. Her work continues through the many she inspired.

By Masako Hamada

Selected References: Kawai Michi, *Japanese Women Speak: A Message from the Christian Women of Japan to the Christian Women of America*, with Ochimi Kubishiro (Boston, MA: Central Committee on the United Study of Foreign Missions, 1933); Kawai Michi, *Sliding Doors* (Tokyo: Keisen Jogakuen, 1950); William Heward Murray Walton, *A Torch in Japan: the Story of Michi Kawai* (New York: Friendship Press, 1949).

4.11 Noguchi Hideyo: Medical Researcher
野口英世：アメリカで花を咲かせた医学研究者

野口英世（1876 - 1928）は、日本人として世界で最もよく知られた医学者の1人である。その伝記の数は400を超し、デンマークやスペインの国王からメダルを授かり、また世界の多くの大学から名誉博士号を受けた。ノーベル賞の候補になったことも1度ならず3度もあった。驚くべきことは、野口は大学を卒業しておらず、正規の医学教育すら受けていないことである。いや、アメリカにくる以前、日本で本格的な医学研究者としてのトレーニングさえも受けたことがない。そのような人が一体どうして世界的な大医学者になったのであろうか。

野口は1876年、日本の東北地方の貧しい農家に生まれた。伝記によると、彼の父親は酒飲みで賭け事に興じていたという。仕方なく野口の母が米や野菜を植え、また川に魚や貝を取りに行って家を支えた。ある日の夕方、母が2歳になる野口をいろりのそばに寝かせ、畑でもう一仕事している時に、一大事が起こった。野口が燃えさかるいろりの中に転げ落ちたのである。このため体の各所にやけどをした。特に左手のやけどがひどく、その後、野口の左手は指を動かすことも、ろくに使うこともできなくなった。そして、このことが彼の一生を大きく変えることになったのである。母は、百姓をすることもできなくなった息子に、「生きる道はよく勉強することしかない」と教えた。

野口はその母の言葉通り猛然と勉強に勤しんだ。あまりに優秀な野口のために

More than four hundred books and articles have been published about Noguchi Hideyo (1886–1928), one of the best known and most widely respected medical researchers of the twentieth century. Among the many honors bestowed upon Noguchi were three Nobel prize nominations, medals from the kings of Denmark and Spain, as well as numerous honorary degrees from universities around the world. These honors are all the more remarkable because Noguchi never attended college or medical school, nor did he receive training as a medical researcher in Japan.

Noguchi Hideyo was born in 1886 on a very poor farm in the northern part of Japan. His father was addicted to alcohol and gambling, leaving Noguchi's mother to feed her family by growing vegetables in her garden and catching fish in the nearby river. One afternoon while his mother was out working on the farm, the two-year-old Hideyo, asleep by the hearthside, rolled into the fire. He sustained burns over several parts of his body, and particularly on his left hand, leaving him unable to move his fingers or use the hand. This accident changed his life. His crippled hand made it impossible for him to take up farming, so Noguchi's mother wisely encouraged him to concentrate on his studies instead.

Noguchi worked extremely hard at school and was a talented student. While he was

教師たちが金を出し合って、その左手の手術をするため医師のもとに送った。幸いにも近くの街に渡部鼎（かなえ）という、外国で医学のトレーニングを受けた医師がいた。そして手術の結果、野口の左手は少しではあるが使えるようになった。そのこともあり、野口は中学を卒業した後、この渡部医師のもとで書生として働くことになった。この間、野口は渡部医師から医学を学び、また、医学書を読むためにドイツ語、フランス語、英語などを独学で修得した。数年後、東京で開業医試験を受けた野口は1次試験に合格、そして翌年には80人中4人の合格率という難関の2次試験にも合格したのである。

医師の免許は得たものの左手のこともあり、野口は北里研究所で働くことになり、幸運にもそこで、一生の恩師サイモン・フレクスナー博士と会うことになった。北里研究所を訪問したフレクスナー博士は、ジョンズ・ホプキンス大学で教鞭をとっていたが、その後ペンシルベニア大学の教授になった人である。当時ドイツ医学が主流を占めていたこともあり、北里研究所には英語のできる人が少なく、英語のできる野口がフレクスナー博士の通訳をすることになったのである。野口はこのチャンスを逃がさなかった。博士にアメリカに留学したいことを述べ、博士は「ザッツ・ファイン」と言う外交的な返事をした。これで博士の許可を得たと一人合点した野口は、数年後の1900年12月、フィラデルフィアまでやって来たのである。

しかし、フレクスナー博士は野口が誰であるのかさえ覚えていなかったし、彼の研究室に空席もなかった。フレクスナー博士は帰りの旅費さえ持たずにやって

Noguchi Hideyo. Courtesy of the author

in middle school his teachers collected funds for him to consult a doctor about his hand. Luckily, there was a foreign-educated doctor in the city, Watanabe Kanae, who was able to operate on Noguchi's hand. After the operation, Noguchi was able to use his left hand again to some extent, and after graduation went to work for Dr. Watanabe as a "drug boy" (*shosei*), the equivalent of an apprentice position. During this time Noguchi not only learned as much as he could from Dr. Watanabe, but taught himself

来た野口のことについて、先輩のワイヤー・ミッチェル博士に相談した。たまたまミッチェル博士が自分の蛇毒の研究を引き継いで研究してくれる人を探していたからである。野口はミッチェル博士から譲り受けた世界中の蛇毒のコレクションをもとに、ボランティアとしてフレクスナー博士の下で蛇毒の研究を始めた。仕事の場を与えられた野口は不眠不休で働き、どんどん研究論文を発表した。彼の才能がここに花開いたのである。野口はその後、当時研究の始まったばかりの免疫学について学ぶため、デンマークのマドセン博士のもとに送られた。そして山羊に蛇毒を反復注射することにより、山羊の血液内に蛇毒に対する抗体が出来ること、この抗体を含んだ血清を与えると、毒蛇にかまれた山羊の命を救えることを発見した研究者の1人となった。

1904年、野口はロックフェラー研究所を発足させるために、フレクスナー博士に付いてニューヨークに行くことになった。野口はここで梅毒の研究を始めた。当時、梅毒は世界で猛威を振るっていたが、この病気の原因や治療法などはまだあまり理解されていなかった。野口は梅毒の診断のための血清診断法を確立し、また、梅毒の原因であるスピロヘータの純粋培養に成功した。そして当時全身麻痺、脊椎に異常をきたし運動失調を起こし死んでいく原因不明の病気は、実は梅毒菌により起こることを証明した。また、野口は免疫学の基礎となり、現在も使われている数多くの実験法を開発し、『梅毒の血清診断法』という本を書いた。こうして野口の研究は世界中で大きな注目を浴びることになり、世界の多くの国から招かれた。

to read German, French, and English in order to read the medical books in his employer's library. In a few years' time Noguchi was able to go to Tokyo to sit for the first of two examinations required to practice medicine. He not only passed the first examination, but in the following year also passed the second, being one of only four out of eighty students who passed.

Early in his professional life he worked at the Kitasato Institute, where he met Dr. Simon Flexner in 1887. Flexner was a visiting professor from Johns Hopkins Medical School, and later taught at the University of Pennsylvania. Noguchi acted as Flexner's interpreter and apparently misunderstood the latter's polite approval of Noguchi's plan to study in America as an invitation. When Noguchi arrived in Philadelphia in December 1900, Flexner did not remember Noguchi, much less have a position for him. He nevertheless allowed Noguchi to work in his laboratory as a volunteer. Noguchi was one of the researchers at the University of Pennsylvania who discovered that the antidote for snakebite could be produced from snake venom. He also established many basic immunological methods that are still used today.

In 1904 Noguchi moved to New York with Flexner to establish the Rockefeller Institute for Medical Research. Noguchi concentrated his research on syphilis, a disease not well understood at that time, and established a simple method for detection of the disease in its many forms, including the so-called "brain syphilis." Noguchi's research won him worldwide recognition, and he traveled extensively to share his knowledge with

しかし、やがて野口は自分の命を奪う最後の旅をすることになった。行き先はガーナであった。当地で流行していた黄熱病の研究をするためだった。そしてそこで自ら研究する黄熱病に感染して、劇的ともいえる死を遂げたのである。筆者はアフリカに多い鎌状赤血球貧血病の診断法や治療法を伝えるグループの1員として、ガーナに行く機会を得た。そしてそこで92歳になるアレキサンダー・ウィリアムズ氏という人に会うことができた。かつて野口の助手として働いた人が、まだ生きていたのである。そしてウィリアムズ氏の口から野口が黄熱病の研究の他、鎌状赤血球貧血病の診断法を開発し、当時その病院で使われていたことを聞いて驚嘆した。その病院も、そしてその研究室も今も残されている。

医学研究の先駆者野口英世の名は、日本やアメリカなどの多くの国で知られている。野口博士の物語は、私を含めて多くの人に医学の道へ進むことを鼓舞した。私が野口博士と同じフィラデルフィアのペンシルベニア大学で医学の道を歩むこととなったのは、野口博士のお陰である。

朝倉稔生

other countries. His final trip was to Africa to investigate yellow fever, where his career came to a dramatic end when he died from yellow fever in 1928. On a trip to Ghana, I met a ninety-two-year old man, Alexander S. Williams, who remembered Dr. Noguchi and his work there on yellow fever. I was astonished to learn that while Noguchi was in Ghana, he also studied sickle cell disease and developed a diagnostic method that was used at the hospital where he worked. The hospital and laboratory used by Noguchi still exist.

Noguchi Hideyo is remembered as a pioneering medical hero both in Japan and in the United States. His life story has inspired many, including myself, to enter the medical field. I feel fortunate to have followed in his footsteps to Philadelphia and the University of Pennsylvania, where Noguchi began his medical research career.

By Toshio Asakura

Selected Reference: Kweku Ampiah, "Icons in Moral Education: Noguchi Hideyo and Modern Japan," *Social Science Japan Newsletter* 13 (Aug. 1998): 29–31.

If you go: The bronze statue of Noguchi Hideyo that stood near 36th and Market Streets when the Noguchi Medical Research Institute operated at the University City Science Center was returned to Japan and installed at Onshinkai Hospital, Fukaishimizuchō, Naka Ward, Sakai, Osaka Prefecture 599-8273, Japan.

4.12 Arishima Takeo: A Novelist's Sojourn in Philadelphia

有島武郎：ハバフォード大学で学んだ小説家

1903年9月のある日の午後、ジョゼフ・エルキントン氏はフィラデルフィアのブロード・ストリート駅のプラットホームに立って、25歳の日本人学生、有島武郎（1878‐1923）を乗せた列車が到着するのを待っていた。

有島がアメリカに来た1番の理由は、フィラデルフィア郊外にあるクエーカーの学校であるハバフォード大学で修士号を得るためであった。それ以前に日本の札幌農学校（現在の北海道大学）で、有島はジョゼフ・エルキントンの義理の兄弟である、新渡戸稲造（1862‐1933）がいる官舎に入っていた。エルキントンと新渡戸はクエーカー（キリスト友会のメンバー）であった。有島より16歳年長の新渡戸は、有島にキリスト教徒になるように説き、改宗させたのだった。

有島は1878年3月4日に東京で生まれた。1903年には札幌農学校を卒業し、すでに学士号を取得していた。父は名門出身で大蔵省役人の有島武、母は幸子である。有島は家庭では伝統的な儒教教育を受けたが、その一方で英語も学び、ミッション・スクールで初等教育を受けた。その学校は生徒のほとんどが外国人で、有島はそこで初めてキリスト教に触れた。

有島が日本を出る決意をした時、新渡戸はハバフォード大学で勉強することを勧めた。そこで有島は師である新渡戸の妻、メアリ・エルキントン・新渡戸から、英語の集中レッスンを受け始めた。

On a September afternoon in 1903, Joseph Elkinton stood on the platform of the Broad Street station in Philadelphia waiting for the train carrying a twenty-five year-old Japanese student named Arishima Takeo (1878–1923).

Arishima had come to the United States, among other reasons, to earn his master's degree at Haverford College, a Quaker institution outside Philadelphia. At the Sapporo Agricultural College, now Hokkaido University in Japan, Arishima had roomed with Nitobe Inazō, Joseph Elkinton's brother-in-law. Both Elkinton and Nitobe were members of the Religious Society of Friends (Quakers) and Nitobe, sixteen years Arishima's senior, convinced Arishima to become a Friend also.

Arishima received an A.B. from the Sapporo Agricultural College in 1903. Born in Tokyo on March 4, 1878, he was the son of a high-born finance minister, Arishima Takeshi, and mother, Arishima Yukiko. While Arishima Takeo received a traditional Confucian-style education at home, he also learned English and received a primary education at a mission school where most of the students were foreign. It was there that he was first introduced to Christianity.

Determined to leave Japan, he was advised by Nitobe to study at Haverford College. Arishima began taking intensive English

Arishima Takeo, 1904. Haverford College Quaker & Special Collections

lessons from Mary Elkinton Nitobe, his mentor's wife, and in July of 1903, he obtained a position as foreign correspondent in the U.S. for the newspaper *Mainichi*. He kept a diary during his journey to America in which he recorded his experiences.

Arishima's classes at Haverford began on September 22. He was only the second Japanese student at the college since its founding in 1833. He studied German, Greek, and Roman history, and economics; he excelled in Greek history. One of Arishima's classmates, Arthur Crowell, invited Arishima to spend Thanksgiving at the Crowell home, a farm south of Philadelphia. The hospitality and warmth of the occasions spent with American families were to remain important memories for Arishima.

Arishima's 254-page thesis for Haverford College, written in his own hand, was entitled, "Development of Japanese Civilization: From the Mythical Age to the Time of Decline of Shogunal Power." Of the thirty-seven authors cited in his bibliography, only six are Japanese, including Nitobe's books, *The Intercourse between the United States and Japan* and his even better-known *Bushido, the Soul of Japan*.

An astute, observant, and insightful commentator, Arishima later wrote in his journal about his experience at Haverford:

My first year in America was spent at a Quaker institution, founded by the Orthodox branch of that sect. It

そして、1903年、毎日新聞のアメリカ特派員の職を手に入れる。アメリカへの旅の間、彼は日記をつけ、体験したことを記録した。ハバフォードで、有島の授業は9月22日に始まった。1833年創立のハバフォード大学の歴史において、有島は2人目の日本人学生であった。有島はドイツ史やギリシャ史、ローマ史、経済学の授業を取り、ギリシャ史では最高の成績を得た。級友の1人アーサー・クロウェルが、家族と一緒に感謝祭を過ごすように招待してくれ、フィラデルフィアの南にある農場で、アメリカ人の家族と共に過ごした。その時の厚いもてなしと温かさは、有島にとって大切な思い出となった。

有島がハバフォード大学に提出した自筆の254頁の論文は、「日本文明の発展－神話時代から将軍家の滅亡まで」と題されている。参考文献一覧表に挙げられた37人の著者のうち日本人は6人だけで、その中には新渡戸も含まれ、『日米交流』や有名な『武士道―日本の魂』も文献一覧に記されている。

明敏で観察力と洞察力に富んだ論説者として、有島はハバフォード大学での経験について、後に日記に次のように書いている。「アメリカで最初の1年は、クエーカーのオーソドックス派によって創立された教育機関で過ごした。そこは宗教的雰囲気がとても強かったと言えるが、幸いなことに、この教派の礼拝形式は非常に自由であった。毎週木曜日午後の礼拝では、説教がなく、賛美歌を歌ったりすることも、教義を朗読することもなかった。心を動かされた者のみが、ひざまずいて祈りを捧げたり、立って話したりした。私はいつも後の席に1人で座り、自分の考えに沈潜した。その沈黙の時は、私にとって大事なものであった。外国へ行った主な目的は、物事を1人で考え抜くことだったので、人に近付く努力はしなかった」。

論文を提出したその日に、有島はペンシルベニア州フランクフォードのフレンズ精神病院（現在のフレンズ病院）で、たぶんボランティアだったと思われるが、付添人として働き始めた。有島は両親への手紙に、「このような場所を選んだ理由は、この国で行われている慈善活動の一部をみたいと思い、また自分より弱い者を手助けし、私の飢えた精神を満たしたいと思ったからです」と書いている。有島は1日15時間働き、ほとんどの時間はドアの外から患者を監視し

is not wrong to say that the religious atmosphere there is very strong. But fortunately the forms of this sect are very free. In the religious meeting that was held every Thursday afternoon, there were no sermons nor hymn singing, nor reading of creeds. Those only whose hearts were moved, knelt and offered prayer, or stood and spoke. I always sat alone on the back seat and sank into my own thoughts...the quiet minutes used to be dear to me...However, because my main purpose in going abroad was to think things out for myself, I did not make an effort to approach people.

On the same day that he handed in his thesis, Arishima also began work as an attendant, probably a volunteer, at the Friends Asylum for the Insane (now Friends Hospital) in Frankford, Pennsylvania. Arishima wrote to his parents, "The reason I chose this sort of place is because I want to observe a part of the philanthropic work done in this country and also to give assistance to those weaker than myself and to satisfy my famished spirit." Arishima worked fifteen hours a day, mostly supervising patients out of doors. During his two months at the hospital, he became a close acquaintance of one of the patients, a Dr. Scott. Arishima's growing disillusionment with Christianity was supported by Dr. Scott's belief that Christianity could not encompass sin, and was deepened by Scott's suicide later that year.

Arishima returned to Japan some time late in 1906 or in 1907. After a brief stint as a lecturer at Sapporo Agricultural College in philosophy, he turned to writing, founding and contributing to the literary magazine

ていた。病院にいた2ヶ月の間に、彼はスコット博士という患者と親しくなった。有島のキリスト教に対する幻滅は膨らみ始めていたが、キリスト教は罪を包み込むことはできないというスコット博士の意見によって強化され、さらにその年のスコット博士の自殺でいっそう深まったのであった。

有島は1906年末から1907年ごろに、日本に戻った。札幌農学校で哲学の講師を短期間務めた後、作家に転じ、文芸同人雑誌『白樺』の創刊に関わり、同人として寄稿した。1911年と1919年の間に、最初の小説『或る女』を書いた。トルストイの作品に強い影響を受け、その頃には社会主義に帰依し、プロレタリア文学に賛同していた。その後、『カインの末裔』(1918)や『宣言一つ』(1922)などの作品を発表し、社会や自然の力に圧倒された個人の悲劇を描いた。

有島の作品は、聖書やトルストイ、無政府主義的な社会主義に基づく考えを用い、感情的に激しく、学究的、人道主義的であった。自分は真の社会主義者にも、真のキリスト者にもなれない、と有島は最終的に思うようになる。創造力の喪失、そして空しさと絶望感に苛まれ、1923年に自らの命を絶った。

ダイアナ・フランズソフ・ピーターソン
今井元子/戸田徹子 訳

Shirakaba. Between 1911 and 1919, Arishima wrote his first novel *Aru Onna (A Certain Woman)*. Deeply influenced by the works of Tolstoy, he had by then embraced socialism and associated himself with proletarian literature. He published other works, including *Cain no Matsuei* (The Descendants of Cain, 1918) and *Sengen hitotsu* (A Declaration, 1922), depicting the tragedy of individuals overwhelmed by the forces of society and nature. His work was emotionally intense, erudite and humanistic, employing ideas from the Bible, Tolstoy, and anarchic socialism. In the end Arishima felt he could be neither a true socialist nor a true Christian. He suffered from a loss of creativity, and a sense of futility and despair, resulting in his suicide in 1923.

By Diana Franzusoff Peterson

Selected References: Paul Anderer, *Other Worlds: Arishima Takeo and the Bounds of Modern Japanese Fiction* (New York: Columbia University Press, 1984); Donald Keene, *Modern Japanese Diaries* (New York: Columbia University Press, 1998), pp. 403–445. Leith Morton, *Divided Self: a Biography of Arishima Takeo* (Sydney: Allen & Unwin, 1988).

If you go: Haverford College, 370 West Lancaster Avenue, Haverford, Pennsylvania, PA 19041; Barclay Hall was the dormitory where Arishima lived, and is still in use. The James P. Magill Library houses the Special Collections, including the original manuscript of Arishima's handwritten thesis.

4.13 Takaku Jinnosuke: Philadelphia's Connection to the Japanese Rescue of Jews?

高久甚之助：ユダヤ難民を助けたJTB

高久甚之助（たかく・じんのすけ）は1886年、三重県伊賀上野（現・伊賀市）の生まれ。1908年に東京外国語専門学校（現・東京外国語大学）英語科を首席で卒業、帝国鉄道庁（後の鉄道省）に入る。1921年に欧米留学を命ぜられ、ペンシルベニア大学でMBAを取得。帰国後、鉄道省運輸局国際課長を経て1928年にジャパン・ツーリスト・ビューロー（現在のJTBの前身）の最高責任者に迎えられる。1942年まで社業のみならず、戦前の日本の観光業界発展に尽くした。戦後は日本ホテル協会会長などを歴任したのち、1953年に病没。享年67歳。

1940年当時、外務本省の訓令に従わず、独断で日本通過ビザを発給して6000人のユダヤ人を救ったと言われる日本の外交官、杉原千畝の話はあまりにも有名であるが、それらのユダヤ難民がどのようにして日本にたどり着き、その後アメリカなどへ渡っていったかを知る人は少ない。いわんや、彼らの逃避行を助けたのが、ジャパン・ツーリスト・ビューロー（JTB）であったことはほとんど知られていない。

1940年のある日、JTBのニューヨーク事務所に1本の電話がかかってきた。現地の旅行会社からで、前年に勃発した第2次世界大戦のあおりを受けてヨーロッパを脱出しようとしているユダヤ人の逃走に、手を貸してやってほしいという内容であった。ドイツが勢力を広げてきたために、シベリア鉄道でウラジオストクまで行き、そこから海路日本に渡り、

Takaku Jinnosuke was born in 1886 in Iga Ueno, Mie Prefecture, now Iga City. Upon graduating with honors from the Tokyo University of Foreign Studies in 1908 with a degree in English, he started his career with the Ministry of Railways. In 1921 Takaku obtained his MBA from the University of Pennsylvania and shortly after his return to Japan, he became manager at the Ministry of Railway's Department of International Relations. In 1928, he became the CEO of the Japan Tourist Bureau (JTB) where he oversaw Japan's tourism industry until 1942. After World War II, he served as President of the Japan Hotel Association and passed away at the age of sixty-seven in 1953.

Sugihara Chiune (1900–1986) is well known for his heroic actions, in defiance of Japan's Ministry of Foreign Affairs, that ultimately saved the lives of 6,000 Jews from the Nazi war machine. However the behind the scenes role that Takaku must have played is little known. Sugihara saw to it that transit visas were issued to the Jews. But it was the Japan Tourist Bureau, under Takaku's leadership, that was responsible for providing the Jews the escape route they needed to flee.

One day in 1940, a phone rang at the New York office of JTB. We can imagine the caller might have said something like this:

Hello. I'm calling from the local travel agency. At the request of the Hebrew

Takaku Jinnosuke at Meiji Shrine, front row, third from left, with Matthew
Ridgway, Allied Commander-in-Chief. June, 1951. Courtesy of Takaku Kōichi
連合軍最高司令官リッジウェイ大将夫妻を明治神宮に案内.
前列左から3人目が高久甚之助. 高久紘一 所蔵.

日本を経由してアメリカに来るというの
が、彼らに残された唯一のルートであっ
た。ウラジオストクから福井県敦賀まで
の海上輸送を引き受けてもらいたいと
の依頼だった。

JTB東京本社では激しい議論が戦わさ
れたが、最終的には人道的見地から要
請を受けることになった。同盟国のドイ
ツの手前、それは大変な英断であった。
戦中戦後の混乱によりJTBには当時の
記録がまったく残されていないが、その
英断の背後には組織のトップとしての
高久の意思があったであろうと想像され
る。

高久は、ドストエフスキーやトルストイ
の人道主義が一世を風靡していた時代
に多感な青年期を送った。ペンシルベ
ニア大学時代には多くのユダヤ人学生

Immigrant Aid Society, we're involved
in the effort of rescuing Jews whose
lives are threatened by the persecution
of Nazi Germany. As you may know,
after the German invasion of Poland
last year, a very large number of Polish
Jews have been trying to escape Europe.
But because Germany has been so
dominant, many escape routes have
been shut down. Now the only route left
is to take the Trans-Siberian Railway to
Vladivostok, cross the sea to Japan, and
then come to America. This is their last
and only resort.

We're asking your company to transport
these people from Vladivostok to
Tsuruga, Fukui Prefecture, and then
from Japan to America. Would you be

との交流を持ち、彼らを通じてユダヤ民族の苦難の歴史を知ったと推測される。日露戦争が起きたのは、高久が18歳の時だったが、その日露戦争を日本が遂行できたのは、ヤコブ・シフというユダヤ人銀行家の資金援助によることももちろん知っていただろう。

当時のJTBがユダヤ難民の輸送を引き受けた背景として、フィラデルフィア時代の高久の姿が浮かんでくる。なお、奇しくも私と高久は郷里を同じくする関係にあることを付言しておきたい。

北出明

参考文献：
『日本交通公社70年史』（株式会社日本交通公社）
『観光文化・別冊2006』（財団法人日本交通公社）
北出明『命のビザ、はるかなる旅路：杉原千畝を陰で支えた日本人たち』（交通新聞社、2012）

willing to help?

After periods of intense discussion and debate with the headquarters in Tokyo, JTB decided to accept their request. As Germany was an ally of Japan, such a bold decision was indeed risky, but ultimately JTB chose to view the situation from a humanitarian standpoint.

My efforts to verify and inspect the information regarding the decision to assist in the transport operation fell short, as no evidence or records were found at the JTB. Therefore, we may only assume—although it is not hard to imagine—that Takaku, who stood at the top of the organization, was behind the verdict.

Takaku grew up in a period when the humanitarianism of the likes of Dostoevsky and Tolstoy were prominent, and their ideas may have influenced the adolescent Takaku. Also, through his close connections with Jewish friends he had developed during his time at the University of Pennsylvania, he learned of the Jewish people's gruesome hardships and history. He was only eighteen during the Russo-Japanese War, but he knew very well that the reason Japan was able to fight the war was largely thanks to Jacob Schiff, a Jewish banker and philanthropist who helped finance Japanese military efforts.

Putting all this in perspective, I believe that the JTB agreed to transport the Jewish refugees because of the relationships Takaku developed during his time in Philadelphia.

By Akira Kitade
Translated by Minako Kobayashi

5 *Philadelphians in Japan*
日本に来たアメリカ人

5.1 James Curtis Hepburn: His Contributions to Japan
ヘボン博士の貢献：宗教、医療、学術教育

ヘボン博士（ジェームズ・カーティス・ヘップバーン、1815 - 1911）の日本への貢献は宗教、医療、学術教育の3つの分野に分けられる。ヘボンは『聖書』を日本語に訳し、プロテスタントの宣教師としてキリスト教布教に専心した。またフィラデルフィアにあるペンシルベニア大学で1836年医学博士を取得し、医師として働いた後、医療宣教師として来日し、西洋医学で日本人の治療に携わった。さらには「ヘボン式ローマ字」を生み、日本で初期のミッションスクールを創設し、学術教育の分野でも知られている。

ヘボンは1815年にペンシルベニア州の田舎町ミルトンで生まれ、1832年から1836年の期間、ペンシルベニア大学に在籍した。19歳で聖霊の覚醒を体験し、その後、生涯敬虔なクリスチャンとなる。1840年に外国伝道のよき理解者であるクララ・メリー・リートと結婚し、2人は中国の伝道に出かける。1846年に帰国し、マンハッタンで医院を開業すると、医者として成功を収め大金持ちになる。一方、不幸にもニューヨーク時代に3人の子供を失い、悲しみの中、ニューヨークを去って、開国直後の当時、攘夷感情がまだ残る日本へ伝道に行く決意する。1859年、ヘボン夫妻は日本の神奈川に上陸し成仏寺に住み始める。ヘボンは近くの施療院で無料医療奉仕をし、住民に大いに尊敬される。ちなみに1862年、生麦村にて、侍が、参勤交代の行列に乱入したイギリス人を殺傷した生麦事件で、その被害者の手当をしたのはヘボンであった。

Dr. James Curtis Hepburn's (1815–1911) great contributions to Japan can be seen through his work in three distinct fields: religion, medicine, and academia. He devoted his life to Protestant missionary work, which included translating the Bible into the Japanese language. After receiving his M.D. degree at the University of Pennsylvania, Philadelphia in 1836 and serving as a medical doctor, he came to Japan as a medical missionary and treated Japanese with Western medical science. Hepburn is also known as an academician who created the "Hepburn romanization system" and founded early mission schools in Japan.

Hepburn was born in 1815 in Milton, a rural area in Pennsylvania, and studied at the University of Pennsylvania from 1832 to 1836. In 1834 when he was nineteen years old, he had a religious awakening and remained a devout Christian throughout his life. In 1840 he married Clara Mary Leete, who shared his interest in missionary work, and they went to China together. When he returned to America in 1846, he opened a clinic in Manhattan, which proved to be highly successful, making Hepburn a millionaire. Unfortunately, his three children died in New York, and in his sadness he decided to leave New York for Japan, which at that time still had anti-foreign sentiment, as the country had just reopened its doors to foreigners.

へボンは1867年に伝道のため総合的な和英辞典である『和英語林集成』を作るが、その辞書に使われているのが「ヘボン式ローマ字」（例えば、富士山をHujiでなく、英語の発音通りFujiと表記）である。そして当時のプロテスタント宣教師の大事な目標であった『聖書』の翻訳が、1880年から1887年にかけて完成するが、その主たる翻訳者はヘボンであった。

James Curtis Hepburn. Presbyterian Historical Society, Philadelphia

その頃、横浜には外国人居留地があり、ヘボンの自宅は居留地の中にあった。その自宅は「ヘボン塾」と知られ、そこでヘボンは医学を、妻のクララは英語を教える。その後「ヘボン塾」はミッションスクールの明治学院とフェリス女学院へと発展する。ヘボンは明治学院の初代総理を務めたが、多くの人がもっと日本に滞在するのを願ったにもかかわらず、自分のミッションは終えたとして1892年に日本を去る。

ヘボン夫妻の3人の子供はニュージャージー州のイースト・オレンジで永眠している。夫妻が1893年にそこに移り、余生を過したのは、緑と教会の多い、この平和で宗教心の強い町であった。日本滞在時代の輝かしい名声とはうって変わり、アメリカでのヘボンの隠居生活は慎ましかった。1911年に亡くなった時に

In 1859 the Hepburns landed in Kanagawa, Japan, and took up residence in Jōbutsuji Temple. Hepburn opened a free clinic near the temple, making him highly respected among local residents. Incidentally, it was Hepburn who treated the victims in the Namamugi Incident in 1862, when a party of Japanese samurai slashed at British subjects who interrupted their procession in the village of Namamugi.

In 1867 Hepburn completed a comprehensive language tool, entitled *A Japanese and English Dictionary (Waei gorin shūsei)*, to aid him in his missionary work. The "Hepburn romanization system," in which readings are based on English pronunciations, was used in the dictionary. For example, Mt. Fuji is used instead of Mt. Huji. Hepburn also served as the principal translator who rendered the Bible into Japanese, an important goal of the Protestant missionaries and the translation was completed between 1880 and 1887.

In that period, Yokohama had a foreign settlement, within which Hepburn's house was located. His residence was known as Hebon-juku (Hepburn School); there he taught Western medicine and his wife Clara taught English. Hebon-juku later developed into the mission schools known as Meiji Gakuin University and Ferris Women's College. Hepburn served as the first president of Meiji Gakuin; however, he felt that he had completed

は、彼の書斎は、必要としている人に全てのものをあげてしまっていて、空だった。ヘボンの家は現在も残っており、著者はヘボン博士の研究をしている時に、その家を調査し、図面付きで「イースト・オレンジにおけるヘボン」(2011)に発表した。

明治政府が日本の近代産業を興すために外国から招聘した「お雇い外国人」はよく知られているが、ヘボンは「お雇い外国人」ではなく、個人的、宗教的理由で来日した。日本に33年にわたり住み、広範囲な分野において多大な貢献をし、ヘボン博士は、日米関係の始まりを眺めた時、知るべき大事なアメリカ人である。

渡辺英男

参考文献：
岡部一興（編）『ヘボン在日書簡全集』
（教文館、2009）
杉田幸子『ヘボン博士の愛した日本』
（いのちのことば社フォレストブック
ク、2006）
渡辺英男「イースト・オレンジにおける
ヘボン」『明治学院大学キリスト教研究
所 紀要』第44号（2011）
渡辺英男「ニューヨークにおけるヘボ
ン」『明治学院大学キリスト教研究所紀
要』第45号（2012）

【参考情報】
明治学院　歴史資料館
〒108-8636　東京都港区白金台
1-2-37
電話：03-5421-5170
http://shiryokan.meijigakuin.jp

his mission in Japan and left in 1892, although many Japanese wanted him to stay.

Three of the Hepburns' children are buried in East Orange, New Jersey, and it was this peaceful and religious town, with much greenery and many churches, that they moved to in 1893 and spent the rest of their lives in.

Although his stay in Japan was filled with outstanding accomplishments that earned him a brilliant reputation, Hepburn lived modestly. His study was stripped of almost all of his books at the time of his death in 1911, for the doctor had given away everything that could be used by others in need. Hepburn's house in East Orange still stands. While doing research on Dr. Hepburn, I surveyed his home and published an article with drawings, entitled "James Curtis Hepburn in East Orange" (2011).

O-yatoi gaikokujin (foreign government advisors), whom the Meiji Government invited from the West to establish modern industries in Japan, are well known; however, Hepburn was not one of them. Personal, religious reasons motivated him to go to Japan. Living in the country for thirty-three years and making lots of contributions in a wide range of fields, Dr. Hepburn is an important American to know when looking at the beginning of the relations between the United States and Japan.

By Hideo Watanabe

If you go: Presbyterian Historical Society owns the archives of the Japan mission: 425 Lombard Street, Philadelphia, PA 19147.

5.2 The Griffis Family of Philadelphia: Taking the Japanese Seriously
日本の紹介者：グリフィス兄弟

第1次世界大戦以前、フィラデルフィアのグリフィス家は、日本を西洋に紹介するのに最も重要な役割を果たした。ウィリアム・エリオット・グリフィス（1843‐1928）はニュージャージー州のニュー・ブランズウィックにあるラトガーズ大学を卒業し、そこでアメリカで学んだ最初の日本人学生たちに出会う。その後、ウィリアムと姉のマーガレット・クアンドリル・クラーク・グリフィス（1838‐1913）は2人とも、初期の明治政府の下で教師として働く。そして1874年に帰国し、ウィリアムは日本や東アジアについて著述や講演をして余生を過ごした。

ウィリアムはジョン・ライムバーナー・グリフィスとアナ・マリア・ヘス・グリフィスの第4子として、1843年9月17日にフィラデルフィアで生まれた。父親は裕福な石炭商で、ヨーロッパやアフリカ、アジアを旅した。ウィリアムは、1850年にフィラデルフィアで、合衆国フリゲート艦サスケハナ号が、父親の石炭置き場の隣にある波止場に進水するのを見たことを覚えていた。このサスケハナ号は後にマシュー・ペリー提督の旗艦となった船だった。

ウィリアムはまた1860年に最初の日本使節団がフィラデルフィアを訪問したのも見学している。グリフィス家の子供たちは地元の小学校で学び、ペンシルベニア州の山々や、ニュージャージー州とデラウェア州の海岸で休暇を過ごすなど、中産階級の幸福な子供時代を送っ

From the first, I took the Japanese seriously. In many respects they were our equals, in others they seemed to be our superiors.

William Elliot Griffis, The Mikado's Empire, Book II, 1906 edition, recalling his first sight of the 1860 delegation in Philadelphia

William Elliot Griffis (1843–1928) was the most important interpreter of Japan to the West before the First World War. Born and raised in Philadelphia, Griffis graduated from Rutgers College in New Brunswick, New Jersey, where he met some of the first Japanese students to study in the United States. Griffis and his elder sister, Margaret Quandril Clark Griffis (1838–1913), both served as teachers in Japan under the early Meiji government. Returning to the United States in 1874, William Elliot Griffis spent the rest of his life writing and lecturing about Japan and East Asia.

William Elliot Griffis, the fourth child of John Limeburner Griffis and Anna Maria Hess Griffis, was born in Philadelphia on September 17, 1843. His father was a prosperous coal trader who traveled to Europe, Africa, and Asia. Years afterwards, Griffis recalled seeing the 1850 launching of the frigate U. S. S. *Susquehanna*, later

た。

信仰の篤いグリフィス家はフィラデルフィアのジョン・チェンバー第1独立教会（長老派）に通い、母親のアナはこの教会の日曜学校で教えていた。しかしながら、父親ジョンの石炭事業は1857年の不況で痛手を負った。ウィリアムは1859年にセントラル高校を卒業すると、チェスナット通りのジョン・キャロー宝石店で数年間、徒弟として働いた。姉のマーガレットはウィリアム・A・パットン牧師（博士）とその妻が経営する名門私立女学校で学んでいたが、同年（1859年）、両親と兄弟姉妹を養うために、テネシーのプランテーションで家庭教師の仕事に就いた。1860年代、グリフィス家はフィラデルフィアで借家住まいだった。この中には南ブロード通り419番や北12番通り1223番などの住所が含まれる。

ウィリアムは1863年に奴隷制の問題でチェンバー教会と対立し、フィラデルフィアのオランダ改革派第2教会に通い始めた。同年の6月、第44ペンシルベニア連隊の兵士となったが、すんでのところでゲティスバーグの戦いを免れた。3ヶ月間の任期を終えると、フィラデルフィアに戻り、ラトガーズ大学入学の準備をした。この当時、ラトガーズ大学は牧師養成を目的とする改革派教会の小規模な私立男子校であった。1865年にラトガーズ大学に入学すると、ウィリアムは伝統的で古典的な教育を受けたが、科学の授業もいくつか履修した。非常に優れた学生であり、大学のリーダーだった。大学新聞『ターガム』を始めたばかりでなく、学業で6つの賞をとり、ファイ・ベータ・カッパの会員だった。

Commodore Matthew Perry's flagship, at the Philadelphia waterfront next to his father's coal yard, and the 1860 visit of the first diplomatic mission from Japan to Philadelphia.

The Griffis children enjoyed a happy, middle-class childhood, attending local primary schools and taking vacations in the Pennsylvania mountains and at New Jersey and Delaware beaches. The pious family attended Presbyterian John Chambers' First Independent Church of Philadelphia, where Anna Griffis taught Sunday school. John Griffis' coal business suffered badly, however, in the financial panic of 1857. After graduating from Central High School in 1859, William Griffis apprenticed for a few years at John Carrow's jewelry firm on Chestnut Street. Also in 1859, Margaret Griffis, who had attended the prestigious girls' private school conducted by the Rev. Dr. William A. and Mrs. Patton, took a position as a governess on a Tennessee plantation to help support her parents and siblings. The Griffis family lived in several rented houses in Philadelphia during the 1860s, including 419 South Broad and 1223 North Twelfth Streets.

In 1863, William Elliot Griffis broke with Chambers over the issue of slavery and began to attend the Second Reformed Dutch Church of Philadelphia. That June he enlisted as a private in the 44th Pennsylvania Regiment, barely missing the Battle of Gettysburg. After completing his three-month term, Griffis returned to Philadelphia and began to prepare for entrance to Rutgers College, at that time a small private men's school affiliated with the Reformed Church, with the ultimate goal of becoming a minister. After

William Elliot Griffis.
Rutgers University Libraries

entering Rutgers in 1865, he followed the traditional classical curriculum but also took a number of science courses. Griffis was an outstanding student and campus leader who won six academic prizes and was a member of Phi Beta Kappa as well as a founder of the campus newspaper, the *Targum*.

After graduating from Rutgers in 1869, William Elliot Griffis studied at the neighboring New Brunswick Theological Seminary for a year before he received, through Reformed Church missionary Guido Verbeck, an invitation to teach chemistry and physics at the domain school in Echizen (today Fukui Prefecture) in the west of Japan. The offer included a house, a horse, and a handsome salary that was particularly attractive to Griffis because of his family's continuing financial difficulties.

As well as introducing Western-style science education in Fukui, Griffis was a witness to the *haihan chiken*, the abolition of the feudal *han* or domain in favor of the prefecture system. After less than a year, however, Griffis relocated to Tokyo, where he became an instructor at *Kaisei gakkō*, one of the forerunners of Tokyo University. In 1872, Griffis was joined by his sister Margaret, who was hired by the Ministry of Education to teach at the first government school for girls. Although the Tokyo Girls' School closed in 1877, it became a model for girls' education in Japan.

In 1874, Griffis left Japan after some conflict with the Ministry of Education over his teaching contract. He settled in New York, where he threw himself into writing and lecturing, publishing his first and most

ウィリアムは1869年にがラトガーズ大学を卒業し、近くにあるニュー・ブランズウィック神学校で1年ほど学んでいたところ、改革派教会宣教師のギドー・フルベッキ（バーベック）を通して、越前（現在の福井県）の藩校から化学と物理を教えてほしいとの招聘があった。住宅と馬、そして高額な給料が提示されており、家族が経済的困難に陥っているウィリアムには魅力的な申し出だった。この間ウィリアムは、福井に西洋の科学教育を導入する役割を果たしながら、廃藩置県 —封建制の藩を廃止し、県制度を採用する—を目撃したのである。しかしながら、1年もしないうちに東京に転居し、東京大学の前身校の1つである開成学校の教師となった。姉のマーガレットが文部省に雇われて、政府が初めて開

Margaret Griffis with Japanese students, Tokyo, c. 1874.
William Elliot Griffis Collection, Rutgers University Libraries

設した女学校で教えることになり、1872年にウィリアムの元にやって来た。東京女学校は1877年に閉校したが、日本の女子教育のモデルとなった。

その後、ウィリアムは雇用契約をめぐって文部省と対立をきたし、1874年に日本を去る。そしてニューヨークに落ち着き、著述と講演に専念し、1876年には最初にして最も有名な『皇国』を出版する。さらに、ユニオン神学校で学んだ後、3つの教会で牧師を務めている。ニューヨーク州のシュネクダディ第1改革派教会（1877‐1886）、ボストンのショームット会衆派教会（1886‐1893）、ニューヨーク州イサカの第1会衆派教会（1893‐1898）である。1879年にシュ

famous book, *The Mikado's Empire*, in 1876. After studying at Union Theological Seminary, Griffis served as a pastor of three churches—the First Reformed Church of Schenectady, New York (1877–1886); Shawmut Congregational Church in Boston (1886–1893); and the First Congregational Church in Ithaca, New York (1893–1898). In 1879, Griffis married Katharine Lyra Stanton (1856–1898) of Schenectady and the couple had three children. Griffis retired from the ministry in 1903 to devote himself fulltime to his research and writing on East Asia.

Margaret Griffis gave up the opportunity to organize the first women's teacher training college in Japan to return to the United

ネクダディのキャサリン・リラ・スタントン（1856‐1898）と結婚し、3人の子供をもうけた。1903年に牧師を辞し、東アジアに関する調査と著述に従事した。

姉のマーガレットは日本で最初の女子教員養成学校をつくる機会を諦めて、弟と一緒にアメリカに戻った。フィラデルフィアでは、マーガレットと彼女の2人の姉妹は、マーガレットが教員の職を見つけるまで、デラウェア出身の家族のところに下宿し、それから北16番通り1226番の借家に引っ越した。1876年、マーガレットはR・E・ジャドキン嬢の女学校—後のフィラデルフィア女子セミナリ（1871年の創設）—に教師として採用され、そこで22年間教鞭をとる。その後もマーガレットは日本に関心を持ち続け、横浜にある女子ミッション・スクールを支援するように教え子たちに勧め、女子英学塾（後の津田塾大学）図書館に書籍を一揃い寄贈している。生涯、病気に苦しんだが、1898年に教職を退き、イサカの弟世帯に同居し、子供たちの育児を助けたり、ウィリアムの調査を手伝ったりして、1913年に亡くなった。

その生涯において、ウィリアムは50冊以上の本を著し、数えきれないほど多くの記事と、百科事典や参考書の項目を書いた。その中にはオランダやアメリカ史などのトピックばかりでなく、日本、東アジア、アメリカ人の太平洋における役割に関するトピックが多数含まれていた。ウィリアムは歴史家として、日本の思想と文化における天皇の重要性に、早い時点で気づいたことで知られている。日本人留学生とその関係者、そして宣教師やお雇い外国人（日本政府に雇われた外国人）を含む日本を相手にして働くようになった西洋人たちのどちらとも、ウ

States with her brother. Back in Philadelphia, Margaret Griffis and her two sisters initially had to board with a family from Delaware until she was able to find a teaching position, enabling them move to a rented property at 1226 North Sixteenth Street. In 1876, Margaret Griffis was hired as a teacher at Miss R. E. Judkin's School for Girls, later the Philadelphia Female Seminary (founded 1871), where she would remain for twenty-two years. Margaret Griffis remained interested in Japan, encouraging her students to support a missionary school for girls in Yokohama and donating a set of books to the library of Joshi Eigaku Juku (later Tsuda College). Suffering throughout her life from ill health, Margaret retired from teaching in 1898 and joined her brother's household in Ithaca, where she helped with the children and his research until her death in 1913.

In his lifetime, William Elliot Griffis authored over fifty books and innumerable journal articles and entries in encyclopedias and reference books, including a great many on Japan, East Asia, and the American role in the Pacific, not to mention the Netherlands, American history, and many other subjects. As a historian, he is known for his early recognition of the importance of the emperor in Japanese thought and culture. A supreme networker, Griffis maintained his contacts both with Japanese students and associates, and with other Westerners involved in work with Japan, including especially missionaries and *yatoi* (foreign employees of the Japanese government).

In 1926–1927, William Elliot Griffis made a return visit to Japan with his second wife, Sarah Frances King Griffis (1868–1959) of

ィリアムは素晴らしいネットワークを築きあげていた。

1926年から1927年にかけて、ウィリアムは2番目の妻であるニューヨーク州プラスキ出身のフランシス・キング・グリフィス（1868‐1959）を伴い、日本を再訪した。ウィリアムはその翌年に亡くなり、彼の膨大な数の本や文書、写真、記録は母校に寄せられ、ラトガーズ大学図書館ウィリアム・エリオット・グリフィス・コレクションの基礎となっている。

ファーナンダ・H・ペロン
戸田徹子 訳

Pulaski, New York. He died the following year and his extensive collection of books, manuscripts, photographs, and documents were donated to his alma mater, where they constitute the foundation of the William Elliot Griffis Collection at Rutgers University Libraries.

By Fernanda H. Perrone

Selected References: Edward R. Beauchamp, *An American Teacher in Early Meiji Japan* (University of Hawaii Press, 1976); Elizabeth K. Eder, *Constructing Opportunity: American Women Educators in Early Meiji Japan* (Lanham, MD: Lexington Books, 2003).

If you go: Rutgers University holds the William Elliot Griffis Collection (Special Collections and University Archives): Rutgers University Libraries, Rutgers, The State University of New Jersey, 169 College Avenue, New Brunswick, NJ 08901.

5.3 The Whitney Family and Japan: Commercial School Connections

ホイットニー家：勝海舟のアメリカ人子孫

1974年、日本の新聞は、フィラデルフィアから勝海舟の「青い目の孫娘」が訪日したことを伝えた。78歳のヒルダ・カジ・ワトキンズが生まれ故郷を再訪したのである。目の色は青くても、ヒルダは確かに、末期の徳川幕府とそれに続く明治新政府において指導的役割を果たした政治家、勝海舟（1823‐1899）の孫だった。勝海舟は、通訳の1人としてペリーとの交渉に携わり、長崎ではオランダ人から海軍の訓練を受けた。

勝は、1860年に咸臨丸がアメリカへ渡航した時に船長を務め、1868年の幕府から朝廷への平和的な権力移譲や日本海軍の近代化にも、功績があったとされる。

ヒルダのもう1人の祖父であるウィリアム・ホイットニーは、ニュージャージー州ニューアークにあるビジネス学校の校長だった。1870年代、そこには初期の日本人留学生たちの何人かがアメリカのビジネス慣習を学びに来ていた。森有礼はワシントンに新設された日本公使館で弁務使（当時の公使の呼称）を務めていたが、この森がホイットニーの学校に注目したのである。森は1873年に学校を訪れて、非常に感銘をうけ、ホイットニーに、日本で国立のビジネス学校の開設を手伝うという5年契約の仕事を申し出た。東京に開設された、この新しい学校に個人で寄付した人の中には、勝海舟も含まれていた。

1875年、ウィリアム・ホイットニー、妻ア

A Japanese newspaper account in 1974 reported on the visit of Katsu Kaishū's "blue-eyed granddaughter" from Philadelphia. The reference was to Hilda Kaji Watkins, then age seventy-eight, revisiting the land of her birth. Although the color of her eyes was green, Hilda was indeed the granddaughter of Katsu Kaishū (1823–1899), a leading statesman during the last shogunal administration and in the succeeding Meiji government. Katsu served as one of the translators for negotiations with Commodore Perry and received naval training under the Dutch at Nagasaki.

Katsu was the Japanese officer in command of a Japanese ship, the *Kanrin Maru*, when it sailed for America in 1860. Katsu is credited with negotiating the peaceful transition of power to the new Meiji government in 1868 and with helping to modernize the Japanese navy.

Hilda Watkins' other grandfather was William C. Whitney, principal of a business college in Newark, New Jersey, where some of the early students from Japan had come to learn American business methods in the 1870's. The school attracted the attention of Mori Arinori, *charge d'affaires* at the new Japanese legation in Washington, who visited Whitney's school in 1873. Mori was so impressed that he offered William Whitney a five-year contract to help start a national business college in Japan. Among the private

Woman's kimono (kosode) worn by Clara Whitney Kaji at the Imperial Court. Collection of the Philadelphia Museum of Art, Gift of Hilda Kaji Watkins, 1985

donors to the new school in Tokyo was Katsu Kaishū.

William Whitney, his wife Anna, and their three children—Willis (age nineteen), Clara (fifteen), and Adelaide (nine)—arrived in Japan in 1875. The commercial college, which eventually developed into Hitotsubashi University, soon underwent changes in management, leaving William Whitney without a means of support for his family. Katsu came to the rescue, offering the family a house in his family compound. There Clara Whitney first met her future husband, Kaji Umetarō, a son of Katsu Kaishū. Clara worked as a teacher of English and Religion at the Meiji Girls' School. She married Kaji Umetarō in 1885, and they had six children, the youngest of whom was Hilda. Clara left Japan and her husband with her children in 1900 and lived in several places in Pennsylvania and in Baltimore, where Hilda received a Bachelor's Degree in History from Goucher College in 1917. In 1919, Clara and Hilda settled in Philadelphia, where Hilda found employment.

Clara died in 1936. A book incorporating excerpts from her diaries was published in Japan and in the U.S. as *Clara's Diary, An American Girl in Meiji Japan*. Hilda's career

ンナ、3人の子供のウィリス（19歳）、クラ ラ（15歳）、 アデレード（9歳）が日本に 到着した。後に一橋大学となったこの商 科大学はすぐに経営が変わり、ウィリア ム・ホイットニーは家族を養う手段を失 ってしまう。勝が援助の手を差し伸べ、 自邸の敷地内にある家をホイットニー の家族に提供した。そこでクララ・ホイッ トニーは、勝海舟の息子で自分の将来 の夫となる梶梅太郎と初めて出会った のである。クララは明治女学校で英語と 宗教の教師として働いていた。その後

1885年に梅太郎と結婚し6人の子をもうけたが、その末の子がヒルダだった。クララは1900年に夫を残して子供たちと一緒に日本を去り、ペンシルベニア州のいくつかの町とボルチモアで暮らした。1917年、ヒルダはボルチモアにあるガウチャー大学で歴史学の学士号を取得する。その後、1919年、クララとヒルダはフィラデルフィアに住まいを定め、ヒルダはそこで職に就いた。

クララは1936年に亡くなったが、本人の日記を抜粋した『クララの明治日記』という本が、日米両国で出版された。また、ヒルダの職歴にはレタリングやファッション関係の挿絵、商業美術が含まれる。さらに1940年まで美容相談欄を執筆したが、これは通信社を通して多くの新聞社に配信された。ヒルダは1930年にウィリアム・ワトキンズと結婚し、2人の娘を育てながら、物語や挿絵を書いた。その後太平洋戦争が始まるまで日本の親戚と連絡を取り続けており、戦後は彼らに慰問品を送った。

1974年、勝海舟の日記が出版され、海舟の生涯がテレビの連続ドラマで放送されるようになる。この年、ヒルダは生まれ故郷を訪問するように招待され、父の梶梅太郎や祖母のアンナ・ホイットニー、祖父の勝海舟の墓参りをした。一橋大学の昼食会では、ウィリアム・ホイットニーの孫娘として礼遇された。ウィリアム・ホイットニーは、大学の図書館に肖像画が掲げられている唯一の外国人である。1997年、ヒルダは101歳でその生涯を閉じた。

グェンドルン・クララ・ワトキンズ・キーファー
今井元子/戸田徹子 訳

included lettering, fashion illustration and commercial art, as well as authoring a syndicated beauty column until 1940. She had married William Watkins in 1930 and continued to write and illustrate stories while raising two daughters. Hilda maintained contact with her relatives in Japan until the war years, and then sent CARE packages to them after the war.

In 1974, a year marking the publication of Katsu Kaishū's diaries and a televised series about his life, Hilda was invited to revisit the land of her birth. There she visited the graves of her father, her grandmother Anna Whitney and her grandfather Katsu. At a luncheon at Hitotsubashi University, Hilda was also honored as the granddaughter of William Whitney, whose portrait hangs in the school library, the only non-Japanese so acknowledged.

Hilda Watkins died in 1997 at the age of 101.

By Gwendolyn Clara Watkins Kiefer

Selected Reference: Clara A. N. Whitney, *Clara's Diary: An American Girl in Meiji Japan*, ed. M. William Steele and Tamiko Ichimata (Tokyo and New York: Kodansha International, 1979).

5.4 Mary Harris Morris:
Devoted Supporter of Japanese Students

メアリ・モリス：日米の架け橋になったクエーカー女性

ときに故郷よりも外国で有名な人がいるものだが、フィラデルフィアのフレンド（クエーカー教徒）であるメアリ・モリス（1836‐1924）はそのような人物の1人である。彼女はフィラデルフィアで多くの有為な日本人学生に出会い、彼らの多くが帰国後、日本の指導者となったことにより、メアリ・モリスの名前は語り継がれているのである。

メアリ・ハリス・モリスはペンシルベニア州センター郡に生まれた。幼くして両親を亡くし、クエーカーの鉄工場主を後見人として育った。長老派教会で洗礼を受けていたが、後見人の影響下でクエーカーとなり、チェスター郡にあるクエーカーの寄宿学校ウェストタウン・スクールで学んだ。

1863年、メアリは裕福なフィラデルフィア・フレンドのウィスター・モリス（1815‐1891）と結婚した。ウィスター・モリスは駐日大使を務めたローランド・S・モリス（41章参照）の従兄弟に当たる。バルブや蛇口などの鉄製品を生産するモリス・タスカー社の創業者で、ペンシルベニア鉄道の重役でもあった。メアリは10代の初めから地域奉仕に関わり、結婚後は、キリスト教婦人矯風会やフィラデルフィア孤児院などの活動に参加した。とりわけフィラデルフィアにあるイースタン刑務所に収監された女性囚人たちに心を寄せ、独房を訪問したばかりでなく、刑務所を出た女性たちが社会復帰するための施設であるハワード・ホームのマネジャーも務めた。

Some people are more famous abroad than in their hometown, and a Philadelphia Friend (Quaker) named Mary Harris Morris (1836–1924) is one of them. She helped promising young Japanese students, many of whom returned to become major figures in Meiji Japan, and her name has been passed down from generation to generation.

Mary Morris was born in Centre County, Pennsylvania. After she lost her parents early in life, a Quaker ironmaster assumed her guardianship. Although she was baptized as a Presbyterian, she became a Friend and attended a Quaker boarding school, Westtown School in Chester County.

Mary married a wealthy Philadelphia Friend, Wistar Morris (1815–1891), in 1863. Wistar was the cousin of Roland S. Morris, the Ambassador of the United States to Japan (1917–1920). He was founder of the Morris, Tasker & Company, which produced ironware such as valves and faucets, and was also a director of the Pennsylvania Railroad.

Mary started dedicating herself to community service early in her teens. After her marriage, Mary became committed to the Women's Christian Temperance Union and the Orphan's Asylum of Philadelphia. She was especially concerned about women prisoners at the Eastern Penitentiary. She would visit them in their cells and later

メアリは1870年に中近東を旅行し、
キリスト教の海外伝道活動に興味を
持った。そして異教女性に伝道し、教
育を与え、クリスチャンの妻や母親を
生み出すために、クエーカー派の伝道
協会(フィラデルフィア・フレンズ婦人
外国伝道協会)を1882年に組織し、
会長となった。この伝道協会は次第に
日本に関心を絞り、1885年から日本
伝道を開始、早くも1887年には東京
に普連土女学校を開設した。

フィラデルフィアにおいて、メアリは
よく日本女性たちの面倒をみた。岡
見京子(25章参照)は日本で最初の
女性医学博士である。米国婦人一致
外国伝道協会が開校した横浜共立
女学校の卒業生で、モリス邸に下宿
してペンシルベニア女子医科大学に
通った。津田梅子にブリンマー大学
入学を勧めたのもメアリ・モリスであ
った。ブリンマー大学はクエーカーに
よって開設された大学で、メアリは大
学幹部と知り合いだった。そこで入
学許可を確保し、津田の2度目の留学
(1889‐1892)が実現できたので
ある。津田が1900年に日本で最初の
女子の高等教育機関である女子英学
塾(後の津田塾大学)を創立したとき、
メアリは財政的にこれを援助した。

Mary Morris in Japan, April 1890. Front row, second from
right. Behind her is Mary's husband Wistar Morris. Friends
School, Tokyo, Japan
普連土学園所蔵

さらにメアリは津田の助言を入れ、後進
の日本女性たちがアメリカ留学できるよ
うに「日本婦人米国奨学金」(別名「ジャ
パニーズ・スカラシップ」)を設けた。こ
の奨学金制度により、1893年から1976
年までの間に25名の日本女性がアメリ
カ留学を果たした。この中には同志社女
学校の校長となった松田道や恵泉女学
校を創設した河井道も含まれる。

became the manager of the Howard Home, a
home for discharged women.

During a visit to the Middle East in 1870,
Mary got interested in foreign missions. In
1882, she organized the Women's Foreign
Missionary Association of Friends of
Philadelphia, of which she became president.
The association was set up for the purpose
of evangelizing "heathen" women, educating
them, and making Christian wives and

Mary Morris in 1890. Friends School,
Tokyo, Japan 普連土学園所蔵

メアリの関心はなにも同性に限定され
ていたわけではなかった。メアリはフィ
ラデルフィア在住の日本人学生を自宅
に招き、月に1回バイブル・クラスを開催
していた。新渡戸稲造が将来の妻、メア
リ・エルキントンと出会ったのはモリス
家の客間だった。アメリカ留学しようとし
たとき、内村鑑三はモリス家を目指して
旅立った。野口英世や岩崎久彌（三菱財
閥第3代目）もモリス邸を訪ね、バイブ
ル・クラスに参加した。これらの人たちか
らメアリは「日本人留学生の母」と慕わ
れた。

メアリ・モリスは1890年と1892年の2
回ほど日本に滞在したが、その動向は
『女学雑誌』などに報じられている。

なおオーバーブルックにある大きな石
造りのモリス邸は1925年にクエーカー

mothers out of them. It gradually focused its
efforts on Japan, where it started a mission
in 1885 and founded the Friends Girls'
School in Tokyo in 1887.

Mary Morris was eager to give a helping
hand to Japanese women in Philadelphia.
Okami Kyōko (also known as Keiko), the
first female medical doctor in Japan, was
very close to the Morrises. Okami graduated
from Yokohama Kyōritsu Girls' School—the
mission school established by the Woman's
Union Missionary Society of America for
Heathen Lands. She boarded at the Morris
home while she studied at the Women's
Medical College of Pennsylvania.

It was Mary Morris who suggested that
Tsuda Umeko should enter Bryn Mawr
College, which was run by Quakers. Mary
had friends in the college administration
and assisted Umeko in gaining admission to
the college. Umeko came to the United States
for the second time in 1889 and majored in
science at Bryn Mawr. When Umeko later
envisioned opening a college for women in
Japan, Mary financially supported her in
opening Women's English School, the present
Tsuda College.

At Umeko's suggestion, Mary Morris set
up the American Women's Scholarship for
Japanese Women to provide an opportunity
for other Japanese women to study in the
States. This scholarship was given to twenty-
five female students from 1893 to 1976,
including Matsuda Michi and Kawai Michi,
who both studied at Bryn Mawr College.
Matsuda Michi later became principal of
Dōshisha Girls School in Kyoto and Kawai
Michi founded Keisen Girls' School.

の学校であるフレンズ・セントラル・スクールに売却され、その校舎の一部となった。そして奇しくも1989年以来、旧モリス邸は毎週土曜日にはフィラデルフィア日本語補習授業校として利用されている。メアリ・モリスと日本とのつながりは今も生きていると言えよう。

戸田徹子

参考文献:
飯野正子・亀田帛子・高橋裕子編『津田梅子を支えた人びと』(有斐閣、2001)

Mary's concern was not limited to women, however. She also invited Japanese students to Bible class at her home in Overbrook once a month. Nitobe Inazō got acquainted with his future wife, Mary Elkinton, in the Morris parlor. When Uchimura Kanzō left Japan for the States, the Morris residence was his first destination. Noguchi Hideyo and Iwasaki Hisaya (the third president of Mitsubishi Cooperation) joined the class at the Morris home in Overbrook. These people appreciated her kindness so much that they called her a "mother for Japanese students in Philadelphia." Mary Morris visited Japan in 1890 and 1892, and her activities were reported in Christian magazines such as *Women's Magazine*.

The Morris' property with its large stone mansion was sold to the Friends' Central School in 1925 and now houses part of the School. Friends' Central School has been the host campus for the Japanese Language School of Philadelphia since 1989. This Japanese Language School holds classes on Saturdays, mainly for Japanese Americans and Japanese families temporarily living in America. The historical connections between Mary Morris and Japan remain alive through the influence of the many Japanese students she befriended and supported.

By Tetsuko Toda

If you go: Friends Central School, 1101 City Avenue, Wynnewood, PA 19096.

5.5 Nitobe Inazō and Mary Patterson Elkinton: An International Marriage Made in Philadelphia
新渡戸稲造と、彼と結婚したフィラデルフィア女性

1891年1月1日、フィラデルフィアの4番通りとアーチ通りの交差点にあるクエーカーのミーティング・ハウスで、異例の結婚式が執り行われた。翌日の『フィラデルフィア・インクワイアラー』紙は、次のような見出しをつけて、その結婚を第1面で報じた。「東洋人を夫に：クエーカーのメアリ・パターソン・エルキントンが日本人の新渡戸稲造と結婚―愛する人のために若い女性が犠牲に―」。この見出しが示唆するように、当時、このような異文化間・異人種間の結婚は稀だった。「犠牲」という言葉には、遠く離れた日本で夫と暮らすというメアリの決意が反映されていた。それはまた、メアリの両親が結婚に反対した主な理由でもあった。そして実際、両親は結婚式に出席しなかった。

明治時代（1868‐1912）には、日本の近代化に貢献しようとする、ひたむきで優れた若者世代が存在した。新渡戸稲造（1862‐1933）は、その世代の1人である。新渡戸は1862年に、現在の岩手県盛岡市で士族の家に生まれた。新渡戸家は、農地開拓によって北日本の経済を発展させようとした一族であった。新渡戸は札幌農学校で学び、ウィリアム・S・クラーク教授の精神的遺産の影響を受けた。クラーク博士は、学生たちはキリスト教に改宗すべきであると主張し、「少年よ、大志を抱け」という有名な激励の言葉を残した。1883年、東京帝国大学に入学するとき、新渡戸は自らの人生の目標を「願わくば、われ、太平洋の懸け橋とならん」という言葉で表現し

On January 1, 1891, an extraordinary wedding took place at the Friends Meeting House at Fourth and Arch Streets in Philadelphia. The next day's *Philadelphia Inquirer* reported it on its front page with the headline: "Weds an Oriental Husband: Mary Patterson Elkinton, Quakeress, Marries Inazō Nitobe, Japanese—A Young Woman's Sacrifice for Love's Sweet Sake." As the newspaper's wording implied, a cross-cultural, interracial marriage of this sort was rare at the time; the "sacrifice" involved Mary's determination to live with her husband in distant Japan. This was also the primary reason Mary's parents were opposed to the union; indeed, they were absent from the ceremony.

Nitobe Inazō (1862–1933) was a member of a remarkable generation of dedicated young Japanese who sought to contribute to the modernization of Japan in the Meiji era (1868–1912). He was born into the samurai class in 1862 in the city of Morioka, in what is now Iwate Prefecture; his family had spearheaded the economic development of northern Japan through land reclamation projects. Nitobe studied at Sapporo Agricultural College, where he was influenced by the legacy of Professor William S. Clark, who had insisted that his students convert to Christianity and had offered them the famous exhortation: "Boys Be Ambitious!" In 1883, as Nitobe entered Tokyo Imperial University, he expressed his own life's goal

た。つまり、相互理解や協力、進歩のた
め、日本文化を西洋に、西洋文化を日本
に伝える役割を果たしたいと説明した
のだった。

1884年、新渡戸は東京帝国大学を休
学し、ジョンズ・ホプキンス大学に入学
した。級友の中にはウッドロウ・ウィルソ
ンやジョン・デューイがいた。新渡戸は
クエーカーとなり、友人への手紙の中で
「私は、クエーカーの質素さとまじめさ
が非常に好きである」と書いているが、
これらは自分の武士気質とも関連して
いた。

1887年5月、新渡戸はフィラデルフィア
郊外のウィスター・モリス夫人の家（現
在はフレンズ・セントラル・スクールのキ
ャンパスの一部となっている）で催され
た会合に招待され、クエーカーのフィラ
デルフィア・フレンズ婦人外国伝道協会
の人々に話をした。その聴衆の中にメア
リ・パターソン・エルキントンがいた。彼
女は女性の福祉と権利の問題に深く関
わっており、日本の女子教育に対する新
渡戸の意見に感銘を受けた。そして、新
渡戸のヨーロッパ留学中に、2人は女性
の諸問題について手紙をやり取りし、つ
いに結婚することになったのである。

メアリ・パターソン・エルキントン
（1857‐1938）は、1857年、フィラデ
ルフィアのクエーカーの名家に生まれ
た。フレンズ・セレクト・スクールで学び、
パイン通り325番地で両親のジョセフ・
エルキントン、マリンダ・エルキントンと
共に暮らしていた。父親は実業家として
成功し、家業をフィラデルフィア・クォー
ツ会社に発展させたほどの人物で、社
会正義に身をささげる、偏見のない寛
大な人だった。彼は常に稲造を称賛して

with the phrase, "I wish to be a bridge across
the Pacific," transmitting Japanese culture to
the West and Western culture to Japan in the
name of mutual understanding, cooperation
and progress.

In 1884, Nitobe took a leave of absence
from his school and matriculated at Johns
Hopkins University, where his classmates
included Woodrow Wilson and John Dewey.
He became a devout Quaker, writing a
friend, "I like very much their simplicity
and earnestness," values he associated with
his own samurai ethos. In May 1887 Nitobe
was invited to speak to the Friends Foreign
Missionary Society at a meeting held at the
home of Mrs. Wistar Morris just outside
Philadelphia, on what is now the campus
of Friends Central School. In the audience
was Mary Patterson Elkinton (1857–1938).
She was deeply involved in issues pertaining
to women's welfare and rights and was
impressed by Nitobe's comments on women's
education in Japan. A correspondence on
women's issues between Mary and Inazō
while he was studying in Europe eventually
developed into a partnership for life.

Mary Patterson Elkinton was born in
Philadelphia in 1857 to a prominent Quaker
family. She was educated at Friends Select
School and lived with her parents, Joseph
S. and Malinda Elkinton, at 325 Pine Street.
Her father, a successful businessman whose
company evolved into the Philadelphia
Quartz Company, was an open-minded
and tolerant man who was devoted to social
justice. He had nothing but praise for Inazō
but did not want to see his beloved daughter
move so far away. The objections of Mary's
parents made it difficult for Mary and Inazō

Mary and Inazō Nitobe. Front row left is Mary; Inazō is behind her.
Haverford College Quaker & Special Collections

to gain their Monthly Meeting's consent to their marriage. When their third application was supported by Mary's three brothers, permission was finally granted. A few days after the wedding Mary's parents gave their blessing to the union, just before the newly-wed couple departed for Japan, where Nitobe was to assume a professorship at his alma mater, Sapporo Agricultural College.

The Nitobe's first and only natural child, Joseph, was born in 1892, only to die tragically within days. The Nitobes adopted a son, Yoshio, and later a daughter, Kotoko, from within the extended Nitobe family, and sent their son to Haverford College. Yoshio graduated in 1915 and worked for a brief time as a journalist at the *Public Ledger* in Philadelphia.

Mary and Inazō Nitobe were colleagues as well as marriage partners. Mary took a strong interest in education and with a small inheritance established one of Japan's first evening schools for adults, the Distant Friends Night School (En'yū Yagakkō) in Sapporo. Nitobe taught at Sapporo, Kyoto

はいたのだが、愛する娘が遠い国に行ってしまうのに耐えられなかった。メアリの両親が反対していたので、クエーカーの所属月会から結婚許可を得ることは難しかった。メアリの3人の兄弟が2人の3回目の結婚申請に賛成した時、やっと許可が下りた。結婚式の数日後、メアリの両親もようやく結婚を祝福したが、それは新婚夫婦が日本に出発する直前だった。稲造は母校の札幌農学校に教授として着任することが決まっていたのである。

1892年に新渡戸の最初の子供で唯一の実子であるジョセフが生まれたが、悲しいことに数日で亡くなってしまった。

新渡戸夫妻は新渡戸の家系から孝夫（ヨシオ）を養子に迎え、後に琴子を養女にし、孝夫をハバフォード大学に送った。孝夫は1915年にハバフォード大学を卒業し、短期間だったが、フィラデルフィアの『パブリック・レジャー』誌でジャーナリストとして働いた。

メアリと稲造は結婚相手であると同時に、仕事上の仲間でもあった。メアリは教育に対して深い関心があり、少額の相続金を使って、日本初の成人向け夜間学校の1つである「遠友夜学校」を札幌で開校した。稲造は札幌で教えたほか、京都大学、東京大学でも教鞭をとり、名門の第一高等学校の校長や東京女子大学の初代学長も務めた。ブリンマー大学の2人の日本人卒業生である津田梅子と河井道が、日本で女子学校を創立するのを援助し、東京の普連土女学校の後援者でもあった。稲造は東洋と西洋の相互理解に尽くしたいと願い、『武士道―日本の魂』という本を書いて、侍の伝統（武士道）を西洋の騎士道に似た精神的道徳的体系として理解しようと試みた。その本は国際的に大成功をおさめ、10ヶ国語を超える言語に翻訳された。稲造の多くの著作の中には、1894年に出版されたウィリアム・ペンの伝記もある。

公職として、新渡戸稲造は国際連盟事務次長を務め、台湾総督府などに勤務したこともあった。1932年6月、ハバフォード大学は新渡戸に法学の名誉博士号を授与した。授与証書には次のように書かれていた。「新渡戸稲造：キリスト教徒の学者であり、日本の魂を世界の人々に説明してくれた。国際連盟では雄弁に国際親善を主唱し、信任が厚かった。アメリカやハバフォードと緊密な絆で結ば

University, and Tokyo University, headed the elite First Higher School, and served as the first president of Tokyo Women's Christian College. He aided two Japanese alumnae of Bryn Mawr College, Tsuda Umeko and Kawai Michi, in establishing women's schools in Japan and was a benefactor of the Friends Girls School in Tokyo. Maintaining his commitment to improve East-West understanding, he wrote a book, *Bushido, The Soul of Japan*, which sought to establish the samurai tradition (bushidō) as a spiritual and moral system resembling that of chivalry in the West. The book was a huge international success, translated into more than a dozen languages. Among his many writings was also a biography of William Penn, published in 1894.

Nitobe's career in public service included a term as Under-Secretary of the League of Nations, and a stint in the colonial administration of Taiwan. In June 1932 Haverford College awarded him the honorary degree of doctor of laws. The citation read: "Inazō Nitobe: Christian scholar and interpreter of the soul of Japan; eloquent and trusted apostle of international good-will in the League of Nations; already connected by close ties with America and Haverford."

In 1933 Nitobe took ill after a conference in Canada and died in Victoria, British Columbia, on September 12. After his state funeral in Tokyo, attended by 3,000 mourners, Mary continued to live in Japan, overseeing the Distant Friends School and helping to establish Japan's first Humane Society. She died in 1938 at the mountain home she had shared with her husband in Karuizawa. Nitobe Inazō continues to be

れている」。

1933年、カナダにおいて、稲造は会議後に病で倒れ、ブリティッシュ・コロンビア州ビクトリアで9月12日に死去した。東京での国葬には、3000人の会葬者が参列した。夫亡き後も、メアリは日本で生活した。遠友学校を監督し、日本初の動物愛護協会設立に力を貸した。彼女は夫と共に暮らした軽井沢の山荘で、1938年に亡くなった。新渡戸稲造は現在でも日本で最初かつ最も有名な国際人の1人とみなされている。1984年には、5000円札に新渡戸の肖像が採用された。

マシュー・ミゼンコ
今井元子/戸田徹子 訳

【参考情報】
盛岡市先人記念館
〒020-0866
岩手県盛岡市本宮字蛇屋敷2-2
電話：019-659-3338
www.mfca.jp/senjin

regarded as one of Japan's first and most prominent internationalists, and in 1984 his portrait was placed on the 5,000 yen bill.

By Matthew Mizenko

Selected References: Nitobe Inazō, *Bushido, The Soul of Japan* (Rutland, VT and Tokyo: Tuttle, 1994); John F. Howes, ed., *Nitobe Inazō: Japan's Bridge Across the Pacific* (Boulder, Co.: Westview, 1995).

If you go: Friends Meeting House, 320 Arch Street, Philadelphia, PA 19106.

Archival materials associated with the Nitobes are housed at Friends Historical Library, Swarthmore College, 500 College Avenue, Swarthmore, PA 19081, and the Quaker Collection, Haverford College, 370 Lancaster Avenue, Haverford, PA 19041.

Elkinton Residence, 325 Pine Street, Philadelphia, PA 19102.

5.6 Anna Hartshorne: Devoted to the Education of Japanese Girls
アナ・ハーツホーン：日本の女子高等教育に貢献したフィラデルフィア女性

アナ・コープ・ハーツホーン（1860‐1957）はフィラデルフィア生まれのクエーカーである。ブリンマー大学在学中の津田梅子と知り合い、彼女を助けるために来日。津田亡き後も日本に残り、草創期から1940年までの約40年間、女子英学塾（現津田塾大学）で教鞭をとった。

アナ・コープ・ハーツホーンは、ヘンリー・ハーツホーン（1823‐1897）と妻メアリの一人娘として1860年にフィラデルフィアで生まれた。父親のヘンリーは医師、教育者、作家と多芸多才な人物で、医学書を通して日本と縁があった。津田梅子の父親、津田仙は佐倉藩士で1867年に渡米する機会に恵まれた。このとき津田仙はヘンリー・ハーツホーンが著わした医学書 (1867) を持ち帰り、この本が桑田衡平訳により『内科要摘』（1875）として出版され、多くの読者を得たのである。

ヘンリーはフィラデルフィア・フレンズ婦人外国伝道協会の名誉会員でもあり、自分が編集を務める週刊新聞『フレンズ・レビュー』に関連記事を掲載するなどの形で、伝道協会に協力していた。当然のことながら、同伝道協会が展開している日本伝道に興味があった。ヘンリーは1886年に妻を亡くし、1893年には『フレンズ・レビュー』の編集長を辞任していた。そこで伝道活動のために日本を訪問することを思いついたようだ。ヘンリーは娘アナを伴い2回（1893年と1995年）ほど来日し、2回目の訪日中の

Anna Cope Hartshorne (1860–1957) was a Philadelphia Quaker. She became acquainted with Tsuda Umeko while Tsuda was studying at Bryn Mawr College. Hartshorne helped Tsuda found Tsuda College by collecting donations and went to Japan in 1902 in order to teach at the college. She outlived her lifelong friend and taught at the college for about forty years, returning to the United States just before World War II broke out.

Anna Cope Hartshorne was born in Philadelphia in 1860 as the only child of a devout Quaker couple, Henry and Mary Hartshorne. Henry Hartshorne (1823–1897) was a multi-talented person, being a doctor, teacher, and writer. He started his career as a doctor, graduating from the medical school of the University of Pennsylvania. His book, *Essentials of the Principles and Practice of Medicine* (1867), was introduced to Japan by Tsuda Sen (Umeko's father). Sen was a samurai belonging to the Sakura Domain (now in Chiba Prefecture). He joined the 1867 delegation to the United States to buy warships for the Tokugawa government. He bought Henry's book, which was translated into Japanese by Kuwata Kōhei, as a souvenir. It was titled *Naika tekiyō* (An outline of internal medicine, 1875) and had a large readership in the early Meiji period.

Henry Hartshorne was an editor of the Quaker weekly, *The Friends' Review*. He was

Anna Hartshorne. Haverford College
Quaker & Special Collections

also an honorary member of the Women's Foreign Missionary Association of Friends of Philadelphia, which started the Japan mission in 1885. He often published articles about its Japan missionary work in the weekly. As Henry naturally developed an interest in Japan, after his wife passed away in 1887, he resigned the editorship in 1893 and went to Japan with Anna in 1893 and 1895.

Anna Hartshorne went to a Quaker girls' school, Howland Collegiate School, in Union Springs, New York. She graduated from the school in 1876 and continued her studies at the Pennsylvania Academy of the Fine Arts. She taught art at a girls' school near her home in Germantown. Hartshorne had reunions with Tsuda twice when Anna visited Japan with her father.

1897年2月に東京で亡くなった。

アナはニューヨーク州ユニオン・スプリングスにあったクエーカーの女子高等教育機関ハウランド学校を、1876年に卒業した。フィラデルフィアにある美術学校(ペンシルベニア・アカデミー・オブ・ファイン・アーツ)で学び、ジャーマンタウンの自宅近くにある女学校で絵

During her second visit to Japan, Anna's father died suddenly, leaving the thirty-seven-year-old Hartshorne alone in a foreign country. Tsuda invited Anna to the seaside resort of Hayama and tried to comfort her. At that time, Tsuda told Anna of her decision to set up a college for girls in Japan and asked

を教えていた。アナはブリンマー大学在学中の津田梅子と出会っており、旧知の間柄だったので、日本で津田と再会する。だが2回目の日本滞在中に父親ヘンリーが突然亡くなり、アナは1人日本に残された。このときアナは37歳だった。この傷心のアナを津田が葉山に招いて慰め、学校開設の夢を語り、援助を頼んだ。アナの回顧によれば、これによって学校がアナの夢に、そして一生涯のプロジェクトとなったという。

アナは1897年11月に帰国した。アメリカにおいて、アナはメアリ・モリスが津田の学校設立を経済的に支援するために組織したフィラデルフィア委員会を手伝った。女子英学塾が開校されたのは1900年9月のことである。アナは津田を助けるために1902年5月に再来日し、女子英学塾で本格的に英語を教え始めた。語学教師として外国語教授法を学び、またテキスト編纂にも取り組んだ。

1923年の関東大震災で女子英学塾の校舎が焼失すると、アナは直ちに渡米し、津田の実妹の安孫子余奈子とともにアメリカ各地を回り、校舎再建のための寄付集めに奔走した。その結果、かねてより小平市に確保していた用地に3階建の立派な校舎が建てられたのである。津田は1929年にこの世を去った（享年66歳）が、アナは日本に留まり太平洋戦争開戦が迫る時期になるまで津田英学塾で教え続けた。

1940年11月には津田英学塾創立40周年記念祝賀式が挙行された。アナはこれに出席した後、11月28日に一時帰国のため出航した。翌年5月には日本に戻る予定であったが、日米関係の悪化により、それは果たせなくなる。1957年10

the grief-stricken Anna to help her. This encouraged Hartshorne to live by giving her some aims and goals.

Returning to the United States in November 1897, Hartshorne joined the Philadelphia Committee that Mary Morris had organized to help establish Tsuda College and engaged herself in collecting funds. Tsuda College was opened in September 1900, and in May 1902, Hartshorne went back to Japan to teach English at the college. As a teacher, she used the Berlitz Method of Language Study and got involved in editing textbooks.

When the Great Kantō Earthquake hit Tokyo in 1923, the college buildings all suffered serious damage. Hartshorne soon returned to the United States and visited various cities with Tsuda's younger sister, Abiko Yonako (1880–1944), to solicit donations to reconstruct the college's buildings. As a result of their great efforts, they succeeded in securing adequate financial resources, and the new campus was reconstructed in Kodaira, Tokyo. Tsuda Umeko passed away in 1929 at the age of sixty-six. However, Hartshorne stayed in Japan and assisted Tsuda's successors by teaching English.

After attending the fortieth anniversary of the college, Hartshorne left Japan on November 28, 1940, intending to make a short-term visit to the United States and return to Japan in May of the next year. However, she had to give up her plan to return to Japan as World War II was impending. She died at a Quaker nursing home in suburban Philadelphia on October 2, 1957, at the age of ninety-seven.

Anna Hartshorne, who came from a wealthy

月2日、アナはフィラデルフィア郊外にあるクエーカーのナーシング・ホームで亡くなった。享年97歳であった。

裕福な家の出身で生活に困らなかったとはいえ、アナは無給で教えていた。そればかりでなく定期的に学校に寄付を続けた。1922年6月に「ミス・ハーツホーン20年勤続祝賀謝恩会」が開催されたとき、アナは「私の如き孤独な者を慰め且つ生甲斐のあるライフを与えてくれた吾が娘達諸姉に対する吾が感謝、吾が親愛こそ表し得可き言葉もない」と語ったという。いまアナ・ハーツホーンの名前は津田塾大学本館の名称(ハーツホーン・ホール)として残されている。また同大学の校歌「アルマ・マータ」はアナの作詞によるものである。

アナには『日本と日本人』(1902)の著書がある。 また自然を愛し、よく観察していたのであろう。津田塾大学にはハーツホーン作成の押し花標本が残されている。さらに日本で貝を収集しており、そのコレクションはフィラデルフィアにあるドレクセル大学の自然科学博物館に収蔵されている。

戸田徹子

参考文献:
亀田帛子『津田梅子とアナ・C・ハーツホーン』(双文社出版、2005)

【参考情報】
津田塾大学
〒187-8577　東京都小平市津田町2-1-1
電話:042-342-5111(代表)
www.tsuda.ac.jp

Philadelphia family, taught at Tsuda College without accepting any pay. In fact, she regularly donated to the college. At the commemoration of her twentieth anniversary on the job in June 1922, instead of accepting the gratitude of others she thanked the college and its people. She told them that she was at a loss to describe how much the college had provided her companionship and a purpose in life. People respected her for her kindness, integrity, and humbleness. Anna Hartshorne's name is well remembered among teachers and students of Tsuda College, whose main building ("Hartshorne Hall") is named after her. She also wrote the lyrics of its college song, *Alma Mater*.

Hartshorne was the author of *Japan and Her People* (1902). She seems to have appreciated nature very much. Tsuda College has her collection of pressed flowers. She was also a shell collector, and her shell collection is now in the Academy of Natural Sciences of Drexel University, Philadelphia.

By Tetsuko Toda

Selected References: Anna C. Hartshorne, *Japan and Her People* (Philadelphia, PA: Henry T. Coates, 1902).

If you go: The Academy of Natural Sciences of Drexel University, 1900 Benjamin Franklin Parkway, Philadelphia, PA 19103.

5.7   Roland S. Morris: Ambassador to Japan
ローランド・モリス：フィラデルフィア出身の駐日大使

ローランド・モリス（1874 - 1945)は、フィラデルフィアの高名な法律家で、20世紀前半に活躍した。彼の先祖は1682年にアメリカに渡り、1700年以前にフィラデルフィアに住みついた。なかにはフィラデルフィアの第2代市長を務めた人物もおり、先祖の多くが指導的地位についた。モリスは父親の仕事の関係で、ワシントン州のオリンピアで1874年3月11日に生まれた。フィラデルフィアに戻った後、ニュージャージー州のローレンスビル高校、プリンストン大学を経て、ペンシルベニア大学の法律大学院を1899年に修了した。数年後、モリスは2人の友人と共同でデュアン・モリス・アンド・ヘックシャー法律事務所を設立した。その法律事務所はフィラデルフィアの有名な大手の法律事務所の1つとなり、今でも存続している。

プリンストン大学の教授であり後にアメリカ大統領になったウッドロー・ウィルソンは、モリスの人生と仕事に大きな影響を与えた。市民はみな義務として政治や市民問題にかかわらなければならないという、ウィルソンの信念に動かされて、モリスは最初は地元で、後には州や国政レベルにおいて、民主党員として活躍した。ウィルソンが勝利を納めた1912年と1916年の大統領選挙戦で、モリスはウィルソンを強力に支持し、親しく信頼のおける助言者となった。そのため、モリスはウィルソン大統領の2期目が始まった1916年に駐日大使に任命されたのである。

Roland Morris (1874–1945) was a prominent Philadelphia lawyer for forty years during the first half of the twentieth century. His family had come to America in 1682 and settled in Philadelphia before 1700. One ancestor had served as the second mayor of the city, and many were among its leading citizens. Morris himself was born on March 11, 1874, in Olympia, Washington, where his father's business had taken him. After returning to Philadelphia he attended the Lawrenceville School in New Jersey, Princeton University, and the University of Pennsylvania Law School, from which he graduated in 1899. Several years later, with two friends, he formed the law firm of Duane, Morris & Heckscher, which became, and remains, one of the largest and most prominent in the city.

Roland Morris' life and career were strongly influenced by Woodrow Wilson, who was a member of the Princeton faculty and later became president of the United States. Motivated by Wilson's belief that it was every citizen's duty to become involved in government and civic affairs, Morris became active in Democratic politics, at first locally and later as a leader at the state and national levels. During Woodrow Wilson's successful campaigns for the presidency in 1912 and 1916, Morris was a strong supporter and became a close and trusted advisor. This led to his appointment as Ambassador to Japan in 1916 at the beginning of the second Wilson

モリスが東京の大使館に勤務した4年間は地政的・軍事的同盟の時代であり、アメリカと日本は、他の列強と同様に、その同盟関係の中に組み込まれていた。そのため、外交上の問題というのは、紛争解決というよりも、主に共通の目標のために利害調整することであった。しかし、モリスはウィルソン大統領から信頼されていたので、日本で幾つかの特殊任務を遂行するよう要請されている。1918年、ロシア革命によってロマノフ王朝支配に終止符が打たれた後、アレキザンダー・コルチャックという白系ロシア人が、シベリアにおいて反革命組織を結成しようとした。そのために、モリスは1918年から1919年にかけての12ヶ月の間に、機密の実情調査で3回もシベリアを訪れる。ウィルソン大統領がコルチャックと反革命活動への対策を決めるのに不可欠な任務だったのである。モリスはまた、同盟国に中国の南満州鉄道の支配権を与える交渉にも一役買ったのである。

ウィルソン政権終了に伴い、モリスはフィラデルフィアに戻り弁護士に復帰。1945年に亡くなるまで、25年間にわたり活躍した。フィラデルフィア弁護士会の会長を務め、市の指導者として多くの重要なポストに就いた。ペンシルベ

Roland S. Morris, late 1920s.
Duane, Morris & Heckscher, Philadelphia

administration.

The four years of the Morris embassy in Tokyo was a period of geopolitical and military alliance that embraced the United States and Japan as well as the other Allied powers. The diplomatic challenges, therefore, were largely those of coordinating efforts toward common goals rather than the resolution of disputes. But because of the confidence Wilson had in him, Morris was called upon to carry out several unusual assignments from his base in Japan. In 1918, for example, after the Bolshevist Revolution ended the rule of the Romanov dynasty in Russia, a White Russian named Alexander Kolchak attempted to organize a counter-revolution from his base in Siberia. Over a period of twelve months in 1918 and 1919, Morris was sent on three secret fact-finding missions to Siberia that were vital in the formation of Wilson's policy toward Kolchak and his activities. Morris was also instrumental in negotiation of an agreement that gave the Allies control of the Chinese Eastern Railway.

At the end of the Wilson administration,

ニア大学では国際法の教授となり、プリンストン大学やカーネギー国際平和基金、ブルッキングス研究所、スミソニアン研究所では理事を務めた。アメリカ哲学協会やウッドロー・ウィルソン財団の会長も務め、多くの企業や慈善団体の理事会のメンバーでもあった。

駐日大使としてのモリスには面白い逸話が残っている。それはモリスの孫の回想である。孫の名もローランド・モリスといい、彼自身もモリス法律事務所の弁護士で、フィラデルフィアの著名人だった。その回想によると、モリス大使が亡くなって何年も経ってから、1人の年老いた日本人がフィラデルフィアを訪れ、モリスの墓への案内を頼んできた。フェアモント公園のイースト・ローレル・ヒル墓地に到着すると、老人はすぐに墓のそばに行って、約20分間、直立の姿勢で、ここ50年間に日本で起きた出来事を大声でしゃべっていた。老人と別れる時、孫のローランド・モリスがいったい何をしていたのかと尋ねると、その訪問客は、大使に最後にお会いしてから長い月日が経ったので、昔の懐かしい友人に、その間に日本で起こったことを全部報告したいと思ったのだ、と返事したという。

ウィリアム・B・イーグルソン・ジュニア
今井元子/戸田徹子 訳

Morris returned to Philadelphia and to his law practice in which he remained active for twenty-five years until his death in 1945. He served as Chancellor of the Philadelphia Bar Association and in many important positions of civic leadership in the city. He held a professorship in international law at the University of Pennsylvania, served as a trustee of Princeton, the Carnegie Endowment for Peace, The Brookings Institution and as a Regent of the Smithsonian Institution. He was president of the American Philosophical Society, the Woodrow Wilson Foundation, and a member of numerous corporate and charitable boards of directors.

There is an interesting footnote to this account of the Morris embassy to Japan that is recalled by his grandson, also named Roland Morris and himself a prominent lawyer in the firm bearing the family name. Many years after Ambassador Morris' death, an elderly Japanese appeared in Philadelphia and asked to be escorted to visit Morris' grave. Upon arrival at East Laurel Hill Cemetery in Fairmount Park he stood stiffly at the graveside for some twenty minutes speaking aloud about events of the last fifty years in Japan. As they departed, the younger Roland Morris asked about what had occurred. His visitor replied that it had been many years since he had last seen the Ambassador and he wanted to inform his old and dear friend about all the things that had occurred in Japan in the intervening years.

By William B. Eagleson, Jr.

If you go: Laurel Hill Cemetery, 3822 Ridge Avenue, Philadelphia, PA 19132.

5.8 Esther Biddle Rhoads: Dedicated to Helping Japanese People in Both Japan and the U.S.
エスター・ローズ：日米で救済活動に尽力した女性

エスター・ビドル・ローズ（1896‐1979）はフィラデルフィアのフレンド（クエーカー）で、日本の女子教育に生涯を捧げ、戦中戦後は日本人のための救済事業や平和活動に精力的に携わった。エスターはキリスト友会（クエーカーの教会名）のフィラデルフィア年会ミッション・ボードの宣教師として、東京の三田にある普連土女学校で教えた。太平洋戦争中はアメリカで強制収容所に入れられた日系人のために働いた。戦後日本に戻ると、教職に復帰するとともに、ララ救援物資の配給で指導的役割を果たした。またエリザベス・バイニングの後任として、明仁皇太子（今上天皇）に英語を教えている。

エスター・ローズは代々続いたクエーカーの家庭に生まれ育った。エドワード・G・ローズ医師とマーガレット・パクストン・ローズの間にクエーカーとして誕生し、1900年から1913年までジャーマンタウン・フレンズ・スクールに通い、最終学年のみチェスター郡にあるクエーカーの寄宿学校ウェストタウン・スクールで勉強した。その後、ドレクセル・インスティチュート（現ドレクセル大学）に進学し、家政学の教職免許を取得した。

エスターは日本に関心を持つように運命づけられていたのかもしれない。母親のマーガレットは、1885年に日本伝道を開始したフィラデルフィア・フレンズ婦人外国伝道協会のメンバーで、エスターは子供の頃、普連土女学校に送るクリスマス・ボックスを用意するのを手

Esther Biddle Rhoads (1896–1979) was a Philadelphia Quaker who devoted her life to Japanese people as a teacher and a social worker. Rhoads was supported by the (Quaker) Mission Board of Philadelphia Yearly Meeting (Orthodox) and taught at Friends Girls' School in Mita, Tokyo. During World War II she stayed in the United States and helped Japanese Americans who were relocated and kept in internment camps. Returning to Japan after the war, she resumed teaching and played a leading role in the LARA (Licensed Agencies for Relief in Asia). Esther succeeded Elizabeth Vining as tutor to Crown Prince Akihito (the present Emperor).

The daughter of Edward G. Rhoads, M.D. and Margaret Paxson Rhoads, Esther was a Quaker by birth and was raised in a Quaker environment. She attended Germantown Friends School from 1900 to 1913 and spent her senior year at Quaker-run Westtown School in Chester County, Pennsylvania. She studied at Drexel Institute (now Drexel University) and got a teacher's certificate in home economics.

Rhoads seems to have been destined to become interested in Japan. Esther's mother was a member of the Women's Foreign Missionary Association of Friends of Philadelphia, which had started a Japan mission in 1885. So, as a child, she sometimes helped in making Christmas boxes to be sent

Esther Rhoads. Haverford College Quaker & Special Collections

to the Friends Girls' School in Tokyo.

Rhoads decided to go to Japan as a Quaker missionary teacher. She arrived there in September 1917 and taught English, the Bible, and foreign cooking at the Friends Girls' School. However, her first stay was only for one year, and she left for home in August 1918. She received a Bachelor of Science from Earlham College in Indiana and returned to Japan in 1921. From that time until her departure in 1940, she worked at the Friends Girls' School in Tokyo.

Beginning in 1931, Japan started enlarging its territories in China, resulting in the Manchurian Incident in 1939. When Rhoads returned home on furlough in April 1940, the American government did not allow her to go back to Japan due to the possibility of war, and in December, 1941 Japan attacked Pearl Harbor. On the West Coast, Japanese Americans were relocated and interned. When the American Friends Service Committee (AFSC) started assisting these Japanese Americans, the Mission Board decided to "lend" Esther to the AFSC

伝った。宣教師として日本に赴任することを決め、エスターは1917年9月に来日した。最初の滞在は短く、普連土女学校で1年間、英語、聖書、西洋料理を教え、1918年8月に帰国した。インディアナ州のアーラム大学で学び理学士を取得し、1921年に再来日。それから1940年に帰国するまで、普連土女学校の教師を務めた。

第1次世界大戦後、日本は中国に進攻

し、1939年には満州事変が起こった。エスターは1940年に恩賜休暇で帰国した。日本に戻る予定であったが、アメリカ政府は戦争の可能性からビザを発行せず、1941年12月に太平洋戦争が勃発。西海岸で日系人の立ち退きが始まると、米国フレンズ奉仕団は日系人支援活動を開始した。ミッション・ボードはエスターを奉仕団に派遣することを決め、彼女はカリフォルニアに赴いた。

日本語の達者なエスターは、奉仕団スタッフとして転住所や収容所で日系人に接した。さらに全国学生転住協議会の事業にも参加し、学生たちが学業を継続できるように転住を促進する仕事にも関わった。また日系人は就職先と安全な生活環境が保障されれば東部や中西部に転居できたので、仕事や住居を探す仕事も引き受けた。そして収容終了が近づくと、戻る場所を失ってしまった日系人に一時的な滞在先を提供するために、ロサンゼルスにエバーグリーン・ホステルを開設した。

1946年6月22日、エスターはついに日本に戻ることができた。米国フレンズ奉仕団の代表となり、持ち前の実行力で、食料や古着などのララ救援物資の注文と配給に手腕を発揮した。この仕事に加えて、エスターはキリスト友会日本年会の再興に尽力し、空襲で跡形もなく破壊された普連土女学校の再建にも乗り出した。普連土女学校はエスターにとって、かけがえの無いものだった。エスターはこの学校に40年間在職し、校長を6年余、理事長を5年務めた。

ララ救援物資は1952年6月に終了し、救援と復興活動は日本政府の厚生省の手に委ねられた。この年、エスターは

and sent her to California.

As she spoke Japanese well, Rhoads worked mainly with Japanese evacuees in assembly centers and internment camps. She also helped college students relocate to other regions to start or resume their educations, a project that was sponsored by the National Student Relocation Council. Finding jobs for those who wanted to move to other places and insuring safe living places for them was another project with which she assisted. When the closing of the internment camps neared, she organized the Evergreen Hostel in Los Angeles as a "halfway house" for those Japanese Americans who had given up their homes and belongings and thus had no place to go.

Rhoads finally returned to Japan on June 22, 1946, supported both by the Mission Board and the AFSC, to work as an AFSC representative to the LARA. She first engaged herself in ordering and distributing food and used clothing, but because of her managerial talent, she became a leader in the LARA program. Esther also became committed to reorganizing the Friends Meetings in Japan (Japan Yearly Meeting of the Society of Friends) and to reviving the Friends Girls' School, whose buildings had been completely destroyed by the bombing. The school had always been her highest priority and she taught there for more than forty years, six years as principal and five years as director.

The LARA program ended in June 1952, when relief work and rehabilitation were taken over by the Japanese government (the National Council of Social Work). In the same year, Rhoads received the Fourth

昭和天皇から勲四等旭日章を授与された。さらに退職と帰国（1960年4月）に際しては、勲三等旭日章をはじめ様々な表彰を受けた。

明仁皇太子の家庭教師を務めたエリザベス・バイニングが日本を離れることになった時、後任として同じジャーマンタウン月会員のエスターを推薦した。エスターは約10年にわたり、皇太子と皇室メンバーに英語を教えている。1978年12月に皇太子夫妻がフィラデルフィアを訪問した時、エスターとバイニング夫人は晩さん会に招待された。翌年の2月4日、エスターは家族との夕食の後、ジャーマンタウンの自宅で静かに息を引き取った。

戸田徹子

参考文献：
エスター・B・ローズ記念出版委員会編
『一クエーカーの足跡』（1980）

【参考情報】
普連土学園
〒108-0073
東京都港区三田4-14-16
電話: 03-3451-4616
www.friends.ac.jp

Order of the Sacred Treasure from Emperor Hirohito. She was awarded many other honors and tokens of appreciation, including the Third Order of the Sacred Treasure.

When Elizabeth Vining retired as the English tutor to the Crown Prince in 1960, she recommended her Quaker friend, Rhoads, to be her successor. Rhoads served as an English tutor to Crown Prince Akihito and later, other members of the Imperial Family, for approximately ten years. Esther Rhoads and Elizabeth Vining dined with Crown Prince Akihito and Crown Princess Michiko when they visited Philadelphia in December 1978. The next year, on February 4, Esther passed away peacefully at home in Germantown after a family dinner.

By Tetsuko Toda

If you go: The Quaker Collection at Haverford College, 370 Lancaster Avenue, Haverford, PA 19041, holds Esther Rhoads' Papers.

5.9　Hugh Borton: A Scholar and "Friend" of Japan
ヒュー・ボートン：対日占領政策立案にかかわった歴史家

ヒュー・ボートン（1903－1995）は日本研究が専門の歴史家。クエーカー宣教師ならびに米国フレンズ奉仕団スタッフとして、20代の3年間を日本で過ごした。コロンビア大学で日本語と日本史を教えていたが、太平洋戦争が始まると国務省に勤務し、対日占領政策立案にかかわった。コロンビア大学に戻り、その後、ハバフォード大学の第8代学長を務めた。クエーカー信仰と専門知識に基づき、友好的な日米関係の構築に尽力した。

ボートンは1903年、ニュージャージー州モレスタウンのクエーカー家庭に生まれた。地元のクエーカーの学校に通った後、ペンシルベニア州チェスター郡にあるクエーカーの寄宿学校、ウェストタウン・スクールで学んだ。ハバフォード大学に進学し、学生自治会や新聞部、討論部、グリークラブ、サッカーなどで活躍した。そして大学で、米国フレンズ奉仕団（AFSC）創設者の1人であるルファス・ジョーンズの授業や説教から大きな影響を受けた。

米国フレンズ奉仕団とはクエーカーの組織で、第1次世界大戦中の1917年に、良心的兵役拒否者に兵役の代替サービスを提供する目的で結成された。この米国フレンズ奉仕団を通して、多くの若いフレンド（クエーカー）がヨーロッパに送られた。彼らはヨーロッパにおいて戦時中は救援活動に従事し、戦争が終わると復興や食糧援助、国際親善などの活動を展開した。

Hugh Borton (1903–1995) was a historian who specialized in Japanese history. In his twenties, he spent three years in Japan as a Quaker missionary and as a staff member of the American Friends Service Committee (AFSC). He taught Japanese and Japanese history at Columbia University. During World War II, he served in the State Department, helping with postwar planning for Japan. He was the eighth president of Haverford College. Through his Quaker beliefs and knowledge about Japan, Borton helped build good relations between the United States and Japan.

Hugh Borton was born into a devout Quaker family in Moorestown, New Jersey in 1903. He attended a local Quaker school and then studied at a Quaker boarding school, Westtown School in Chester County, Pennsylvania. He entered Haverford College and made the most of his college life, taking part in student council, the news board, debating society, glee club, and soccer. At college, he was greatly influenced by the preaching and lectures of Rufus Jones, one of the founders of the AFSC.

The AFSC was a Quaker organization founded in 1917 to help victims of World War I and to provide conscientious objectors with non-combatant work in lieu of military service. Many young Friends (Quakers) were sent to Europe with the help of the AFSC.

Hugh Borton. Haverford College
Quaker & Special Collections

They were engaged in relief work during the war, and then got involved in reconstruction, food aid, and international goodwill activities after the war.

In the Philadelphia Yearly Meeting, a new generation of Quakers was coming to the fore in the first two decades of the twentieth century. These youths were influenced by the AFSC and interested in domestic social problems and international issues. Hugh Borton represented this generation. Although he himself was brought up in a wealthy family, he developed sympathy for socially vulnerable people, participating in settlement activities during his summer vacations.

After graduating from college in 1927, Borton married Elizabeth Dean Wilbur. The couple sought a way to make a living compatible with their Quaker beliefs. They looked to the AFSC, which provided them with teaching posts at a small boarding school in the Great Smoky Mountains of Tennessee.

Borton's father (Charles Walter Borton) was one of the executive members of the Foreign Missionary Association of Friends of Philadelphia, so Japan probably was not an unfamiliar country to the son. Borton decided to go to Japan as a Quaker missionary and as a staff member of the AFSC.

1910年代から1920年代にかけてフィラデルフィア年会では、平和や国際問題、国内の社会問題などに関心を持つ新しい世代のフレンドが出現しつつあり、ボートンはその代表格だった。自分自身は恵まれた家庭で育ったが、社会的弱者に共感を示し、夏休みにはセツルメント運動などに参加していた。

大学卒業後、ボートンはエリザベス・ディーン・ウィルバーと結婚した。2人はクエーカーの信仰に適った生き方を求め、米国フレンズ奉仕団スタッフとして、

193

南部の山岳地帯にある寄宿学校で2年間ほど教えた。

ボートンの父親(チャールズ・ウォルター・ボートン)はフィラデルフィア・フレンズ外国伝道協会の役員で、日本に関心を寄せていた。それゆえ息子にとっても、日本は遠い国ではなかったのかもしれない。ヒュー・ボートンは日本赴任を希望し、クエーカー宣教師 兼 米国フレンズ奉仕団スタッフとして日本に派遣されたのである。

ボートン夫妻は1928年に来日。東京において、ボートンは主に2つの仕事に従事しなければならなかった。1つはフレンズ日本伝道の主任であるギルバート・ボールズの平和活動を手伝うことであり、もう1つは柯南寮の管理人として男子大学生たちの指導をすることだった。一方で、ボートンは日本語と日本史を学び始めたのだが、次第に学問的関心を深め、イギリス大使館の参事官であったジョージ・B・サムソンから週に1回、日本文化史を教えてもらうようになった。帰国するとコロンビア大学の大学院に進学し、それからオランダのライデン大学で学び、「徳川時代の農民一揆」と題された論文を書き、博士号を授与された。

ボートンはコロンビア大学で教鞭をとるようになっていた。太平洋戦争が始まると、クエーカーの平和主義に基づき良心的兵役拒否者であったボートンは、1942年から1948年まで国務省に転出した。そこで日本の専門家として、対日占領政策立案に従事した。ボートンは「戦後日本の設計者」の1人とみなされているが、穏健な立場を堅持し、一貫して日本の間接統治と天皇制の維持を

Mr. and Mrs. Borton arrived in Tokyo in 1928. Borton had two main missions in Japan. One was to assist Gilbert Bowles, the superintendent of the Friends mission, with peace activities. The other was to mentor male college students as a supervisor at Longstreth Memorial Dormitory. As he learned the Japanese language and about Japanese history, his academic interest in Japan grew and he began studying Japanese cultural history with Sir George B. Samson of the British Embassy.

After returning to the United States, Borton attended the graduate school of Columbia University. He furthered his study at Leiden University in the Netherlands and received his Ph.D. degree from Leiden in 1937 with a dissertation titled, "Peasant Uprisings in Japan in the Tokugawa Period."

Borton was professor of Japanese and Japanese history at Columbia University from 1937 until 1957. However, he took a leave of absence from 1942 until 1948. A Quaker, he had registered himself as a conscientious objector to military combat. During the war years of 1942 to 1948, he went to Washington, DC to work with the State Department, where he became one of the principal architects of United States policy toward Japan. As a specialist on Japan, he committed himself to preparing postwar policies for Japan. He took a moderate position, insisting on the policy of indirect occupation and the continuation of the Emperor system.

Returning to the academic world after the war, Borton devoted himself to developing the fields of Japanese and Asian Studies. He nurtured the new East Asian Institute

主張した。

学問の世界に戻ると、ボートンは大学ならびに学会において日本研究とアジア研究の発展に寄与した。コロンビア大学では新しい東アジア研究所の充実を計り、後にそのディレクターとなった。またボートンはアジア学会の創立メンバーの1人であり、1957年から1958年まで会長を務めた。さらにジョン・F・ケネディ大統領と池田隼人首相によって1961年に創設された日米教育文化会議（カルコン）のアメリカ側代表となった。

ボートンは1957年から1967年までの10年間、母校であるハバフォード大学の第8代学長を務め、1963年に学生数を450名から700名に拡大した。また1966年にはクエーカー礼拝への強制出席の廃止を決めたが、これは学生の90％はすでにクエーカーではないという現実に即した決断であった。

学長を辞めると再びコロンビア大学に戻り、東アジア研究所で日本近代史の研究を再開した。退職後はマサチューセッツ州コンウェイに転居し、この地で1995年8月11日に亡くなった。享年92歳であった。

戸田徹子

参考文献：
ヒュー・ボートン『戦後日本の設計者：ボートン回想録』（朝日新聞社、1998）

at Columbia University and later became its director. He was one of the founding members of the Association for Asian Studies (AAS) and served as its president from 1957 to 1958. He also participated in the United States-Japan Conference on Cultural and Educational Interchange (CULCON), which was organized in 1961 by President John F. Kennedy and Prime Minister Ikeda Hayato for the purpose of strengthening cultural and intellectual ties between their two countries. Borton was appointed the chairman of the United States delegation.

Hugh Borton served as the eighth president of Haverford College from 1957 until 1967. During his presidency, he guided the college through some major changes, including increasing its student population from 450 to 700 and doing away with compulsory attendance at Quaker meetings for students, as ninety percent of the students were not Quaker.

After serving at Haverford, Borton resumed his research on modern Japanese history at Columbia University. He moved to Conway, in western Massachusetts, to retire and passed away on August 11, 1995, at the age of ninety-two.

By Tetsuko Toda

Selected References: Hugh Borton, *Spanning Japan's Modern Century: The Memoirs of Hugh Borton* (Lanham, MD: Lexington Books, 2002).

If you go: Haverford College, 370 Lancaster Avenue, Haverford, PA 19041.

5.10 Elizabeth Gray Vining: Tutor to the Crown Prince
エリザベス・バイニング：明仁皇太子の家庭教師

エリザベス・グレイ・バイニング（1902‐1999）は、今上天皇が明仁皇太子だった時の家庭教師として、フィラデルフィアと日本の皇室を結びつける重要な役割を果たした。父はスコットランド移民のジョン・ゴードン・グレイ、母はクエーカーとして育てられたアン・イザード・グレイで、エリザベスはその末っ子として生まれた。バイオレットという名前の姉がおり、長い間、フィラデルフィアとウォリングフォード（ペンシルベニア州）で一緒に暮らした。エリザベスはフィラデルフィア近郊にあるブリンマーと、ジャーマンタウンのクィーン・レーン地区で育ち、ブリンマー大学に通った。

卒業後はノース・カロライナ大学で図書館司書として働き、そこでモーガン・バイニングと出会い結婚する。だが1933年、夫が自動車事故で早すぎる死を迎えたため、フィラデルフィアに再び戻り、児童文学作家となる。出版したなかには『旅の子アダム』という本もあり、この作品によって1943年に念願のニューベリー賞を獲得した。全部で20冊近い本を書いたが、その中にはウィリアム・ペンの伝記や、強い信念を持つクエーカー教徒ルーファス・ジョーンズの伝記、さらには『皇太子の窓』（1952）、『日本への再訪』（1960）、『天皇とわたし』（1970）など、本人の日本滞在の経験を語った3冊の本も含まれる。

明仁皇太子の家庭教師に任命されていた頃のことは『皇太子の窓』に詳述されており、この東京で過ごした4年間の回

As the tutor to then Crown Prince, and now Emperor Akihito, Elizabeth Gray Vining (1902–1999) provides one of the most important connections between the Philadelphia region and imperial Japan. The youngest child of Scottish immigrant John Gordon Gray and a mother of Quaker upbringing, Anne Iszard Gray, Elizabeth had one older sister, Violet, who lived with her for many years in Philadelphia and Wallingford, Pennsylvania. Raised in Bryn Mawr and the Queen Lane section of Germantown in Philadelphia, Elizabeth attended Bryn Mawr College. She subsequently accepted a post in the library at the University of North Carolina in Chapel Hill, where she met and married Morgan Vining. After her husband's untimely death in an automobile accident in 1933, she returned to Philadelphia. There Elizabeth Vining enjoyed a career as an author of children's books, including *Adam of the Road*, winner of the respected Newberry Award in 1943. In all, Vining authored nearly twenty books, including biographies of William Penn and Quaker stalwart Rufus Jones, as well as three volumes recounting her experiences in and with Japan: *Windows for the Crown Prince* (1952), *Return to Japan* (1960), and *Quiet Pilgrimage* (1970).

The story of her appointment and tenure as the tutor to Crown Prince Akihito is described in detail in *Windows for the Crown Prince*, Vining's best-selling memoir of her four years in Tokyo. Her background as a Quaker,

Elizabeth Vining with Crown Prince Akihito in the center.
Haverford College Quaker & Special Collections

想録はベストセラーとなった。宮内庁が大勢の候補者の中からエリザベス・バイニングを選んだ理由には、本人がクエーカー教徒であり、教養があるけれども学究的過ぎるというわけでもないという背景や、成功と悲劇の両方を経験しているということがあった。バイニングの任務には皇太子の個人授業だけでなく、学習院での英会話の授業や皇太子の姉妹に対する授業も含まれていた。多くの公式の場で昭和天皇と皇后に会い、皇太子の教育について天皇や皇后と打ち解けた会話を交わすこともあった。

バイニングのアメリカ占領時代に関す

well-educated but not strictly academic, and her experience of both success and tragedy played a part in the Imperial Household Agency decision to choose Mrs. Vining over a number of other applicants. In addition to private lessons with the Crown Prince, her duties included English conversation classes at the Peers' School and lessons for Akihito's sisters as well. She met the Shōwa Emperor and Empress on numerous formal occasions, and even held informal conversations with them about the education of their son.

Vining's account of the years of American occupation of Japan (1945–52) is insightful,

る記述は、洞察力に満ちており、他では得られない視点からの報告や意外な事実が含まれている。アメリカ占領総司令部の役人のほかに日本の閣僚とも接触したため、多くの歴史的瞬間について非常に信憑性の高い内容を、特に1970年の自伝『天皇とわたし』の中に書いている。例えば、バイニングは、当時首相であった鈴木貫太郎などから聞いた話に基づき、1945年の御前会議の最後の記者会見について詳述しているが、この記者会見こそが天皇の降伏宣言の草案作成を促したものだった。(英語版、229頁)

1950年にフィラデルフィアに戻ってからも、バイニングは日本の皇室と親しい関係を続けた。明仁皇太子は、1953年の訪米の際に、フィラデルフィア郊外のマウント・エァリーにある夫人の家に滞在したが、皇太子が個人宅に宿泊することは、たいへん稀なことであった。バイニングは1957年に講演と観光を兼ねて日本を再訪し、1959年には明仁皇太子の結婚式にも参列した。90代を迎えた彼女のもとに、皇族方や大使、使節が皇室からのお心遣いの言葉だけでなく、絹の反物から、挨拶や祝辞の和歌に至るまで、様々な贈り物を携えて訪問し続けた。

フランク・チャンス
今井元子/戸田徹子 訳

with revelations and reports from a viewpoint that remained otherwise inaccessible. Her contact with members of the Imperial cabinet, as well as with the Allied Occupation General Headquarters and other officials, allowed Vining to write authoritatively about many historical moments, particularly in her 1970 autobiography, *Quiet Pilgrimage*. She recounts, for example, the final press conferences of the Imperial War Council in 1945, leading up to the drafting of the Imperial Rescript announcing surrender, based on her discussions with the then-Prime Minister Suzuki Kantarō and others.

After returning to Philadelphia in 1950, Vining continued to maintain a close relationship with the Japanese Imperial Family. Her home in the Mt. Airy section of Philadelphia is one of the few private dwellings where the current Emperor has stayed, notably during a visit in 1953. Vining visited Japan as a lecturer and tourist in 1957, and attended the Crown Prince's wedding in 1959. Ambassadors, envoys, and members of the Imperial Family continued to visit Mrs. Vining in her ninth decade, bearing the good wishes of the family as well as gifts ranging from bolts of Imperial silk through poems of greetings and good wishes.

By Frank L. Chance

Selected References: Elizabeth Gray Vining, *Windows for the Crown Prince* (Philadelphia, PA: Lippincott, 1952); Shelia K. Johnson, *The Japanese Through American Eyes* (Stanford, CA: Stanford University Press, 1988).

Continuing Connections

現代につながっている交流

6 Benjamin Franklin's Descendents and Japan
フランクリンの子孫たちと日本

6.1 Robert W. Irwin: Benjamin Franklin's Descendants in Japan

ロバート・アーウィン：日本に生きたベンジャミン・フランクリンの子孫

歴史には興味深い話がたくさんある。その1つがロバート・ウォーカー・アーウィン（1844 - 1925）の物語である。彼の父親は、かつてペンシルベニア選出の国会議員であったウィリアム・ウォーレス・アーウィン。母親は、ベンジャミン・フランクリンの第4代直系子係である、フィラデルフィア出身のソフィア・アラベラ・ベイチだった。ロバートの父親は有名な弁護士で、ピッツバーグ市長やコペンハーゲンでデンマーク駐在米国代理大使などを務めたことがあった。母親はフィラデルフィアの多くの慈善団体で活躍し、フランクリン家の伝統に誇りをもっていた。ロバートの姉妹のアグネス・アーウィンとソフィ・アーウィンはフィラデルフィアでよく知られ、評判の高いアグネス・アーウィン女学校の創始者である。そして、アグネスが1894年にラドクリフ大学の初代学部長の職を引き受けると、ソフィがアグネス・アーウィン女学校を運営した。

しかし先祖のベンジャミン・フランクリンとロバートの姉妹たちがフィラデルフィアを拠点とし、時々ヨーロッパへと旅行したのに対し、ロバートは西へ向かい、ハワイや日本に旅行した。兄に励まされて、ロバートは太平洋郵船会社に就職した。会社が横浜まで航路を延ばすことになり、1866年、ロバートは横浜駐在代理人として日本に派遣された。

1872年まで、ロバートはウォルシュ・ホール商会の横浜事務所で活躍し、益田孝と知り合った。益田は会社の通訳とし

History has many interesting tales to tell. One is the story of Robert Walker Irwin (1844–1925), the son of William Wallace Irwin, a one-time Pennsylvania representative in the United States Congress, and Sophia Arabella Bache of Philadelphia, a fourth-generation direct descendant of Benjamin Franklin. Robert's father was a prominent lawyer whose career included service as the mayor of Pittsburgh and *charge d'affaires* in Copenhagen. His mother was active in many charitable organizations in Philadelphia and wore her Franklin heritage proudly. Robert's sister Agnes Irwin became the first Dean at Radcliffe College in 1894.

But while ancestor Benjamin Franklin and his own sisters made Philadelphia their capital with intermittent sojourns in Europe, Robert Irwin looked west to Hawaii and Japan. Encouraged by an older brother, he obtained employment with the Pacific Mail Steamship Company, which in 1866 sent him to Japan as its agent to open a Pacific Mail Steamship service to Yokohama. Robert remained in touch with his Philadelphia family even when he was far away in Japan.

By 1872 Robert Irwin was active in the Yokohama firm of Walsh, Hall and Company. There he became acquainted with Masuda Takashi, who had been working for the firm as interpreter and had left to become an official in the Ministry of Finance. It

て働いていた
が、会社を辞め
て大蔵省の役
人になった。ロ
バートが井上馨
という人と出会
ったのは、おそ
らく益田を通じ
てだったと思わ
れる。井上は、明
治時代の近代
化と発展を担う
ことになる将来
の指導者たちの
中でも、新進の
期待の星であっ
た。1873年、ロ
バートは益田と
井上ともう一人
の仲間が、輸出
促進のため、特
にロンドンへの
米の輸出を促進
するために、先
収会社を設立
するのを手伝っ

Robert and Iki Irwin, 1889.
Courtesy of Yukiko Irwin

た。その会社は、1876年に益田を社長
として三井物産会社（三井貿易会社）と
して再組織された。

井上は政府の仕事をするため会社を辞
め、政府の高官となった。最初は工部卿
（通産大臣）を、その後は外務卿（外務
大臣）を務めた。ロバートと井上は親し
い友人となり、1876年に、井上とその妻
と娘が約20人の補佐役や学生と共にア
メリカへ旅行する手配をした。井上の主
な目的は、金融市場や貿易、通貨・金融
システムを研究することだった。ロバー
トは旅行の間、井上の案内役を務め、サ
ンフランシスコ、ネバダ、シカゴ、ナイア

was probably through Masuda that Irwin met one Inoue Kaoru, a rising star among future leaders of Japan's Meiji era of modernization and expansion. In 1873 Irwin assisted Masuda, Inoue, and another partner in organizing a company, the Senshū Kaisha, to promote exports, especially the export of rice to London. The company was reorganized in 1876 as Mitsui Bussan Kaisha (The Mitsui Trading Company), with Masuda as president.

Inoue left the firm to enter government service and became a highly-placed government official, first as Minister of Industry and eventually as Foreign Minister. Irwin and Inoue became close friends, with Irwin arranging a trip for Inoue, his wife and daughter, as well as about twenty assistants and students, to the United States in 1876. Inoue's main purpose was to study financial markets, trade, financial, and currency systems. Robert Irwin acted as Inoue's guide during the trip, which took them to San Francisco, Nevada, Chicago, Niagara Falls, and Philadelphia. The Inoue party arrived in August 1876, during the Philadelphia Centennial Exhibition.

Several years later Inoue undertook the task

Robert Irwin Family. Courtesy of Yukiko Irwin

ガラ滝、フィラデルフィアを回った。

　ロバートは遠く日本にいる時でも、家族と連絡を取り合っていた。1876年8月、フィラデルフィアで開催されていた独立100周年記念万国博覧会の期間中に、井上の一行と共にフィラデルフィアに到着した。日本に帰国して数年後、井上はロバートにふさわしい日本人の妻を探し出す役割を引き受け、先祖に武士や商人をもつ武智イキという女性を見つけた。これは、完全な日米間の法的処理に基づく、最初のアメリカ人と日本人の結婚であり、1882年3月15日に最後の法律書類にサインがなされるまで、手続きに1年以上が費やされた。

　1880年代半ば、ロバートはハワイ政府

of searching for and finding a suitable and proper Japanese wife for Irwin, eventually identifying Takechi Iki, whose ancestry included both samurai and merchants. Their marriage was the first American-Japanese union to be based on formal legal arrangements between the United States and Japan, taking more than a year before the final papers were signed on March 15, 1882.

In the mid 1880s Robert Irwin was invited by the Hawaiian government to assist with the importation of Japanese workers to Hawaii as contract laborers for the sugar plantations. He took on the job energetically and, as it turned out, with great skill, becoming the principal architect of Japanese immigration to Hawaii. Contemporary records indicate

に招かれ、日本の労働者を砂糖農園の契約労働者としてハワイに連れて行く仕事に従事した。彼はその仕事に精力的に取り組み、優れた手腕を発揮し、結局、日本人のハワイ移住の重要な企画者となった。当時の統計によると、1894年までに、日本から、2万3071人の男性、5487人の女性、そして133人の子供が、アーウィンの考案したやり方（官約移民）で、ハワイに来たということである。アーウィンは日本に対する貢献により、日本政府から旭日章と瑞宝章の2つの勲章が授与された。

ロバートとイキの夫婦には6人の子供があり、全員が日本とアメリカの両方で教育を受けた。一番年長のソフィア・アラベラは1917年東京に保母（保育士）養成の玉成保姆養成所と付属幼稚園を開設した。彼女は父親から相続した資金で1947年に学校を拡張し、その学校はアルウィン学園玉成高等保育学校から玉成保育専門学校と名称変更して、存続している。

ヒラリー・コンロイ
今井元子／戸田徹子 訳

【参考情報】
渋川市指定史跡　ハワイ王国公使別邸
群馬県渋川市北橘町真壁　2372-1
渋川市教育委員会文化財保護課
電話: 0279-52-2102
www.city.shibukawa.lg.jp/kankou/
rekishi/hawaikousibettei.html

JICA横浜：海外移住資料館
神奈川県横浜市中区新港　2-3-1
電話：045-663-3257
www.jomm.jp

that 23,071 Japanese men, 5,487 women and 133 children came to Hawaii under Irwin's system by 1894. Irwin was awarded both the Order of the Rising Sun and the Order of the Sacred Treasure by the Japanese government for his services to Japan.

Robert and Iki Irwin had six children, all of whom were educated in the United States and Japan. The eldest, Sophia Arabella, established the Gyokusei School for nursery school teachers and an adjoining kindergarten in Tokyo in 1917. She expanded the school in 1947 with funds inherited from her father, and it continues today as Irwin Gakuen.

By F. Hilary Conroy

Selected References: Yukiko Irwin and Hilary Conroy, "Robert Walker Irwin & Systematic Immigration to Hawaii," in *East Across the Pacific: Historical and Sociological Studies of Japanese Immigration and Assimilation*, eds. Hilary Conroy and T. Scott Miyakawa (Santa Barbara CA: ABC-Clio Press, 1972), pp. 40–55; Christine M.E. Guth, *Art, Tea, and Industry: Masuda Takashi and the Mitsui Circle* (Princeton, NJ: Princeton University Press, 1993).

If you go: The Benjamin Franklin Museum, 317 Chestnut Street, Philadelphia, PA 19106.

Summer Residence of the Minister of the Kingdom of Hawaii Historic Site, Kita Tachibana-chō, Makabe 2372-1, Shibukawa-shi, Gunma Prefecture.

6.2　Benjamin Franklin's Maxims Published in Japanese: Frugality for All

日本語に訳されたベンジャミン・フランクリンの格言

1733年から1758年にかけて、ベンジャミン・フランクリンは『貧しいリチャードの暦』を出版した。歴史や科学上の知識、詩、ジョーク、調理法、諺などが書かれた年鑑である。アメリカ独立革命前の出版物で影響力があり、フィラデルフィア、ペンシルベニア植民地ならびに近隣の植民地、さらにはヨーロッパ、特にフランスで読まれた。

各版には貧しいリチャードの名言と題して、多くの格言や諺が書かれているが、これはベンジャミン・フランクリンの格言としても知られていた。題材の多くは古典や聖書からとられているが、その当時のものやフランクリン自身の創作によるものもある。次のような格言が含まれている。「日の照っているうちに干し草を作れ（チャンスを逃すな）」「一銭の節約は一銭のもうけ」「早寝早起きは、人を健康で金持ちで賢くする（早寝早起きは三文の得）」。

1996年に、参議院議員の真島一男氏がフランクリンの格言を日本語に訳し、『プーア・リチャードの暦』という小さな本を出版した。そこには貧しいリチャードの名言に加えて、10点の面白い漫画が描かれている。

クィンシー・ウィリアムズ
今井元子/戸田徹子 訳

注：
フランクリンの『自伝』にある12の徳目に触発されて、明治天皇の妻である昭

From 1733 through 1758, Benjamin Franklin published *Poor Richard's Almanack*, an annual almanac containing historical and scientific observations, verses and rhymes, jokes, recipes, and proverbs. The *Almanack* was an influential pre-revolutionary publication in Philadelphia, in Pennsylvania and neighboring colonies, and ultimately in Europe, notably France. Each edition contained a number of maxims or proverbs, entitled Poor Richard's Sayings. Poor Richard's Sayings are also known as Franklin's Maxims. Much of this material had a classical or Biblical origin: "Make hay while the sun shines," "A penny saved is a penny earned." A minority, such as this last example, were contemporary and/or original: "Early to bed and early to rise make a man healthy, wealthy and wise."

In 1996 Majima Kazuo, a member of the House of Councillors (the upper house of the Diet), translated Franklin's Maxims into Japanese and published a small book, *Poor Richard's Almanack*, that contains ten amusing cartoons in addition to Poor Richard's sayings.

By Quincy Williams

Note: Franklin's ideas inspired the Meiji Empress Shōken (1849–1914) to write thirty-one syllable *waka* poems on the twelve virtues he touted in his *Autobiography*, such

Japanese version of *Poor Richard's Almanack.*
Courtesy of Quincy Williams

as this one on Frugality: *Kuretake no hodo yoki fushi o tagaezuba sueha no tsuyu mo midarezaramashi* (If we stay ourselves like nodes of black bamboo, ever steady, Even the dew on the tips of the leaves will surely not spill).

"Tips of the leaves" was an expression for "descendants"; the verse suggests that if we live prudently, our children will not be wasteful either.

Linda H. Chance

If you go:

Franklin Court, site of the former Franklin home, first post office, and printing shop, 312–322 Market Street, Philadelphia, PA 19106. The Post Office still operates as a U.S. Post Office.

The Benjamin Franklin Museum, 317 Chestnut Street, Philadelphia, PA 19106 is part of Independence National Historical Park. The Park's Independence Visitor Center is at 525 Market Street, Philadelphia, PA 19106.

憲皇后（1849‐1914）は和歌を作った。例えば、「節約」について次のように詠んでいる。

呉竹の　ほどよきふしを　たがへずば
　　末葉の露も　みだれざらまし

「末葉の露」とは子孫を表わしており、この和歌は、もし私たちが贅沢をせずに生活をすれば、おのずと子孫も贅沢を慎むようになると詠っている。

リンダ・チャンス

6.3 Yukiko Irwin: Perpetuating the Bonds Between the United States and Japan
アーウィン・ユキコ：ベンジャミン・フランクリンの日本人子孫

アーウィン・ユキコは1925年に東京で生まれた。リチャード・アーウィンと渡部市子夫妻の娘である。ユキコの祖父、ロバート・ウオーカー・アーウィンはベンジャミン・フランクリン5代目の子孫で、ハワイ王国の総領事として、そして後には同国の公使として、1880年代に日本人のハワイ移住を推進した。(ロバート・アーウィン記事、45章を参照のこと)。

アーウィン・ユキコの父、リチャード・アーウィン(1890-1928)は、ロバート・ウオーカー・アーウィンと、武智いきの子供で、日本で生まれ育ち、日米両国で教育を受けた。リチャードはプリンストン大学とハーバード大学ロースクールを卒業している。弁護士の資格を取得後、スタンダード石油会社の極東副支配人として日本に帰国した。1920年に渡部市子(普連土女学校卒)と結婚した。市子の父、渡部鼎博士は医学者で、カリフォルニア大学の医学部で学んでいる。父親のリチャードが亡くなった時、ユキコはわずか4歳であり、兄と一緒に父方の親戚に育てられた。その兄は第二次世界大戦で日本のために戦い、戦死した。

アーウィン・ユキコは東京女子大学で国文学を学び学士を取得し、さらにアメリカのインデイアナ大学で社会福祉学を専攻し卒業した。ユキコはアーウィン一族の歴史や日米交流関係などについて書いており、主な出版物に『フランクリンの果実』(1988年)や、ヒラリー・コンロイとの共著『ロバート・ウオーカー・

Yukiko Irwin, the daughter of Richard Irwin and Ichiko Watanabe, was born in Tokyo in 1925. Yukiko Irwin's grandfather, Robert Walker Irwin, was a fifth generation descendant of Benjamin Franklin. As Consul General, then as Minister of the Kingdom of Hawaii to Japan, Robert Irwin was instrumental in promoting Japanese immigration to Hawaii in the 1880s. (Please see the entry on Robert Irwin.) Yukiko Irwin's father, Richard Irwin (1890–1928), one of the children of Robert Walker Irwin and Takechi Iki, was born and raised in Japan and attended schools in both Japan and the United States before graduating from Princeton University and Harvard Law School. After becoming a lawyer, he returned to Japan as a Vice President of the Standard Oil Company. In 1920, he married Ichiko Watanabe, whose father, Kanae Watanabe, was a medical doctor who had pursued his studies at the medical school of the University of California and eventually served in the the House of Representatives of the Japanese Diet and as Surgeon General. Yukiko was only four years old when her father died, and she and her brother, who would later die during World War II while fighting for Japan, were sent to live with her father's relatives.

Yukiko Irwin graduated from Tokyo Women's Christian College with a B.A. in Japanese Literature and from Indiana University with a B.A. in Social Work. She has written extensively about her family's history and

Yukiko Irwin. Courtesy of Yukiko Irwin

the history of Japanese American relations. Among her publications are her book *Franklin no kajitsu*, published by Bungei Shunjū in 1988 and an article, "Robert Walker Irwin and Systematic Immigration to Hawaii" in *East Across the Pacific* (with Hilary Conroy) published by the ABC-Clio Press in 1972.

In addition to the prominent role she has played in promoting friendship between the United States and Japan, Yukiko Irwin is a renowned shiatsu and acupuncture therapist. Shiatsu is a health-maintaining art that is the product of 4,000 years of Asian medicine, therapy and philosophy. Her book, *Shiatzu: Japanese Finger Pressure for Energy, Sexual Vitality and Relief from Tension and Pain*, published by the Penguin Group in 1976, received broad acclaim and was published in many foreign languages.

Yukiko Irwin became interested in shiatsu as a young girl in Tokyo in the late 1940s, when she came to know an elderly practitioner who was treating her aunt for debilitating tension headaches that had lasted for months. After intensive shiatsu therapy intended to relax her muscles, ease tension, and improve the flow of blood throughout her body, her aunt was permanently cured of her headaches. As Mrs. Irwin noted in the introduction to *Shiatzu*: "The therapist encouraged me to learn from him. I was profoundly moved by his skill, sincerity and inner serenity and wanted to experience these things for myself."

アーウィンとそのハワイへの官約移民』（1972）などがある。

日米交流に寄与する一方、ユキコは高名な指圧・針治療のセラピストでもあった。指圧は健康管理の技であり、4000年にわたる東洋の医学やセラピー、哲学が生み出したものである。ユキコの著書、『指圧：健康維持のための日本の指圧』（1976）は広い支持を受け、多くの外国語に翻訳、出版されている。

ユキコは1940年代後半、まだ女学生だった頃、年配の指圧セラピストが叔母の数カ月も続く偏頭痛を治療しているのを見て、指圧に興味を持つようになった。集中的な指圧セラピーにより、筋肉をリラックスさせ、緊張を和らげ、体全体の血液の循環を良くしたおかげで、叔母は偏頭痛から完全に快復した。ユキコは著書『指圧』の冒頭で、「セラピストは私

に指圧を習うように勧めた。セラピストの技術、誠意、そして内面の平静さに大いに感銘を受け、自分自身で同じような体験をしてみたいと思った」と述べている。

ユキコは2年間日本指圧学校で勉強し、1951年に日本の厚生省から指圧セラピストの資格免許を取得した。インディアナ大学卒業後、ニューヨークに来て、1964年には医者達の協力の下、指圧と針治療のセラピストとして仕事に就いた。そしてハークネス・バレエ・カンパニーの専属セラピストとなった。また、ニューヨーク市の理学療法委員会のメンバーも務めた。ユキコの患者の中にはニューヨークビジネス界の著名人、その親族、ヨーロッパの貴族や王族も含まれて

In her book *Franklin no kajitsu*, Yukiko Irwin further explained: "I looked for the purpose of life for a long time and I found it by introducing shiatsu (which was originally from China and which bloomed in Japan) to America. Shiatsu's basic principle is based on the spirit of love and service." Yukiko is mindful of the Irwin family motto, "Contribute to Society." She strongly believes her grandfather's dream that Japan and the United States would become like siblings has been both her guiding light and a source of great mental and moral support.

Yukiko Irwin studied at the Nippon Shiatzu School for two years, and after graduation, she received accreditation in shiatsu therapy from the Japanese Ministry of Health in 1951.

Yukiko Irwin introducing shiatsu to European royals in Majorica Island, Spain, 1987.
Courtesy of Yukiko Irwin

いる。ユキコは、末期癌で苦しんでいる患者たちに身体的ならびに精神的な慰めと平安を与え、慢性疾患で苦しんでいる患者たちの痛みを和らげることのできる人物として有名になった。

ユキコは『フランクリンの果実』の中で、次のように述べている。「長いこと生きる目的を探していた私は（中国で始まり日本で開花した）指圧をアメリカに紹介することに、生きがいを見出すようになった。指圧の根本には愛と奉仕の精神がある。」ユキコはアーウィン一族の「社会に貢献せよ」という教えを尊重し、祖父ロバートの「日本とアメリカが兄弟のように親しくなるという夢」を心の支えにしている。

1970年にユキコはアメリカ独立宣言署名者子孫の会の正式メンバーとなった。また、1982年には米国名門家族人名録、『名士録（Social Register）』に登録された。1999年にはフィラデルフィアを訪れ、日米協会の『フィラ・ニポニカ：フィラデルフィアと日本を結ぶ歴史的絆』（初版）の出版祝賀会に出席した。現在は仕事を引退し、ニューヨークで静かな隠居生活を過ごしている。

浜田昌子訳

参考文献：
ユキコ・アーウィン『フランクリンの果実』
（文芸春秋出版、1988）

After completing undergraduate studies at the University of Indiana, Mrs. Irwin came to New York and began to practice as a shiatsu and acupuncture therapist professionally in 1964, working closely with a number of western doctors. She served as resident therapist for the Harkness Ballet Company and was on the New York State Board for Massage Therapy. Her clients included prominent New York City business leaders and their relatives and members of important European aristocratic and royal families. She was renowned for being able to bring comfort and peace, both physically and spiritually, to a number of her patients suffering from terminal stages of cancer, and to cure or provide long term relief to many suffering from long-standing chronic ailments.

In 1970, Yukiko Irwin became a member of The Society of the Descendants of the Signers of the Declaration of Independence. In 1982, she was listed in the Social Register, a directory of members of prominent American families. In 1999, she visited Philadelphia to attend the Publication Reception for the first edition of *Phila-Nipponica: An Historic Guide to Philadelphia and Japan*. Yukiko Irwin is now retired and living a quiet life in New York City.

By Steven M. Berzin

Selected Reference: Yukiko Irwin with James Wagenvoord, *Shiatzu: Japanese Finger Pressure for Energy, Sexual Vitality and Relief from Tension and Pain* (Philadelphia: Lippincott, 1976).

6.4　The Agnes Irwin School: Founded by a Fifth Generation Descendant of Benjamin Franklin

アグネス・アーウィン・スクール：フランクリンの子孫が創立したフィラデルフィアの学校

アグネス・アーウィン・スクールは、1869年、アメリカにおける最初の女子教育機関のひとつとしてフィラデルフィアに開校された。創立者のアグネス・アーウィン（1841‐1914）はロバート・W・アーウィンの姉で、2人はベンジャミン・フランクリンの末裔である。アグネスは伝統的なカリキュラムの下で広範な学科を学び、女子が成長できる場を提供したいと考え、「しっかりとした、明確な思考」を重んじる学校を目指した。

創立者ならびに校長として、28歳のアグネスは、生徒たちがハーバード大学主催の女性教員資格認定試験を受けることを奨励した。1885年にブリンマー大学が開学すると、生徒たちにより多くの教育機会が開かれると判断し、カリキュラムを大学進学を前提としたものへと改革する。数学、科学、芸術分野の授業科目を増やし、体育や健康のためのプログラムも新設した。

その実績により、アグネスは、1894年、ボストンのラドクリフ大学で初の学部長に就任した。アグネスが去った後、校長の後任には妹のソフィア・ダラス・アーウィンが着任し、個人の人格形成に重点を置き、生徒たちが大人に成長して行く様子を見守った。1933年、キャンパスはフィラデルフィア郊外のウィンウッドへと移転する。1943年には、さらに敷地が拡張され、幼稚園から高校3年まで一貫した女子教育が可能となった。

1961年、アン・バートル校長がキャンパ

The Agnes Irwin School was founded in Philadelphia in 1869 as one of the first establishments in the United States devoted to the education of girls and young women. Agnes Irwin (1841–1914) wanted to provide a place for girls where they could flourish while exploring a conventional curriculum that included a wide range of study, so she created the institution to emphasize "disciplined and precise thinking."

The twenty-eight-year-old founder and headmistress encouraged her students to

Agnes Irwin. The Agnes Irwin School

Agnes Irwin School on Delancey Place in Philadelphia. The Agnes Irwin School

challenge themselves and take the examinations offered by Harvard University to certify women for teaching. When Bryn Mawr College opened in 1885, she realized that there would be more opportunities for her students to continue their educational studies, so she revised her curriculum, transforming it into a more progressive, college preparatory course of study. This included expanding its offerings in mathematics, science, and the arts, as well as creating programs dedicated to excellence in athletics and physical wellness. Twenty-five years after she established this legacy, Agnes Irwin left to become the first Dean of Radcliffe College in 1894. Her sister, Sophia (Sophy) Dallas Irwin, assumed leadership of the school upon Agnes's departure. Her contribution was to place special emphasis on the development of each girl's character, watching her students grow into mature individuals.

スを現在のローズモントに移転させた。ここは理想的な場所で、この移転によって各部門がそれぞれのスペースを確保できるようになった。1980年代後半には、メアリ・E・ケスラー校長が、全日制幼稚園プログラムと総合的な共学サマー・プログラムを開始した。M・ペニー・モス校長は、1988年から2005年まで

In 1933, the Agnes Irwin School moved to a suburban estate in Wynnewood, and after expanding its campus in 1943, the school began to educate girls from kindergarten through twelfth grades. Headmistress Anne Bartol brought the school to its current ideal location in Rosemont in 1961, allowing more space for the academic

の在任中、レノックス・アート・センター
を改築し、新しいハミルトン・サイエン
ス・センターを完成させ、幼稚部・小学
部の拡張を実現した。

現校長であるメアリ・F・セパラの指揮
の下、女子発達センターが設立された。
このセンターでは研究、画期的なプロ
グラム、地域貢献を通して、女子生徒に
必要な4つの分野(リーダーシップ、健
康、グローバル市民、21世紀の教育と
学び)に焦点をあてた教育を試みてい
る。2013年秋には、アスレチック・セン
ターと生徒会館のために、8万5000平
方フィート(約8000平方メートル)のス
ペースが新しく設けられた。

アグネス・アーウィン・スクール
ホーク奈々子 訳

programs.

Head Mary E. Kesler initiated a full-day
kindergarten program and a comprehensive
co-educational summer program in the late
1980s. Head of School M. Penney Moss saw
the completion of an enhanced Lenox Arts
Center, new Hamilton Science Center, and
expanded Lower School during her tenure
from 1988 to 2005.

Under the guidance of Head of School Dr.
Mary F. Seppala, The Agnes Irwin School has
established the Center for the Advancement of
Girls, an educational initiative that focuses—
through research, innovative programming,
and community engagement—on four
domains of girls' lives: leadership, wellness,
global citizenship, and teaching and learning
in the twenty-first century. In the fall of 2013,
the school opened 85,000 square feet of new
space in an Athletic Center and Student Life
Center.

By The Agnes Irwin School

If you go: The Agnes Irwin School, 275 S.
Ithan Avenue, Bryn Mawr, PA 19010.

6.5 Irwin Gakuen: Founded by a Sixth Generation Descendant of Benjamin Franklin

アルウィン学園：フランクリンの子孫が創立した日本の学校

アルウィン学園（アルウィン学園では "Irwin" を「アーウィン」ではなく「アルウィン」と表記している）の創設者ソフィア・アラベラ・アルウィン（1883‐1957）は、1883年11月24日、東京のハワイ王国公使館内で誕生した。ベンジャミン・フランクリンの6代目の子孫にあたる。父は初代日本駐在ハワイ公使となったアメリカ人、ロバート・ウォーカー・アルウィン、母は日本女性の武知イキであった。

ソフィア・アルウィンは12歳までは日本で教育を受け、その後フィラデルフィアのマダム・サトンの女子寄宿学校に入学、主席で卒業し、1901年に日本に帰国する。

1904年頃から父の別荘のあった伊香保（群馬県）で日曜学校を開いて子どもたちと交わるなかで、幼児教育こそ神から賜った自分の使命だと感じられるよ

Sophia Arabella Irwin (1883-1957), a sixth generation descendant of Benjamin Franklin, was the founder of the Irwin Gakuen in Tokyo. She was born in 1883 in the Hawaii legation in Tokyo, where her father, Robert Walker Irwin, had been appointed the Kingdom of Hawaii's Minister to Japan. Her mother was a Japanese woman, Takechi Iki. Sophia was educated in Japan until the age of twelve and then entered a boarding school for girls from middle and upper class families run by Madam Sutton in Philadelphia. She graduated from the school as a top student and returned to Japan in 1901.

In 1904 Sophia (also known as Bella) opened a Sunday school for local children at Ikaho (in Gunma Prefecture), where her family's summer house was located. That residence in Ikaho is now designated as an Historic Site in Japan and is open to the public as a small

Irwin Gakuen in 1905. The building was burned down during World War II アルウィン学園所蔵

Sophia Bella Irwin with her father Robert Irwin.
Irwin Gakuen アルウィン学園所蔵

A young Sophia Bella Irwin.
Irwin Gakuen アルウィン学園所蔵

うになる。この伊香保の別荘は1985年に、日本からハワイに官約移民が渡って100年になることを記念し、外交資料として、史跡に指定され、現在に至るまで保存されている。

1906年再びフィラデルフィアに渡り、カロライン・ハート女史の「幼児教育専門学校」で学び、また在学中にコロンビア大学で「フレーベル研究講座」を受講し、ボストン、ニューヨークの大学課程で学んだ。さらに全米各地の幼稚園を視察した後、フレーベルの遺したフレーベル学園（ドイツ）、モンテッソーリ女史の「子どもの家」（イタリア）で実践法を修得し、1914年に日本に戻る。

museum to the Irwin family and Japanese immigration to Hawaii. Through her interaction with the children, Irwin came to feel that educating children was her mission from God.

Irwin returned to Philadelphia in 1906 to study at Miss Hart's Training School for Kindergartners, which was run by Caroline M.C. Hart. During her study in America, Irwin attended the "Froebel Research Seminar" on education at Columbia University as well as taking courses at a college in Boston. In addition to visiting various kindergartens in America, she also visited the Froebel School

早速、幼稚園創設へと行動を開始し、1916年2月、東京麹町に玉成（ぎょくせい）保姆養成所と幼稚園を設立、1952年東京都杉並区松庵に場所を移した。現在はアルウィン学園玉成保育専門学校、保育センターこどもの木かげ（認定子ども園玉成幼稚園・野のはな空のとり保育園）として、保育者の養成と保育実践を一体化して取り組んでいる。

2016年に、アルウィン学園は100周年を迎える。

大塚兼司

【参考情報】
アルウィン学園玉成保育専門学校
〒167-0054 東京都杉並区松庵1丁目9番33号
電話: 03-3332-5345
www.gyokusei.jp

渋川市指定史跡　ハワイ王国公使別邸
群馬県渋川市北橘町真壁　2372-1
渋川市教育委員会文化財保護課
電話: 0279-52-2102
www.city.shibukawa.lg.jp/kankou/rekishi/hawaikousibettei.html

in Germany and the "House for Children" run by Maria Montessori in Italy to learn about their practices.

In 1914 Irwin returned to Japan and made preparations to open a kindergarten. Two years later, in February 1916, she founded both a Kindergarten and the Gyokusei Kindergarten teacher training school in Kōjimachi in Tokyo. In 1952 she moved both institutions, which integrate kindergarten teacher training and childcare practice, to Suginami Ward in Tokyo. The schools are now known as the Irwin Gakuen Gyokusei Kindergarten Teacher Training School and the Childcare Center (*Kodomo no Kokage*). 2016 will mark the one hundredth anniversary of the founding of the school by Sophia Arabella Irwin.

By Ohtsuka Kenji
Translated by Masako Hamada

If you go: Summer Residence of the Minister of the Kingdom of Hawaii Historic Site, Kita Tachibana-chō, Makabe 2372-1, Shibukawa-shi, Gunma Prefecture.

7 *Educational Exchanges*
教育機関の交流

7.1 Rutgers University and Japan: From the Dutch Connection Forward

ラトガーズ大学：幕末の日本人たちが学んだ学校

ラトガーズ大学と日本との特別な関係は19世紀中期に始まる。ラトガーズ大学はオランダ改革派教会の牧師養成校として1766年、ニュージャージーのニュー・ブランズウィックに創設されたが、1870年には宗教色のない私立学校になっていた。鎖国中の日本で、オランダが長崎に貿易基地を持っていたことにより、アメリカで学んだ最初の日本人留学生たちは、オランダに縁のあるラトガーズ大学に来たのである。

徳川時代末期、少数の者たちが西洋の知識を学ぼうと海外に飛び出した。その若者たちの中には、若いオランダ人技術者で宣教師だったギドー・フルベッキ（バーベック）が長崎で開いた語学学校で学んだ人たちもいた。最初にニュー・ブランズウィックに来たのは熊本出身の横井兄弟で、改革者である横井小楠の甥だった。横井兄弟は伊勢佐太郎、沼川三郎の変名を名乗り、禁を破り出国した。ニューヨークにあるオランダ改革派教会海外伝道局の主事（事務局長）であったジョン・フェリス宛ての紹介状を携えて、横井兄弟は1866年にアメリカに到着した。フェリスは2人をニュー・ブランズウィックに送り、当時はラトガーズ大学の一部であったラトガーズ・グラマー・スクール（後の私立ラトガーズ予備学校）で学ばせた。横井佐平太はアナポリスにある合衆国海軍学校に転学し、横井大平は日本に戻り、熊本洋学校設立に尽力するが、間もなくして亡くなった。

The special relationship between Rutgers University and Japan dates from the mid-nineteenth century. Founded in New Brunswick, New Jersey, in 1766 to train pastors for the Dutch Reformed Church, by 1870 Rutgers was an independent, secular institution. It was this connection with the Dutch, who had retained a trading post in Nagasaki during Japan's period of "isolation," which made Rutgers a destination for some of the first Japanese students to study in the United States.

In the last years of the Tokugawa era (1603–1868), a few individuals ventured abroad to acquire Western knowledge. Several of these young Japanese men initially attended the language school in Nagasaki established by Guido Verbeck (1830–1898), a Dutch engineer and missionary. The first to come to New Brunswick were the Yokoi brothers from Kumamoto, the nephews of reformer Yokoi Shōnan. They left Japan without permission under the names Ise Satarō and Numagawa Saburō. The brothers arrived in 1866 with a letter of introduction to John Ferris, Secretary of the Board of Foreign Missions of the Dutch Reformed Church in New York. Ferris sent them to New Brunswick to study at the Rutgers Grammar School—later the independent Rutgers Preparatory School—at that time part of Rutgers College. Yokoi Saheida (1845–1875) subsequently transferred to the U.S. Naval Academy at Annapolis, while Yokoi Daihei (1850–1871)

Japanese students and friends at Rutgers, 1870. Rutgers University

横井兄弟の後に、聡明な日下部太郎が続いた。日下部は越前（現在の福井県）出身の武士で、「国際法と普遍的原理の観点から日本と外国との関係の欠陥を明らかすることによって、朝廷に対する義務を果たす」との使命に燃えて、1867年に到着した。学年で1番の成績を収めた日下部は、ラトガーズ大学を卒業した最初の日本人、そしてファイ・ベータ・カッパの最初の日本人メンバーとなった。日下部とアマースト大学で学んだ新島襄は、アメリカの大学を卒業した最初の日本人だった。悲劇的なことに、日下部は卒業式を目前にして肺結核で亡くなり、他の7人の若い日本人と共にニュー・ブランズウィックのウィロー・グローブ墓地に、埋葬されている。

returned to Japan, where he was able to help establish a School of Western Sciences in Kumamoto before his early death.

The brothers were followed by the brilliant Kusakabe Tarō, a young samurai from the province of Echizen—later Fukui Prefecture—who arrived in 1867 fired with the desire to "fulfill my duty to the Imperial realm by clarifying the defects in the relations between us Japanese and the foreigners in the light of the international law of all nations and universal principles." Ranked number one in his class, Kusakabe became the first Japanese to graduate from Rutgers College, the first to become a member of Phi Beta Kappa, and, along with Joseph Hardy

Kusakabe Tarō, 1867. Rutgers University

明治初期、日本人留学生にとってラトガ
ーズ大学は実に有難い学校だった。ラト
ガーズ大学は1864年に理学部を開設
し、日本人学生の多くはこの学部に在籍
した。小規模で柔軟な体制をとり、年3
学期ある中でどの学期からでも入学可
能だった。またグラマー・スクールを併
設していたので、大学入学の準備勉強
もできた。さらに指摘すれば、ラトガーズ
大学は教員数12名、学生数81名にすぎ
なかったので、学生を必要としていたの
である。

ラトガーズ大学で学んだ学生たちは日
本に帰国し、教育や産業、商業の分野
で指導者となった。例えば、鹿児島出
身の畠山義成(1844 - 1986)はラトガ
ーズ大学では杉浦弘蔵の名で科学を

Neesima at Amherst, the first to graduate from an American college. Tragically, Kusakabe died of tuberculosis on April 13, 1870, only weeks before commencement. He is buried in the Willow Grove Cemetery in New Brunswick along with seven other young Japanese.

Indeed Rutgers was an important destination for *ryūgakusei* (foreign students) during the early Meiji period. In 1864, Rutgers established a Scientific School, in which most of the *ryūgakusei* enrolled. The small college had a flexible structure that allowed students to be admitted in any of three terms, while the presence of the Grammar School accommodated those who required additional preparation. Furthermore, with only eighty-one students and twelve faculty members, Rutgers needed students.

Many of those who studied at Rutgers returned to Japan to become leaders in education, industry, and commerce. For instance, Hatakeyama Yoshinari (1844–1876) from Kagoshima, who used the name Soogiwoora Kozo at Rutgers, studied science until he was recalled to Japan in 1870. He served as an officer in three departments of the new Meiji government before becoming the director of Tokyo University during its foundational period. Sadly, like his friend Kusakabe, Hatakeyama contracted tuberculosis and died while returning to Japan from the Philadelphia Centennial Exhibition. Hattori Ichizō (1851–1929), a samurai from Yamaguchi in Chōshū, also studied science at Rutgers. Upon graduation in 1875, he took a post in the Education Ministry (*Monbushō*), and later served as an administrator at Tokyo University. Between

Kusakabe Tarō (center row, third from right) and his class, c. 1867. Rutgers University Libraries

学び、1870年に召還されて帰国した。畠山は新しい明治政府において3つの部局で役人として働き、その後、草創期の東京大学（開成学校）で校長になった。友人だった日下部と同様に、畠山も肺結核を患い、フィラデルフィアで開催されたアメリカ独立100周年記念万国博覧会から日本への帰路で命を落とした。長州藩山口出身の武士である服部一三（1851‐1929）もまた科学を学んだ。1875年に卒業し、文部省の役人となり、後に東京大学の幹事として働いた。服部は1891年から1916年まで岩手県、広島県、長崎県の3つの県で県知事を務め、1903年には貴族院勅選議員に任命された。

1891 and 1916, he served as governor of four prefectures—Iwate, Hiroshima, Nagasaki, and Hyōgo—and in 1903 was appointed to the House of Peers.

By the late 1880s, the number of Japanese at Rutgers declined as more opportunities became available in their own country. Among these later students was Matsukata Kōjirō (1865–1950), the third son of Matsukata Masayoshi, Japan's first modern finance minister. Matsukata entered Rutgers College in 1885 but transferred to Yale a year later. Returning to Japan in 1890, he devoted himself to business and served as president or director of several corporations, including

Engraving of Rutgers College, 1879. Rutgers University Libraries

日本国内で教育が受けられるようになったので、ラトガーズ大学の日本人数は1880年代後半には減少した。後期の留学生には松方正義（日本で最初の大蔵大臣）の3男である松方幸次郎（1865–1950）がいる。松方は1885年にラトガーズ大学に入学、1年後にエール大学に転学した。1890年に日本に戻ると、経済界に身を投じ、川崎重工の前身である川崎造船所などの会社で社長や取締役を務めた。松方は美術パトロンとなり、西洋美術ならびに日本の浮世絵を収集し、著名な松方コレクションを形成した。1868年から1926年の間に、ラトガーズ大学には全部で25名の日本人が在籍していたことが記録されている。これ以外にグラマー・スクールに通った学生や、この地域で家庭教師のもとで学んだ学生もいた。この期間、ニュー・ブランズウィックに来た日本人は200人に達するかもしれない。

日本で、教育者や顧問、宣教師として働いたラトガーズ大学の教員や卒業生もいた。ラトガーズの天文学なら

Kawasaki Shipyards, the forerunner of Kawasaki Heavy Industries. Matsukata became a patron of the arts, building renowned collections of Western art and Japanese woodblock prints.

Overall, twenty-five Japanese students have been documented as having been enrolled at Rutgers between 1868 and 1926. Others attended Grammar School or studied with private tutors in the area. As many as two hundred Japanese may have passed through New Brunswick during this period.

Meanwhile Rutgers faculty and alumni found positions as educators, advisors, and missionaries in Meiji Japan. Rutgers professor of astronomy and mathematics David Murray (1830–1905) was invited to Japan in 1873 to serve as Superintendent of Education, where he played an important role in organizing a Western-style educational system. William Elliot Griffis introduced Western science education in Kusakabe's home prefecture,

びに数学の教授、デイビッド・マレー（1830‐1905）は1873年に日本に招かれ、教育顧問を務めた。マレーは西洋式の教育制度を整備するのに重要な役割を果たした。ウィリアム・エリオット・グリフィス（36章を参照）は日下部の出身地である福井に西洋の科学教育を導入し、日本について著述と講演をして余生を過ごした。ウィリアムの友人で同級生だったエドワード・ウォーレン・クラーク（1849‐1907）は静岡の藩校と東京大学の前身の1つである開成学校で教鞭をとった。1872年卒業のマーティン・N・ワイコフ（1850‐1911）は福井でグリフィスの後継者として働いた。ワイコフは後に宣教師として日本に戻り、最終的に明治学院で教えた。彼の著わした『英作文初歩』（1885）は大きな影響力を持った。

ラトガーズ大学と日本との関係は戦争の間は途絶えていたが、1950年代後半にラトガーズ大学の政治学の教授アーダス・バークスによって再発見された。この時、ラトガーズ大学は公立の大規模な研究大学になっていた。その後、大学は日本の言語、文学、歴史、映画、そして文化のコースを開設するようになった。2014年の時点で、100人以上の学生が日本語を学習し、ラトガーズ大学日本学生会（RONS）に参加している。ラトガーズ大学は京都の立命館大学、九州の立命館アジア太平洋大学、東京の国際基督教大学、山梨県の都留文科大学と交流プログラムを持っている。ニュー・ブランズウィック市は日下部太郎の出身地である福井、ならびに山形県の鶴岡と姉妹都市関係にある。

フェルナンダ・H・ペローネ
戸田徹子　訳

Fukui, and then spent the rest of his life writing and lecturing about Japan. Griffis' friend and classmate Edward Warren Clark (1849–1907) taught at the Shizuoka clan's school and at the Kaisei Gakkō, forerunner of Tokyo University, while 1872 graduate Martin N. Wyckoff (1850–1911) served as Griffis' successor in Fukui. Wyckoff later returned to Japan as a missionary, ultimately becoming the director of Meiji Gakuin and the author of an influential textbook, *English Composition for Beginners Prepared for Japanese Students* (1885).

The relationship between Rutgers and Japan lapsed during the war period but was rediscovered in the late 1950s by Rutgers professor of political science Ardath Burks. By that time, Rutgers had evolved into a major public research university. In the ensuing years, the university developed courses on Japanese language, literature, history, film, and culture. In 2014, over one hundred students were studying Japanese language each year and participating in the Rutgers Organization of Nippon Students (RONS). Rutgers maintains exchange programs at Ritsumeikan University in Kyoto, Asia Pacific University in Kyushu, International Christian University outside Tokyo, and Tsuru University in Yamanashi Prefecture. The City of New Brunswick has active Sister Cities relationships with Fukui, the home of Kusakabe Tarō, and Tsuruoka in Yamagata Prefecture.

By Fernanda H. Perrone

Selected References: Marilyn Bandera, "A Case Study in Educational Motivation: Ryugakusei and Rutgers College, 1866–

1895" (Unpublished M.A. thesis, University of Hawaii, 1970). Ardath Burks, ed., *The Modernizers: Overseas Students, Foreign Employees, and Meiji Japan* (Boulder, CO: Westview Press, 1985).

If you go: Rutgers, The State University of New Jersey, 169 College Avenue, New Brunswick, NJ 08901.

7.2 Japan and the University of Pennsylvania: Academic Foundations

ペンシルベニア大学と日本：近代化のパイオニアたちを輩出した大学

ペンシルベニア大学は、創設者ベンジャミン・フランクリンにより、当時のスコットランドの一流大学を模範として1740年に創立された。1756年にはアメリカ植民地で初の医学部を開設し、1790年には初のアメリカ法の教授が就任した。

ペンシルベニア大学と日本とのつながりは、1868年の大政奉還後、日本で国際交流を含む大規模な教育改革が行なわれた時期に始まった。大学での学位取得を目的として渡米した初めての日本人留学生が今立吐酔（いまだてとすい）である。今立は1875年にフィラデルフィアに到着した。その後1879年にペンシルベニア大学にて理学士号を取得し、後に清の日本公使館において重要な任務に就いた。今立は同大学内において限られた学生しか入会できない友愛会の一員でもあった。ペンシルベニア大学における2人目の日本人留学生は名倉納で、1880年に医学博士号を取得している。

ペンシルベニア大学のウォートン・スクールは1881年に創設された、世界で最初の大学レベルのビジネス・スクールであるが、ウォートン・スクールも日本とのつながりがある。最初の卒業生はたった4人だったが、その中の1人は日本人の柴四朗であった。その後も多くの日本人がここで学び、日本人の割合が高い傾向は今日まで続いている。

第1期生であった柴は、位の高い武家の4男として、1852年に生まれた。明治維

Modeled by its founder Benjamin Franklin on the leading Scottish universities of the time, the University of Pennsylvania was established in 1740, opened the first medical school in the American colonies in 1765, and in 1790 had the first professor of American law.

The University's ties with Japan began after the Meiji emperor ascended the throne in 1868 and major educational reforms were instituted in Japan, including the encouragement of international exchanges. The first student from Japan to pursue and receive a university degree in America arrived in Philadelphia in 1875. In 1879 Imadate Tosui earned a Bachelor of Science degree from the University of Pennsylvania, where he was a member of a fraternity. He later became a key member of the Japanese legation in China. The second Japanese student at Penn was Nagura Osamu, who received a doctor of medicine degree in 1880.

Japan has been linked with the University of Pennsylvania's Wharton School since its founding in 1881 as the first collegiate school of business in the world. Although there were only a total of four students in that class, the presence of a Japanese among them established a pattern that has persisted up to the present.

The Japanese student in Wharton's first class was Shiba Shirō, born in 1852 as the fourth

新によって苦境に立たされたが、英語を
学び、後にサンフランシスコ領事となる
柳谷謙太郎の下で働いていた。柴は柳
谷と共に渡米した後、フィラデルフィア
に転居し、ウォートン・スクールで学び
学位を取得した。日本へ帰国後は、農商
務大臣の下で働き、国会議員に当選し
たが、政治活動で収監されたこともあっ
た。またフィラデルフィアの独立記念館
の場面で始まる16巻の小説を書いた。

1903年には、ペンシルベニア大学の日
本同窓会が、1894年卒業の杉浦貞次郎
によって東京で設立される。その後、ウ
ォートン・スクールの1895年卒業生で
ある松本健次郎が同窓会長となった。
松本は後に貴族院勅選議員や、石炭・
鉄鋼の企業である明治鉱業株式合資会
社の創始者として名声を得て、1936年
にペンシルベニア大学より名誉博士号
（法学）を授与された。

ペンシルベニア大学から最初に名誉学
位を授与された日本人は、1906年に名
誉博士号（理学）を授与された高木兼寛
男爵である。高木は優れた医師で、日本
海軍の軍医総監を務めた。翌年にはもう
1人の医学研究者、日本においては英雄
である野口英世がペンシルベニア大学
より名誉学位を授かった。野口は1902
年から1903年にかけてペンシルベニア
大学で研究した。最近ではソニーの創
業者、盛田昭夫が1990年に名誉博士号
（法学）を授与された。国連難民高等弁
務官や国際協力機構（JICA）理事長など
を務めた緒方貞子も2003年に名誉博
士号を授与されている。

第2次世界大戦前の数十年間、日米の
学生と教員のつながりは発展し続けた。
戦後になると、日本人学生は再びペン

Statue of Benjamin Franklin at the University of
Pennsylvania. Courtesy of the author

son of an elite samurai family that came
upon hard times with the Meiji Restoration.
Shiba Shirō learned English and worked for a
man who was named Japanese Ambassador
to the United States. Shiba came to the U.S.
with Ambassador Yanagiya Kentarō and
stayed to earn his undergraduate degree at
Wharton. After his return to Japan, Shiba
worked for the Minister of Agriculture, was
elected to the Japanese Diet, was incarcerated
for political activities, and wrote a sixteen-
volume novel, the opening of which takes
place in Independence Hall in Philadelphia.

In 1903, the Alumni Society of the University
of Pennsylvania in Japan was established in

Matsumoto Kenjirō in 1930 on his visit to Penn with classmate U.S. Supreme Court Justice Owen Roberts. University of Pennsylvania

Tokyo by Sugiura Isaku Sadajirō, Class of 1894. One of his successors as the head of the Penn alumni in Japan was Matsumoto Kenjirō, Wharton Class of 1895. Matsumoto went on to a distinguished career in Japan as a member of the House of Peers and head of the coal and steel firm, Meiji Mining Corporation. Matsumoto received an honorary LLD degree from the University of Pennsylvania in 1936.

The first honorary degree awarded by Penn to a Japanese was the doctor of science bestowed in 1906 on Baron Takaki Kanehiro, a distinguished physician and surgeon general of the Japanese navy. The following year another prominent Japanese medical researcher, Dr. Noguchi Hideyo, received an honorary degree from Penn, where he had studied during 1902–03. More recently Akio Morita, founder of Sony Corp., received an honorary LLD degree from the university in 1990. Sadako Ogata, who had served as the United Nations High Commissioner for Refugees and was at the time Japan's Special Representative for Afghan Assistance, was honored in 2003.

シルベニア大学やウォートン・スクールで学ぶようになった。1950年代半ばには、将来を嘱望されている若者たちがウォートン・スクールのMBAプログラムに入学したが、その中の1人に寺澤芳男がいる。寺澤は1958年に卒業し、野村證券で優れた実績を上げ、世界銀行に勤務し、参議院議員となり、羽田内閣で閣僚を務めた。

もう1人の1958年卒業生である小林陽太郎は、帰国して富士ゼロックスに勤務し、さらに日米欧三極委員会や太平洋経済委員会、日米経済協議会の一員としても活躍した。またペンシルベニア大学初の日本人理事であった。

1956年の金沢大学を皮切りに、ペンシ

Student and faculty ties continued to develop in the decades before the Second World War. After the war, Japanese students started attending the University of Pennsylvania and Wharton once again. In the mid-1950s, a group of young men destined for greatness enrolled in the Wharton MBA program. Among them was Yoshio Terasawa, who graduated in 1958 and went on to a distinguished career at Nomura Securities. He also saw service at the World Bank, in the upper chamber of the Japanese Diet, and in the Cabinet of Prime Minister Hata. Another

ルベニア大学は東京大学、早稲田大学、慶応大学など15以上の教育機関と交換留学提携を結んでいる。その中には九州を拠点とし、ペンシルベニア大学出身の教員がいる国際東アジア研究センターも含まれている。また、二重学位プログラムのあるローダー・インスティテュートでは毎夏、学生を日本へ送り、学生たちは企業でのインターンシップや日本語集中講座に参加している。現在、ペンシルベニア大学には12の学部ならびに大学院に約230名の日本人学生が、そして様々な分野の客員研究員が130名以上在籍し、フィラデルフィアと日本の重要なつながりを築いている。

もう1つの大切な絆は、ペンシルベニア大学にある東アジア研究センター、フィラデルフィア世界情勢協議会、およびフィラデルフィア学区の公立学校による共同事業として1996年に始まったフィラ・ニッポニカ・プログラムである。このプログラムは米日財団から資金を得ており、毎年春、フィラデルフィア地域の中学校、高校教員が集まる場となっている。まず、ペンシルベニア大学の教員による数回の研修を経て、一行は約3週間日本に滞在する。この絆はペンパルや、さらなる訪日、よりよい理解、そして2011年の東日本大震災の後には、フィラデルフィア地域の学校による復興支援プログラムとして、成果を挙げている。

マーチン・メイヤーソン/ジェフェリー・A・シーハン/フランク・チャンス　追記
今井元子 訳
ホーク・菜々子 追訳

of the 1958 graduates, Yotarō Kobayashi, returned home to join Fuji Xerox Co., Ltd. He also served as a member of the Trilateral Commission, the Pacific Basin Economic Council, the U.S.-Japan Businessmen's Conference, and the first Japanese Trustee of the University of Pennsylvania.

Starting with Kanazawa University in 1956, the University of Pennsylvania has had exchange arrangements with more than fifteen Japanese institutions, including Tokyo University and Keiō University. Among them is also the Kyushu-based International Centre for the Study of East Asian Development, which includes Penn faculty members. In addition, the Lauder Institute of Management and International Studies, in its double degree program, sends a group of graduate students to Japan each summer for company internships and intensive language study. Penn also participates in the Kyoto Consortium for Japanese Studies, which hosts undergraduates each year at Dōshisha University. At present there are about 230 students from Japan in the twelve faculties of the University, and over 130 visiting scholars in various disciplines, continuing to provide a vital link between Philadelphia and Japan.

By Martin Meyerson, Jeffrey A. Sheehan, and Frank L. Chance

If you go: The University of Pennsylvania campus is located in West Philadelphia, and the Wharton School is on campus at 3730 Walnut Street, Philadelphia, PA 19104. A convenient entrance to Locust Walk, the heart of campus, is 34th and Walnut Streets, Philadelphia, PA 19104.

7.3 Temple University and Japan: Groundbreaking Partners in International Education

テンプル大学と日本：日本初のアメリカ大学キャンパス

テンプル大学は日本と多くの関係を持っているが、特に注目すべきことが2つある。1つは、1982年に東京にテンプル大学の分校として日本校が設置されたこと。もう1つは、テンプル大学で教鞭をとっていた著名な芸術家、アーサー・L・フローリーが、日本の版画家たちと共にした先駆的な仕事である。

テンプル大学日本校（TUJ）は、その30年の歴史を通して日本の人々にアメリカ流の大学レベルの教育を受ける機会を提供することで、日米間の教育交流と相互理解に大いに貢献してきた。今までに数千人の日本人学生が、東京でテンプル大学の学部や大学院の学位を取得している。また、日本で学部の勉強を始めて、それからテンプル大学の他のキャンパスに編入する学生も大勢いる。テンプル大学のフィラデルフィア本校から100人を超す教員たちが日本校に教えに行ったが、アメリカに戻った後も日本研究への関心を持ち続ける者も多い。

TUJの計画は日本の企業や政府の指導者たちが、日本の高校卒業生のために英語学習プログラムを設置しようとテンプル大学を招致したことから始まった。テンプル大学日本校が1982年6月5日に開校した時、250人の学生が大学入学前のコースで単位取得を目的としない英語集中コースに正規に入学した。同年、日本の英語教師のために、TESOL（英語教授法）の修士課程プログラムが始まる。これら2つのプログラムの後、1983年には、より国際的な大

Temple University's connections to Japan are many, but two that are particularly notable include the establishment in 1982 of Temple's branch campus in Tokyo (Temple University, Japan Campus) and the groundbreaking work that Temple faculty member and well-known artist Arthur L. Flory did with Japanese printmakers.

Throughout its thirty-two-year history, Temple University, Japan Campus (TUJ) has been providing an American-style education to the residents of Japan and those around the globe with an interest in Japan, and contributing to educational exchange and mutual understanding between Japan and the United States. Over 5,000 students have earned their Temple undergraduate and graduate degrees in Tokyo to date, while many others began their undergraduate programs in Japan and then transferred to one of Temple's other campuses. Over 250 faculty members from Temple's Philadelphia campus have taught at TUJ, including many who have gone on to pursue Japanese research interests upon their return to the United States.

Temple University Japan began with an invitation to Temple from Japanese business and government leaders to establish an English language program for Japanese high school graduates. When TUJ opened in 1982, 250 students were enrolled in a

学レベルの教育を求める学部生のためのプログラムが開始された。1988年にはTESOLの博士課程が加わり、2005年には文部科学省より、日本にキャンパスを置く、初めての外国大学として認定され、TUJとして学生ビザのスポンサーとなることができるようになる。結果として、アメリカをはじめとして世界中から学生たちを受け入れることができるようになった。 現在、TUJには1900人の学生が学び、さらに準学士号、学士号、修士号、博士号が取得できる課程も設置されている。また単位取得とは別に生涯学習コースも開設され、同校で学べる学問領域は多岐にわたるようになった。

Temple University Japan Campus. Temple University

このような学問上の交流が正式なプログラムとして設置される以前にも、テンプル大学の教職員は日本と関係をもっていた。その1人が非常に評判の高い著名な芸術家、アーサー・L・フローリー（1914‐1972）である。フローリーは1939年にフィラデルフィア美術館の美術学校を卒業、その後ナショナル・アカデミー・オブ・デザインで絵画を勉強した。さらにアルフレッド大学で陶磁器の授業を受けた後、テンプルのタイラー美術学校の教師となり、グラフィック・アートと版画を教えるようになった。タイラー美術学校では、1950年から1968年にかけて教鞭をとっている。

1950年代の終わりに、日本の版画家の斎藤清（1907‐1997）が国務省の後援で渡米し、フィラデルフィアも訪れた。その際、フローリーがタイラー美術学校の施設を案内した。斎藤は見学後、リトグラフ（石版画）を作成したいと言い、フローリーのアトリエで夜通し共に制作に取り組み、初の自作のリトグラフを日本に

full-time, pre-college, non-credit intensive English language program. In the same year, the Master's in Teaching English as a Second Language (TESOL) program was also started for English teachers in Japan. Following the opening of these two programs, TUJ began offering an undergraduate program in 1983 for those who were seeking an international university-level education, and in 1988 a doctoral program in TESOL was added. In 2005, TUJ was designated as the first Foreign University, Japan Campus, by the Ministry of Education, Culture, Sports, Science and Technology, enabling TUJ to sponsor student visas for the first time, and to extend its outreach to students from the United States and around the world. Currently, TUJ enrolls approximately 1,900 students, and its academic offerings have expanded to include a wide variety of disciplines leading to associate, bachelors, masters and doctoral degrees, as well as non-credit continuing education programs.

Well before Temple Japan was established, however, Temple University faculty members

持ち帰ったのであった。

この斎藤のタイラー訪問が成功したおかげで、関野準一郎(1914‐1988)や棟方志功(1903‐1975)などの日本人芸術家に対しても、タイラー美術学校から招聘の依頼がなされた。1959年、棟方はニューヨーク日本協会ギャラリーに展示した際に、フィラデルフィアのタイラー美術学校を訪問した。棟方の1週間にわたる訪問のために、タイラー美術学校の学生はリトグラフ用の石を7つ準備したが、棟方は、新しい制作材料を試してみるのに夢中になり、一瞬たりとも止まらないで作業を続け、最初の一晩で石を全部使ってしまう。誰もが棟方の制作のスピードに驚嘆した。フローリーはこの石を使った棟方の最初の労作を版画にし、棟方がタイラーで制作した7枚のリトグラフのセットは、本人によりフィラデルフィア美術館に寄贈された。

1960年、フローリーにロックフェラー財団助成金が授与されると、その助成金でニューヨーク日本協会が新たに始めた交流プログラムにおける、最初のアメリカ人芸術家として来日した。フローリーは東京にリトグラフ印刷を教えるアトリエをオープンし、自分の印刷機と1つの重さが約50ポンド(約22.7キログラム)のババリア石灰石20個を、フィラデルフィアから取り寄せた。1960年から1961年にかけて日本で過ごすが、その間、一緒に仕事をした日本人芸術家仲間から、フィラデルフィアに寄与する多くの友人が生まれた。フローリーの芸術に日本からの影響があることは、彼の「俳句に表れた四季」という題の1963年の作品にはっきりと表れている。

アーサー・フローリーや棟方志功がした

had ties to Japan. One such teacher was the highly respected and well-known artist Arthur L. Flory (1914–1972), who taught at Temple's Tyler School of Fine Arts from 1950 to 1968. Flory graduated from the Philadelphia Museum School of Art in 1939 and subsequently studied painting at the National Academy of Design. After additional course work in ceramics at Alfred University, he joined the Tyler faculty to teach graphics and printmaking. In the late 1950s the Japanese printmaker Saitō Kiyoshi (1907–1997) came to the United States under the auspices of the State Department. Saitō visited Philadelphia and toured Tyler's printmaking facilities, where Arthur Flory showed him around. Saitō expressed a desire to make a lithograph, and after working with Flory in the latter's studio through the night, Saitō went back to Japan with his first lithograph.

The success of the Saitō visit prompted requests for other Japanese artists to come to Tyler, including Sekino Junichirō (1914–1988) and Munakata Shikō (1903–1975). The latter came in 1959, in conjunction with an exhibition of his work at Japan Society Gallery in New York. In preparation for Munakata's week-long visit, Tyler students prepared seven lithograph stones. But Munakata was so enthralled with experimenting in a new medium that he used all the stones the very first night. Everyone was amazed at the speed with which he worked, never stopping for a minute. Arthur Flory printed Munakata's first efforts in this medium, and the set of seven lithographs he made at Tyler was given by Munakata to the Philadelphia Museum of Art.

交流のように、非公式に始められた芸術交流の形式をとるにせよ、テンプル大学日本校のように、より公的で組織的な大学交流の形をとるにせよ、そのような努力により、日米両国が相互に学び合うという長い歴史的伝統が引き継がれ、両国の文化に相互利益をもたらしている。

デニス・A・コナティ/フェリス・フィッシャー
今井元子/中村英恵 訳

【参考情報】
テンプル大学ジャパンキャンパス
〒106−0047
東京都港区南麻布2-8-12
電話: 0120-86-1026
www.tuj.ac.jp/jp

Arthur Flory was awarded a Rockefeller Foundation grant in 1960 to become the first American artist participating in a new exchange program established under the aegis of the Japan Society. Flory opened a lithography teaching studio in Tokyo and had his press and twenty pieces of Bavarian limestone, weighing about fifty pounds each, sent from Philadelphia. Flory spent the 1960–1961 academic year there and made many friends for Philadelphia among the Japanese artists with whom he worked. The influence of Japan on Flory's art is evidenced by works such as his 1963 series entitled "The Four Seasons Expressed in Haiku."

Whether they take the form of artistic exchanges begun informally, such as those of Arthur Flory and Munakata Shikō, or more formally structured academic exchanges, such as the Temple University Japan programs, such efforts continue the long historic tradition of Americans and Japanese learning from each other, to the mutual benefit of both cultures.

By Denise Connerty and Felice Fischer

If you go: Temple University Main Campus, Broad Street and Montgomery Avenue, Philadelphia, PA 19122 ; Tyler School of Art, 2001 North 13th Street, Philadelphia, PA 19122.

7.4 Friends School (Furendo Gakuen): A Japanese School Built on Quaker Principles
普連土学園：日本唯一のクエーカー学校

普連土（フレンド）学園は東京にある中高一貫の女子校で、フィラデルフィア・フレンズ婦人外国伝道協会によって1887年に普連土女学校として創設された。「普連土」という漢字名を考案したのは津田梅子の父親、津田仙である。

アメリカでは南北戦争後、婦人外国伝道運動（女性による、異教女性を対象とする伝道運動）が高まった。女性の回心こそが海外伝道の鍵であり、キリスト者である妻と母親を生み出すことによって、異教社会へのキリスト教伝道は達成されると考えられていたのである。この運動に触発されて、フィラデルフィア年会（正統派）のクエーカー女性たちの一部が、1882年にフィラデルフィア・フレンズ婦人外国伝道協会を結成した。

この伝道協会は日本を宣教地に選び、1組のクエーカー夫婦（ジョゼフ・コサンド夫妻）を派遣することを決めた。さらに、ちょうどアメリカ留学中だった新渡戸稲造と内村鑑三の勧めもあって、女子校を開くことにした。普連土女学校は1887年に麻布本村町の津田仙邸内にあるコサンド宅で教員6名と生徒3名をもって開校し、1889年に現在地である港区三田の聖坂に校舎を新築し、移転した。1902年に失火により校舎が全焼したが、再建された。

戦前、日本のいわゆる「ミッション・スクール」のほとんどは資金を海外に頼った。普連土女学校も例外ではなく、運営費の約半分から4分の3までを伝道協会

Friends School in Tokyo, formerly known as Friends Girls School. is a junior and senior high school (seventh to twelfth grades) for girls. Founded by the Women's Foreign Missionary Association of Friends of Philadelphia in 1887, it is the only Quaker school in Japan. The Chinese characters for its name were chosen by Tsuda Sen, Tsuda Umeko's father.

In the United States, the women's foreign mission movement (whereby American women supported foreign missions for women) gradually gained force after the American Civil War. The supporters of this movement believed that women were the key to successful foreign missions and that Christian missions in "heathen" societies could be achieved only by converting mothers, who would presumably have a positive influence on their spouses and children. Responding to this movement, some women of the Philadelphia Yearly Meeting (Orthodox) set up the Women's Foreign Missionary Association of Friends of Philadelphia in 1882.

The members of the Philadelphia organization found promising opportunities in Japan and decided to send a Quaker missionary couple, Mr. and Mrs. Joseph Cosand, there. They also planned to open a school for girls at the suggestion of Nitobe Inazō and Uchimura Kanzō, who were studying in the United States at that time. As a result, Friends Girls

Biology class, 1922. Friends School, Tokyo　普連土学園所蔵

に依存していた。しかしながら、普連土女学校は外国人校長を置かない少数のミッション・スクールの1つであり、学校側と経営側の宣教師がよく協力しあったと伝えられている。開学してから約半世紀の間、3人の日本人（海部忠蔵、平川正寿、冨山とき）が校長を務めた。いずれもクエーカーである。海部忠蔵はコサンド夫妻の弟子で、インディアナ州にあるクエーカー派のアーラム大学を卒業した。平川正寿は茨城県立土浦中学校教頭を務めていたところ、普連土女学校の校長に請われた。冨山ときは普連土女学校の卒業生で、日本女子大学卒業後、渡米しウエストタウン・スクール（チェスター郡にあるクエーカーの寄宿学校）とコロンビア大学教育学部で学んだ。

太平洋戦争中、冨山校長の下で普連土

School was established in 1887 with six teachers and three students at the Cosand's home, which was located on Tsuda Sen's estate in Azabu-Honmura. The school's first permanent structure was built in 1889 at its present location on Hijirizaka in Mita, Minato-ku. The school compound was totally burnt down in 1902, but was subsequently rebuilt by the missionary association.

Before World War II, many so-called "mission schools" in Japan depended financially on foreign missionary organizations, and Friends Girls School was no exception. About half to three quarters of its expenses were paid for by contributions from Philadelphia Friends.

Friends Girls School was one of the few

Biology class, 1936. Friends School, Tokyo　普連土学園所蔵

女学校は大変な苦労を重ねた。まず少しでも西洋色を薄めるために、学校名を「聖友女学校」に変更した。さらに空襲により校舎が壊滅状態となった。戦後、フィラデルフィア年会ミッション・ボードは早々に学校再建のために、資金調達を始めた。学校は強力な指導者を必要とし、エスター・B・ローズが第4代校長に任命された。ローズは校舎再建プロジェクトが終了する1955年まで、校長の職責を担った。この間、クエーカーで外交官、そして後に東京外国語大学の初代学長となった澤田節蔵が理事長を務めた。

1947年の新教育制度（6・3・3制）の導入に伴い、校名を「普連土学園」に変更し、中高一貫教育を行う女子校となっ

mission schools that had never had a foreign principal, but nevertheless has always had a strong spirit of cooperation between the Japanese and the American missionaries who ran the school. During its first fifty years, the school had three principals—Kaifu Chūzō, Hirakawa Seiju, and Tomiyama Toki, who were all Quakers. Kaifu Chūzō, a student of the Cosands, graduated from Earlham College, a Quaker institution in Indiana. Hirakawa Seiju was recruited for the position while he worked as an assistant principal at Tsuchiura High School in Ibaraki Prefecture. Tomiyama Toki was a Friends Girls School graduate, who, after going to Japan Women's College, attended a Quaker boarding school in Pennsylvania, Westtown School, before continuing her studies at Teachers College,

た。1974年のフィラデルフィア年会日本委員会解散により、普連土学園は財政的に自立した。

普連土学園は建学以来変わらず、礼拝、奉仕、国際理解を大事にしている。現在も、毎朝の礼拝を守り、終拝（讃美歌と沈黙の時間）で1日が終わる。クリスチャンは少ないが、生徒は全員が聖書を学び、クエーカー精神を学んでいる。学習指導にも力を入れ、ほぼ全生徒が進学する。

フィラデルフィア・フレンドは日本で様々な伝道事業を展開したが、普連土女学校および普連土学園の維持は常に最優先であった。学校を財政的に支えたばかりでなく、常時、教員を派遣した。この中には、メアリ・M・ヘインズ、サラ・M・ロングストレス、エスター・ボルダストン（ジョーンズ）、マーガレット・W・ローズ、エリザベス・ボートン、サリー・スミス、メイ・テイラー、シャーロット・コンロイ、キャサリン・テイラー（水野）など、多くのフィラデルフィア・フレンドが含まれている。

戸田徹子

参考文献：
普連土学園百年史編纂委員会編『普連土学園百年史』（普連土学園、1987）

【関連情報】
普連土学園
〒108-0073
東京都港区三田4-14-16
電話: 03-3451-4616
www.friends.ac.jp

Columbia University.

Under the leadership of Tomiyama, the school had a very hard time during World War II, so it temporarily changed its name to "Seiyū" Girls School, which sounded less westernized. The buildings were completely demolished by a major air raid. After the war, the Mission Board of the Philadelphia Yearly Meeting quickly began collecting funds to reconstruct the school compound. The school needed strong leadership, which was found in Esther B. Rhoads, who was appointed as the fourth principal and served until 1955, overseeing the building projects for Friends School. Meanwhile, Sawada Setsuzō, a Quaker diplomat and the first president of Tokyo University of Foreign Studies, served as chairman of the Board of Trustees.

In 1947, the school adopted a new (6-3-3) educational system and changed its name from "Friends Girls School" (Furendo Jogakkō) to "Friends School" (Furendo Gakuen). Even though the school removed the word "Girls" from its name, it remained a secondary school only for girls. With the dissolution of the Japan Committee of Philadelphia Yearly Meeting in 1974, Friends School became independent.

Few students are Christians, but, having been established on Quaker traditions, Friends School respects Quaker teachings. The curriculum emphasizes worship, service, and international friendship as well as academic studies. Students read the Bible as part of the curriculum. Each day, the school starts with meeting for worship and ends with the singing of a hymn and a moment of silence. The school now has a strong academic curriculum, and almost all its students go on to university.

Although the Philadelphia Friends undertook various missionary programs in Japan, the Friends Girls School was always their first priority. They not only supported the school financially, but, except during World War II, consistently provided teachers, many of whom were Philadelphia Quaker women, including Mary M. Haines, Sarah M. Longstreth, Esther Balderston (Jones), Margaret W. Rhoads, Elizabeth Borton, Sally Smith, May Taylor, Charlotte Conroy, and Kathryn Taylor (Mizuno).

By Tetsuko Toda

7.5　Ishii Ryōichi and Fudeko: True "Angels" for Intellectually Disadvantaged Children
滝乃川学園とエルウィン：社会福祉の先駆者

2012年9月下旬、滝乃川学園職員の一行がフィラデルフィア郊外エルウィンにある福祉施設「エルウィン」を訪問した。エルウィンの歴史は長く、1852年開校の知的障害者訓練学校に由来する。「ペンシルベニア知的障害者訓練学校」や「エルウィン・インスティチューツ」などと名前を変えてきたが、エルウィンは今では様々な障害に対処し、あらゆる年代の人たちを対象とする総合的な社会福祉施設として、指導的な役割を果たしている。

一方、滝乃川学園は日本で最初の知的障害児の福祉施設であるが、その創設者（石井亮一・筆子）は施設開設に当た

In late September, 2012, a delegation from Takinogawa Gakuen visited Elwyn, a human services organization in suburban Philadelphia, to strengthen ties and commemorate the 120th anniversary of the founding of Takingogawa Gakuen, which provides similar services in Japan. Elwyn opened in 1852 as a private school for children with intellectual disabilities. It has had various names over its history, including the "Pennsylvania Training School for Feeble Minded Children" and the "Elwyn Institute." Elwyn is now one of the leading providers of welfare services for people of all ages with special needs.

Takinogawa Gakuen is the oldest educational institution for intellectually disabled children in Japan. Its founders, Ishii Ryōichi and Fudeko, visited Elwyn prior to establishing their organization in 1891.

To modernize Japan, the Meiji Government encouraged the development of new industries and educational systems, but it left social welfare to the care of the private sector, such as benevolent and religious groups. Takinogawa Gakuen was started by Mr. and Mrs. Ishii to meet an unserved social need in Japan.

Ishii Ryōichi (1867–1937) was born into a samurai family in Saga and studied at Rikkyō College. He became a Christian and worked as a deputy schoolmaster at Rikkyō

Fudeko Ishii.
Takinogawa Gakuen 滝乃川学園

239

って、エルウィンを参考にした。それゆえ滝乃川学園は学園創立120周年を記念して、歴史的な絆を確かめるために、訪問団を派遣したのである。

明治政府は近代化のために殖産興業を重視し、教育制度の整備を急いだ。だがその反面、社会福祉には積極的に取り組まず、慈善や宗教団体などの民間セクターに委ねたままだった。そのような環境で、滝乃川学園は石井亮一・筆子夫妻の個人事業として始まった。

滝乃川学園の創始者、石井亮一（1867‐1937）は現在の佐賀県の、武士の家に生まれた。立教大学に学び、クリスチャンとなり、立教女学校の教頭をつとめていた。濃尾大地震（1891）の時、孤児となった娘たちが売春宿に売られそうになっているのを救い、彼女たちを収容し教育するために東京に孤女学院を開いたが、そのなかに知的障害児が含まれていた。これを契機に、亮一は知的障害児教育にかかわるようになり、後に孤女学院を滝乃川学園と改称し、知的障害児の福祉と教育を始めた。

一方、石井筆子（1861‐1944）は今の長崎県で生まれた。武士の娘で、知性と美貌に恵まれた女性であった。11歳で東京に引っ越し、日本で最初の官立女学校である東京女学校（竹橋女学校）で学んだ。クララ・ホイットニーとは友人関係にあり、彼女から英語を習った。1880年から82年まで、長岡護美（旧藩主の娘の夫）が外交官としてヨーロッパ（ハーグ）に赴任するのに同行し、そこでフランス語を学んだ。帰国すると、1885年から華族女学校でフランス語を教え始めた。このとき同僚で英語担当だったのが津田梅子である。

Girls School. When a big earthquake hit the Nōbi area (Aichi and Gifu), he rescued orphan girls who were about to be sold for prostitution and helped them enter the Holy Trinity Girls' Orphan School (Kojo Gakuin). The school's aim was to provide female orphans with an education so they could become independent. One of the girls had a mental disability, which led to Ryōichi's commitment to the education and welfare of intellectually disabled children.

Meanwhile, Fudeko (1861–1944) was born in Nagasaki, also to a samurai family. At the age of eleven, she moved to Tokyo, where she had the best and most advanced education at the time, attending the first governmental Tokyo Girls' School (a.k.a. Takebashi Girls' School) and learning English from Clara Whitney. She lived in Europe from 1880 to 1882 as an attendant of Nagaoka Moriyoshi, a diplomat at The Hague, where Fudeko learned to speak French. Nagaoka's wife was from the family whom Fudeko's family had served. After returning to Japan, she began teaching French at the Peeress' School in 1885. Tsuda Umeko, who taught English, was her colleague.

In 1884, Fudeko married Ogashima Tasuku, a promising government official. They had three daughters, who were, unfortunately, all ill or intellectually disabled. The second daughter died early in her life, followed by Fudeko's husband's death at the age of 25, and that of her youngest daughter in 1898.

While she was searching for someone who could look after her children, Fudeko met Ryōichi and they soon decided to marry and devote their lives to the education and

Ryōichi Ishii.
Takinogawa Gakuen 滝乃川学園所蔵

Fudeko Ishii, c. mid 1890s.
Takinogawa Gakuen 滝乃川学園所蔵

1884年に筆子は将来を嘱望された官吏、小鹿島果と結婚した。果との間に3人の娘が生まれたが、次女は夭折。他の2人は知的障害をもっていた。1892年には夫が35歳で亡くなり、筆子は未亡人となった。さらに1898年には3女も亡くなってしまう。

筆子は娘たちの教育を委ねられる人を探していて、石井亮一に出会った。2人は結婚すること、そして知的障害児のために福祉事業を始めることを決意した。施設開設の参考にすべく、亮一はアメリカに福祉事業の視察に出かけた。亮一の訪米とほぼ同時期に、筆子はデンバーで開催される婦人倶楽部万国大会（1898）に日本代表として、津田梅子とともに出席した。大会後、筆子はしばらく

welfare of intellectually disabled children. Before setting up their institution, Ryōichi visited the United States to see the latest developments in education and social services firsthand. He so respected what he saw at the Pennsylvania Training School that he used it as a model for his new institution in Japan.

During almost the same period as Ryōichi's visit, Fudeko was also in the United States representing Japan, along with Tsuda Umeko, at the 1898 Convention of the General Federation of Women's Clubs in Denver, Colorado. After the conference, Fudeko traveled around the States to observe a number of respected social welfare service institutions. During her travels she came to

Mr. and Ms. Ishii. Takinogawa Gakuen 滝乃川学園所蔵

アメリカにとどまり、各地で福祉事業を視察した。フィラデルフィアではエルウィンにあるペンシルベニア知的障害児訓練学校を見学し、施設が農園を経営し、障害者たちに仕事を提供していることに強い印象を受けた。この時、筆子が滞在先としたのはメアリ・モリス宅であった。また夫ウィスター・モリスはこの学校の副会長を務めていた。

帰国後、2人は本格的に知的障害児教育に取り組み始めた。滝乃川学園は日本で最初の知的障害者施設として、モデルとなった。1928年、学園は農業のできる広い土地を郊外に求めて、現在地の国立市に移転した。今日、学園は多機能化し、地域支援部やグループホーム、ケアホーム、認知症高齢者施設などの福祉事業も展開している。学園の本館

Philadelphia and stayed at the Morris's home to visit the Pennsylvania Training School in Elwyn, of which Mary's husband, Wistar Morris, was a vice president. She was very much impressed by the school, which ran a farm to provide work for the children.

Ryōichi and Fudeko became totally committed to Takinogawa Gakuen. As the first institution in Japan specializing in helping intellectually disabled children, it functioned as a model for later institutions serving this population. In 1928, Takinogawa Gakuen moved to its present location in Kunitachi, Tokyo, acquiring enough space for vegetable gardens. Today it offers various social welfare services including community support, a consultation center, a group home, and a home for people with dementia.

は、2002年に国登録有形文化財指定された。滝乃川学園はその歴史を後世に伝えるべく、この建物を「石井亮一・筆子記念館」と改称し、亮一の図書や筆子が弾いたピアノ（「天使のピアノ」）等を保管、展示している。

エルウィンはより長い歴史を誇り、多くの貴重な記録、文献、写真を保有しており、これらの資料を収蔵する「エルウィン歴史資料博物館」が設けられている。

日米でそれぞれに社会福祉分野で指導的な役割を果たしてきた2つの施設は、今後、交流を深め、学び合うことになろう。

戸田徹子

参考文献：
津曲裕次『福祉に生きる49　石井筆子』（大空社、2001）
津曲裕次『福祉に生きる51　石井亮一』（大空社、2002）
滝乃川学園監修・編集『滝乃川学園百二十年史（全2巻）』（大空社、2011）

【参考情報】
社会福祉法人　滝乃川学園（石井亮一・筆子記念館）
〒186-0011
東京都国立市谷保6312
電話: 042-573-3950
www.takinogawagakuen.jp

Takinogawa's main building was registered as a national asset in 2002, and at that time was renamed "the Memorial Hall for Ishii Ryōichi and Fudeko." It holds Fudeko's piano (called the "Angel's Piano") and historical records such as Ryōichi's books and manuscripts.

Established in 1852 and 1891, respectively, Elwyn and Takinogawa can each be proud of their history and contribution to providing important social services to an underserved segment of society at a time when few recognized the need. Elwyn's Historical Archives and Museum has preserved its history with documents, archival photographs, and social welfare and educational resources related to its mission.

Their mutual history demonstrates the enormous potential in the relationship between Takinogawa and Elwyn, two organizations that serve as models for how two different social service institutions can learn from each other to meet the needs of their respective societies.

By Tetsuko Toda

Selected Reference: Elwyn Institutes' Historical Archives and Museum (Pamphlet).

If you go: Elwyn, 111 Elwyn Road, Elwyn, PA 19063.

8

Modern Philadelphia
現代のフィラデルフィア

8.1 The Philadelphia Area Japanese American Community: Loving Civil Liberties

アメリカの人権運動に貢献した日系人たち

1860年から1920年にかけて、アメリカ合衆国にさまざまな国から移民が渡ってきた。そのうちの24万6400人、すなわち0.0086%が、日本からの移民だった。1920年の調査によれば、アメリカ生まれの子どもを含め、日本人は11万1010人と記録されている。初期の日本からの移民は、留学、もしくは日本との貿易事業を始めるためにアメリカに渡ってきた者たちで、東海岸においては、1905年までには、ペンシルベニア大学やブリンマー大学など、フィラデルフィア地域のエリート校に留学する学生たちもいた。

事業を始めるためにアメリカに移住した日本人は、見合いで結婚した妻たちと新しい家族を形成していった。初期のフィラデルフィア住民の中では、ヨウスケ・W・ナカノが、1916年にペンシルベニア大学で建築学の修士号を取得し、ジェファーソン病院とアーキテクツ・ビルなどの建設に携わった。ウィリアム・ヨサブロウ・オカモトとリチャード・トキゾウ・オカモト兄弟は、チェスナット通りの1011番地に店をかまえ、絹シャツの仕立屋を営んだ。第2次世界大戦以前のフィラデルフィアの日本人住民には他に、医者、歯科医、写真家、彫刻家、大工などがいた。1952年までアメリカ市民になることは法律で認められていなかったが、なかにはアメリカ人女性と結婚した日本人が少数おり、地域社会にとけ込んでいる家族も20世帯ほどあった。

日本とアメリカの間に戦争が勃発し、

Between 1860 and 1920, immigrants from many countries arrived in the United States. Of these, 246,400, or .0086%, were from Japan. The 1920 census counted 111,010 Japanese, including their American-born children. The early Japanese immigrants came to study or engage in trade with Japan. By 1905, a number of students of Japanese heritage came to the elite schools in the Philadelphia area, including the University of Pennsylvania and Bryn Mawr College.

Others came to start businesses, and wives whose marriages had been arranged came to establish new families. Among early Philadelphia residents was Yosuke W. Nakano (1887-1961), who received his Masters of Architecture from the University of Pennsylvania in 1916 and was responsible for construction of the Architects Building, work on Jefferson Hospital's main building, and numerous other significant projects. The brothers William Yosaburo and Richard Tokizo Okamoto had a store at 1011 Chestnut Street, selling custom silk shirts. Other resident Japanese in Philadelphia before World War II included doctors, dentists, a photographer, a sculptor, and a carpenter. Although by law ineligible to become American citizens until 1952, a few of the Japanese immigrants married American women, and there were about two dozen families in the area, assimilated into various communities.

Philadelphia JACL national convention 1998, award ceremony;
from left: Norman Mineta, Robert Matsui, Grayce Uyehara,
James Wright (former Speaker of the House). Celebrating the
10th anniversary of the Civil Liberty Act of 1988
(redress act). Courtesy of Hiro Nishikawa

After the outbreak of hostilities between Japan and the United States, President Franklin D. Roosevelt signed Executive Order 9066 on February 19, 1942, leading to the relocation and incarceration of 115,000 persons of Japanese descent (Nikkei) of whom some 75,000 were American born. During the incarceration, a number of Quaker missionaries visited the War Relocation Authority (WRA) camps to help Nikkei young adults obtain leave and come to Philadelphia for jobs and/ or schooling. Thus, even before the Supreme Court decision in December 1944 [*ex parte Endo*] to close the camps, the eastward diaspora of formerly West Coast Nikkei had begun. Many came to southern New Jersey to work for Seabrook Farms. Charles Seabrook, founder of the world's largest frozen food industry, appealed to the camps for badly needed manpower, and over 2,300 Japanese had settled in Seabrook by 1946.

A lesser-known but significant agriculture-related profession in Pennsylvania was chick sexing. Based on discoveries in 1924 in Japan, a method for distinguishing the gender of day-old chicks was developed. Owing to the Immigration Exclusion Act, which prevented Japanese immigration, Nikkei went to Japan to learn the skill and bring it

フランクリン・D・ルーズベルト大統領は、1942年2月19日、大統領行政命令9066号に署名した。それは、7万5000人のアメリカ生まれの日系人を含む、11万5000人を強制移動し、収容するというものだった。強制収容所が稼働していた間、クエーカーの宣教師たちは、WRA（戦時転住局）を訪れ、日系の若者たちが収容所を出て、フィラデルフィアで働けるように、もしくは学校に通えるように働きかけた。このようにして、収容所を閉鎖するという最高裁判決が1944年12月に下される前に、かつて西海岸に住んでいた日系人の東海岸への移動はすでに始まっていた。世界最大の冷凍食品産業の創立者であるチャールズ・シーブルックが、労働者を求めて熱心に収容所へ働きかけた結果、1946年までに、2300人以上の日本人がニュージャージー州南部にあるシーブルック農場に住み着いた。

あまり一般に知られてはいないが、ペンシルベニア州において鶏のひなの性判別は重要な農業関係の職業であった。1924年の日本での発見をもとに、生後1日の鶏のひなの性別を識別する方法が開発された。日本からの移民を禁止する、排日移民法が施行されたことによって、日本へ戻った日系人は、その技術を学び、アメリカに持ち帰った。S・ジョン・ニッタが、日本でその訓練を受けた先駆者であった。ニッタはその後、1937年に、訓練校(アメリカ鶏雛性判別)をロサンゼルスに開いた。1942年にペンシルベニア州ランズデールに移転し、全米のひなの性判別事業を取り込んで、アメリカ鶏雛性判別協会となった。この日系人独自の職業は、アメリカの鶏肉業界の経済発展に多大な影響をもたらした。この技術で生後1日のひなを雄と雌に離して生育させることにより、卵と鶏肉の生産を分けることができたからである。

長年、多くの社会福祉機関や教会などと協力して、フィラデルフィア地域住民に様々な社会活動を提供していた日系人グループ(メアリ・D・ムラカミ、グレイス・K・ウエハラ、ヒロシ・ウエハラ、テツヤ・イワサキなどを含むフィラデルフィア2世協会)は1947年に、JACL(日系アメリカ人市民同盟)のフィラデルフィア支部を設立した。JACL は、1924年に、ワシントン州シアトルで創立された全米で最古、かつ最大のアジア系アメリカ人の市民団体である。アメリカ全土で100以上の支部、1万5000人の会員を数え、ワシントンD.C.とサンフランシスコに本部を置く。

JACLフィラデルフィア支部は、1980年代の補償請求運動で重要な役割を果たした。この運動の成果として、1988年に

back to the States. S. John Nitta was among the pioneers who trained in Japan, then in 1937 started a training school, American Chick Sexing, in Los Angeles. In 1942 it was moved to Lansdale, Pennsylvania, and expanded to include sexing services around the U.S., becoming the American Chick Sexing Association. This Nikkei-dominated profession had a profound impact on the economic development of the American poultry industry, which benefited from being able to gender segregate day-old chicks for egg production vs meat production.

In 1947 a group of Japanese Americans (Mary D. Murakami, Grayce K. Uyehara, Hiroshi Uyehara, Tesua Iwasaki, and others) who had organized community activities through the Philadelphia Nisei Council and had worked with numerous social service agencies, such as the Nationalities Service Center and churches, formed the Philadelphia chapter of the Japanese American Citizens League (JACL). The JACL, the oldest and largest Asian American civil rights organization, was founded in 1929 in Seattle. Now with over one hundred chapters and some 15,000 members throughout the country, its headquarters are in Washington, DC and San Francisco.

The Philadelphia JACL chapter played a prominent role during the 1980s Redress campaign, which culminated in the Civil Liberties Act of 1988 signed by President Reagan. This resulted in a letter of apology and a restitution check to some 80,000 Nikkei who had survived the WRA camp incarceration during World War II. Fighting against overwhelming odds, Grayce Uyehara, a retired social worker from the Philadelphia

Judge William Marutani. Courtesy of Marutani Family

レーガン大統領が市民自由法（通称、日系アメリカ人補償法）に署名した。これにより、第2次世界大戦中の強制収容所から生還した8万人の日系人への謝罪と補償金の支払がなされたのである。多くの反対派をよそに、フィラデルフィアに住む、ソーシャル・ワーカーを定年退職したグレイス・ウエハラは、JACL LEC（立法教育委員会）を率いて、補償金の支払いに対する法案の可決を求め、議会に対しロビー活動を行った。

また、他の特筆すべきJACLの会員は、ウィリアム・マルタニ判事である。マルタニは、1975年に、ミルトン・シャップ知事に

area, headed the JACL Legislative Education Committee to lobby Congress to pass bills for redress.

Another JACL member of note was Judge William Marutani, who was appointed to the Philadelphia Common Pleas Court in 1975 by Governor Milton Shapp. He was the first judge of Nikkei descent in a state east of the Mississippi. Earlier, in 1967, as a JACL lawyer, Marutani had been the first Nikkei to present an amicus brief before the U.S. Supreme Court. The case was *Loving vs. State of Virginia*, in which the court struck down anti-miscegenation laws remaining

DOR (Day of Remembrance) 2000 program. from left, William Marutani, Teresa Maebori, Grayce Uyehara, Tak Moriuchi. Courtesy of Hiro Nishikawa

より、フィラデルフィア民事訴訟裁判所の裁判官に指名された。ミシシッピ川以東の州で、日系で最初の裁判官であった。JACLの弁護士を務めていたマルタニは、1967年に、日系人として初めて米国最高裁判所で法廷助言を行った。訴訟は「ラビング夫妻対バージニア州」で、当時まだ17の州に残っていた、異人種間の結婚を禁止する法律が無効になった。1980年に、マルタニは、カーター大統領によって、第2次世界大戦中の強制収容所に関する情報を収集するために設立された、CWRIC（戦争中の一般市民の転住と拘留に関する調査委員会）の委員に選ばれた、ただ1人のアジア系アメリカ人であった。1983年にCWRICは、調査で明らかになったことを、『否定された個人の正義』という本にまとめ、

in seventeen states at that time. In 1980 Marutani was the only Asian American appointed to the Commission on Wartime Relocation and Internment of Civilians (CWRIC), established by President Carter to gather information about World War II concentration camps in America. In 1983 the CWRIC published its findings in a book, *Personal Justice Denied*, which became the basis for the 1988 Civil Liberties Act.

Ed Nakawatase, chapter president in 1994–97, had an unusual amount of experience in activism as a young man. As a Sansei (third generation Japanese American) born in a Poston, Arizona concentration camp in 1943, he grew up in Seabrook, New Jersey, a son of plant workers at Seabrook Farms. At

それは1988年の市民自由法（日系アメリカ人補償法）の礎となった。

エド・ナカワタセは、1994年から97年まで、JACLフィラデルフィア支部の会長だったが、同胞の若者の中では、異例な活動経験をもっていた。ナカワタセは、日系アメリカ人３世として、1943年に、アリゾナ州ポストンの強制収容所で生まれた。その後、ニュージャージー州シーブルック農場の工場労働者の息子として、同町で育った。20歳で大学を中退し、ジョージア州アトランタにあった、SNCC（非暴力学生委員会）に参加した。ナカワタセは、SNCCの指導部であったジョン・ルイス、ジュリアン・ボンドと共に活動した。

ナカワタセはレストランに行った際、仲間に黒人がいたことを理由に給仕を拒否されたことに反発したために逮捕され、クリスマスを刑務所で過ごした。SNCCで1年半活動した後、ナカワタセはニュージャージーに戻って大学を終えたが、再度60、70年代の反戦運動に参加し、その後は日系人への補償請求活動に入る。さらに、アメリカ・フレンズ奉仕団の、アメリカ・インディアンに関する業務代表を30年以上務めた。

今日、日系アメリカ人は、様々な地域で、多様な職業に従事し活躍している。ロータリー、キワーニス、ライオンズなどの社会奉仕団体に属したり、教会の長老を務めたりしている。多くの日系人は、日本文化を先祖伝来の文化として受け継ぎながらも、アメリカの主流として活躍しながら、同時に生け花、折り紙、日本料

age twenty he dropped out of college and joined the Student Nonviolent Coordinating Committee (SNCC) in Atlanta, Georgia. Ed worked as an intake person in the Atlanta office with SNCC luminaries such as John Lewis and Julian Bond. He spent a Christmas in jail for "criminal trespass" when he and his colleagues were arrested at a local restaurant for protesting after they were refused service because of black individuals in their group. At the end of a year and a half with SNCC he returned to finish college in New Jersey, but then moved into the anti-war movement of the 1960s and 1970s, followed by activism in Nikkei Redress. He spent more than three decades as the national representative for Native American Affairs for the American Friends Service Committee.

Today Japanese Americans are active in all facets of the community and in all professions. They belong to service clubs such as Rotary, Kiwanis, and Lions, or serve as elders of their community churches. As part of mainstream America, yet with Japanese culture as part of their heritage, many talented Nikkei share their skills and knowledge with other Americans in areas such as flower arrangement, origami, and Japanese cuisine.

By Grayce K. Uyehara and A. Hirotoshi Nishikawa

Selected References: http://home.comcast.net/~terrychinn/poultry_sorters/index.html; *The Japanese American Experience*, catalogue of an exhibition held at The Balch Institute for Ethnic Studies, June 15–September 7, 1985; Leslie T. Hatamiya, *Righting a Wrong: Japanese Americans and*

理などを指導して、日本に伝統関する伝統と知識を広めている。

グレイス・ウエハラ/ヒロ・ニシカワ
今井元子/中村英恵 訳

the Passage of the Civil Liberties Act of 1988 (Stanford, CA: Stanford University Press, 1993).

If you go: The Balch Institute for Ethnic Studies is now part of the Historical Society of Pennsylvania, 1300 Locust Street, Philadelphia, PA 19107.

Architects Building, 117-21 South 17th Street, Philadelphia, PA 19103, now housing the Palomar Hotel.

8.2   George Nakashima: "The Soul of a Tree"
ジョージ・ナカシマの足跡：「木のこころ」

ジョージ・ナカシマは1905年、ワシントン州スポケーンで日本人移民の両親のもとに生まれた。ワシントン大学で林学と建築学を学んだ後、エコール・デ・ボザールとハーバード大学への奨学金を獲得した。マサチューセッツ工科大学で1930年に建築学の修士号を取得して、まもなくパリへ行く。

1934年に東京へ渡ると、フランク・ロイド・ライトの弟子であるチェコ人の建築家、アントニン・レイモンドの下で働いた。1936年にはインドのポンディシェリへ派遣され、インドで初の鉄筋コンクリートとなる建物のデザインと建設を指揮した。この間に、スリ・オーロビンドに弟子入りすることとなった。戦争のため、インドを1939年に出ると、ナカシマは東京にしばらく滞在し、同じくワシントン州シアトル育ちで、後に妻となるマリオン・オカジマと出会う。2人はアメリカに別々に帰国し、1941年にロサンゼルスで結婚した。その地でフランク・ロイド・ライトの建物の建設現場を見て、ナカシマは建築をやめる決意をした。原材料、デザインそして組み立てまで一貫して品質管理のできる家具を製作することにし、シアトルに戻って家具事業を始めた。木材加工を男子に教えることを条件に、レオポルド・ティベサー牧師から、メリノール宣協会にある機械類の使用許可を得る。

1942年、真珠湾攻撃や太平洋戦争のため、西海岸に住む日系人はすべて強制収容所に送還された。ナカシマ一家も

George Nakashima (1905–1990) was born in Spokane, Washington, to Japanese immigrant parents and studied Forestry and Architecture at the University of Washington. His talent for architecture enabled him to gain a scholarship to study in France at the École Americaine des Beaux-Arts in 1928. While studying in France, he won the Prix Fontainebleau for excelling academically. After graduating from the University of Washington, Nakashima enrolled in the Harvard Graduate School of Design. He received a Master's degree in Architecture from MIT in 1930, returned to Paris shortly thereafter, and then went to Tokyo in 1934, where he entered the employ of Frank Lloyd Wright's protégé, the Czech architect Antonin Raymond. He was sent to Pondicherry, India, in 1936 to oversee the design and building of the first reinforced concrete building in that country and became a disciple of Sri Aurobindo in the process. Because of the war, he left India in 1939, spent some time in Tokyo, where he met his future bride, Marion Okajima, who was also brought up in Seattle, Washington. They returned separately to the United States and were married in Los Angeles in 1941. After observing some Frank Lloyd Wright buildings under construction there, Nakashima decided to leave architecture and to create furniture so he could control the quality of his creation all the way from raw materials through design and construction. After Nakashima moved back to Seattle to

Conoid Studio. Courtesy of the author

まずワシントン州ピュアラップへ、次にアイダホ砂漠のミニドカへ送られ、最初の家具事業は中断を余儀なくされた。デザインや建築技術をかわれたジョージは、日本で修業したゲンタロウ・ヒコガワと共に、手に入る材料を活用し、バラック内の生活状態を改善するように頼まれた。

1943年、以前の上司で、東京からペンシルベニア州ニューホープに移っていたアントニン・レイモンドは、ジョージのマサチューセッツ工科大の恩師の1人に頼まれて、ナカシマ一家のスポンサーとなる。レイモンドは自分の農場に一家を住まわせ、ジョージを養鶏業者として雇った。1年くらい経ったころ、ナカシマ一家は小さな小屋を賃借りし、ガレージ

start his furniture business, Father Leopold H. Tibesar allowed Nakashima to use the machinery at Maryknoll Mission in exchange for teaching the boys woodworking. Later Tibesar accompanied the Japanese-American community to U.S. government internment camps.

In 1942, all Japanese-Americans on the West Coast were incarcerated because of Pearl Harbor and the war in the Pacific. The entire Nakashima family was sent first to Puyallup and then Minidoka in the Idaho desert, interrupting Nakashima's first furniture making endeavor. Because of his design and building skills, George was given the task, alongside the Japanese-trained carpenter Gentaro Hikogawa, of improving the living

Goerge Nakashima leaning on a tree, c. 1980s.
Courtesy of the author

conditions inside the barracks by utilizing available materials. During the process, he gained knowledge of Japanese carpentry techniques as well as the ability to adapt his design ideas to the materials at hand.

In 1943, at the request of one of Nakashima's professors at MIT, his former employer Antonin Raymond, who had moved to New Hope, Pennsylvania from Tokyo, sponsored the Nakashima family to live on his farm, where George was employed as a chicken farmer. After a year or so, the Nakashimas rented a small cottage, making furniture in the garage, and later bartering a small piece of property in exchange for labor on a neighboring farm. Working from an old army tent, Nakashima designed and built a simple workshop and small house with his own hands, continuing to build and add property as his furniture business grew. In 1948, he joined Hans and Florence ("Shu") Knoll and their design team and created a small line of furniture for Knoll Studios while retaining the right to make the same designs at his workshop. In 1958, he designed an extensive line of furniture manufactured by Widdicomb-Mueller in Grand Rapids, but, like the Knoll venture, it did not last more than a few years before Nakashima became dissatisfied with the quality control issues of mass-produced furniture.

George Nakashima designed a Catholic church in Karuizawa, Japan in 1934 and the disciples' dormitory Golconde for the Sri

で家具製作を始めた。その後、周辺農場で働き、引き換えに小さな土地を得た。ジョージ・ナカシマは、こうしてまず古い軍用テントから出発し、自らの手で簡易作業場や小さな家を建て、家具事業が拡大するのに応じて、所有地を広げ、建物を増やしていった。1948年には、ハンスとフローレンス（シュウ）・ノールとそのデザイン・チームに加わり、ノール・スタジオ用に家具を製造し、自宅の作業場でも同じデザインの家具を作る権利を得た。1958年、ミシガン州グランラピッズのウィディコーム・ミュラー社の製造家具のデザインを多く手掛けたが、ノール事業の時と同じように大量生産による家具の品質管理問題のため、数年で辞めてしまった。

ナカシマは1934年に軽井沢のカトリック教会、1936年にスリ・オーロビンド・アシャムの弟子たちの寮であるゴルコンドのデザインを手掛けた。また1965年には神聖な場所への関心から、京都に

Goerge Nakashima in his shop. Courtesy of the author

Aurobindo Ashram in India in 1936, and he continued his interest in sacred spaces by building the reinforced concrete hyperbolic paraboloid shell roof Church of Christ the King in Kyoto in 1965. He also built adobe chapels and monasteries for the Benedictine communities at Christ in the Desert, Abiquiu, New Mexico in 1972 and La Soledad in San Miguel de Allende, Mexico in 1975.

ある鉄筋コンクリート製HPシェル屋根、チャーチ・オブ・クライスト・ザ・キングを手がけた。1972年にはニューメキシコ州アビクィウのクライスト・イン・ザ・デザート、ベネディクティン・コミュニティーにアドベ（日乾煉瓦）のチャペルや修道院を、1975年にはメキシコのサン・ミゲル・デ・アレンデにあるラ・ソレダッドを建築した。

1964年、ジョージ・ナカシマは彫刻家の流政之と出会い、四国の讃岐民具連に加入した。その結果、家具の個展を東京で10回開催し、世界で唯一、ナカシマ・デザインの使用認可を受けた桜製作所との生涯にわたる関係を築いた。1983年には唯一の著書となる『木のこころ』を出版し、木工の技術や工具ばかりでなく、木工を支えている哲学について記述している。

無宗派の「平和の祭壇」を世界の各大陸

In 1964, George Nakashima met the sculptor Masayuki Nagare and joined the Minguren group ("People's Tool Guild"), an association of designer-craftsmen in Shikoku, Japan, which led to the creation of ten one-man furniture shows in Tokyo and a lifelong relationship with Sakura Seisakusho, the only company in the world licensed to create Nakashima designs. In 1983, he published his only book, *The Soul of a Tree*, in which he describes the philosophical underpinnings, as well as the tools and techniques, of a woodworker.

In 1984, dreaming of making non-denominational "Altars for Peace" for each of the continents of the world, he purchased an immense walnut log and created the first one for the Cathedral of St. John the Divine in 1986. Among the numerous honors he received are the Gold Craftsmanship Medal

に1台ずつ製作することを夢見て、1984年に巨大なクルミ材を購入し、1986年にニューヨーク大聖堂に納める最初の1台を製作した。授与された数々の栄誉の中には1952年のアメリカ建築家協会による職人部門の金賞、1980年の日系アメリカ人市民同盟による「日系アメリカ人ビエンナーレ・アート部門賞」、1983年の日本国政府からの勲三等瑞宝章が挙げられる。1990年には、ナカシマによる最初で最後となった家具の回顧展「フル・サークル」が終了してまもなく、ワシントン大学より最優秀名誉卒業生賞が授けられた。ナカシマが永眠したのは、その1週間後のことであった。

残された家族には、妻マリオン（2004年に他界）、息子のケビン、娘のミラがいる。マリオンは忠実な職人たちと共にナカシマの家具事業を引き継いでいる。熟練職人の技、自然なフォームと素材の美しさを尊重する一方で、現代社会の利己主義や実利主義、大量生産を疑問視するという哲学は健在である。「平和の祭壇」もその後2台完成し、それぞれ1996年にインドのオーロビル、2001年にはモスクワへと送られた。ナカシマは生涯にわたり、15の独創的な建物を敷地内に建てたが、これらは2008年に、アメリカ合衆国の国家歴史登録財に認定され、そのうち3棟は2014年ワールドモニュメント財団によるウォッチリストに指定されている。ナカシマ・スタジオ及びナカシマ平和基金は、ジョージ・ナカシマが大切にした平和、建物及び家具のデザインを後世に受け継いでいきたいと願っている。

ミラ・ナカシマ
ホーク・奈々子 訳

from the American Institute of Architects (1952), the Gold Medal and title of "Japanese American of the Biennium in the Field of Arts" from the Japanese American Citizens' League in 1980, and the Third Order of the Sacred Treasure from the Government and Emperor of Japan in 1983. His first and last retrospective furniture show ("Full Circle") closed in 1990, shortly before he received his award as "Alumnus Summa Laude Dignatus" from the University of Washington. He died one week later.

He was survived by his wife Marion, who died in 2004, his son Kevin, and daughter Mira, who, along with his faithful craftsmen, have continued his furniture business and philosophy of questioning egotism, materialism, and mass-production of the modern world while honoring hand-craftsmanship and the inherent beauty of natural forms and materials. Two more "Altars for Peace" were constructed and sent to Auroville, India in 1996 and to Moscow in 2001. During his lifetime, Nakashima designed and built fifteen unique structures on the Nakashima property, included on the National Register of Historic Places since 2008, with three of them on the 2014 World Monument Fund Watch List. The Nakashima Studio and Foundation hope to continue his legacy of peace, as well as architectural and furniture design, for future generations.

By Mira Nakashima

Selected References: George Nakashima, *The Soul of a Tree: A Woodworker's Reflections* (Tokyo and New York: Kodansha International, 1981); Mira Nakashima, *Nature, Form, & Spirit: The Life and Legacy*

文献:
ジョー ジ・ナカシマ著　神代雄一郎・佐藤由巳子訳『木のこころ：木匠回想記』
（鹿島出版、1983）

【参考情報】
ジョージ ナカシマ記念館
GEORGE NAKASHIMA MEMORIAL
GALLERY
〒761-0122 香川県高松市牟礼町大
町1132-1
電話: 087-870-1020
www.sakurashop.co.jp/nakashima

of George Nakashima (New York: Harry N. Abrams, 2003).

If you go: George Nakashima Woodworker, 1847 Aquetong Road, New Hope, PA 18938.

8.3 Musical Ties between Philadelphia and Japan: The Philadelphia Orchestra

フィラデルフィア管弦楽団：音楽の絆

フィラデルフィア管弦楽団には、非常に熱烈な日本人ファンがいる。フィラデルフィア管弦楽団は1900年に創設され、最初の指揮者はフリッツ・シェールであった。シェールは、1906年、セオドア・ルーズベルト大統領のために、ホワイトハウスで開催されたコンサートの指揮を執っている。同じ年、ルーズベルト大統領は、日露戦争を仲介して終結させたことによって、ノーベル平和賞を受賞した。1921年に、レオポルド・ストコフスキーが指揮者となり、国際的な評価を得る楽団となった。

その後、1936年にユージン・オーマンディが後継者となった。フィラデルフィア管弦楽団は、指揮者オーマンディに率いられて、1967年に初めて来日し、大阪、金沢、名古屋、東京で演奏を行った。ウィリアムとロバート、ジョセフのドパスクェル3兄弟（みなフィラデルフィア管弦楽団の団員）とジョージ・ハーパム（2年後に管弦楽団に加わった）で構成されたドパスクェル弦楽四重奏団は、特別に招かれ、日本の四重奏団と合同室内演奏会をもち、天皇・皇后両陛下の前で演奏した。特にドパスクェル弦楽四重奏団が演奏したドボルザークの弦楽四重奏曲「アメリカン」は好評を博した。

フィラデルフィア管弦楽団と指揮者オーマンディは1972年に再来日し、東京、名古屋、大阪、広島、倉敷、札幌で演奏会を行った。1978年の3度目の来日は、「日本のオデッセイ：オーマンディとオーケストラ」というテレビ・ドキュメンタリ

The Philadelphia Orchestra has extremely devoted and loyal fans among the people of Japan. The Orchestra was founded in 1900 with Fritz Scheel as its first music director. He led the ensemble in a concert at the White House for President Theodore Roosevelt in 1906, the same year Roosevelt won the Nobel Peace Prize for negotiating an end to the Russo-Japanese War. In 1912 Leopold Stokowski took the podium and led the Orchestra to international fame. Eugene Ormandy succeeded him in 1936.

Maestro Ormandy took the Orchestra on its first tour of Japan in 1967, with concerts in Osaka, Kanazawa, Nagoya, and Tokyo. The dePasquale String Quartet, consisting of William, Robert, and Joseph (three brothers, all members of The Philadelphia Orchestra), and George Harpham (who joined the Orchestra two years later), received the extraordinary invitation to perform for the Emperor and Empress in a joint chamber concert with a Japanese quartet. The dePasquale Quartet performed Dvořák's "American" String Quartet, which seemed particularly appropriate.

The Orchestra and Ormandy returned to Japan in 1972 for concerts in Tokyo, Nagoya, Osaka, Hiroshima, Kurashiki, and Sapporo, and its third tour in 1978 was videotaped for a television documentary, "Japanese Odyssey: Ormandy and the Orchestra." Three

Philadelphia Orchestra, Charles Dutoit conducting. Courtesy of the Academy of Music

ーとして放映された。3年後、オーマンディとリカルド・ムーティがアジア演奏旅行中に合同で指揮をとった時、日本の聴衆はオーケストラ指揮者の「交替式」を見る機会に恵まれたのである。1985年にムーティはフィラデルフィア管弦楽団を率いて、東京、横浜、松戸、名古屋、鹿児島、福岡、大阪で演奏し、1989年に再来日している。

1986年の東京サントリー・ホール開館に当たり、NHK交響楽団の名誉指揮者であり、多くの日本人ファンがいるヴォルフガング・サヴァリッシュがベートーベンの交響曲第9番を指揮した。1993年にフィラデルフィア管弦楽団の指揮者に任命され、その1年後、サヴァリッシュは、指揮者としてフィラデルフィア管弦楽団を率いて、初めてのアジア演奏旅行として日本を再訪した。1996年には、サ

years later Japanese audiences got a view of the Orchestra's changing of the guard when Eugene Ormandy and Riccardo Muti jointly conducted the Orchestra during its Asia Tour. In 1985 Muti led the Philadelphians in Tokyo, Yokohama, Matsudo, Nagoya, Kagoshima, Fukuoka, and Osaka, and they returned again in 1989. For the 1986 opening of Tokyo's Suntory Hall, the NHK Symphony performed Beethoven's Ninth Symphony. The conductor for that performance was the NHK Symphony's honorary conductor and a musical hero to many Japanese, Wolfgang Sawallisch. A year after his appointment as The Philadelphia Orchestra's music director, he took the Orchestra back to Japan for their first Asian tour together. They returned in 1996, when Maestro Sawallisch and the Philadelphians presented a week-long Beethoven Festival in celebration of

ヴァリッシュとフィラデルフィア管弦楽団がサントリー・ホール開館10周年を祝って、1週間におよぶベートーベン・フェスティバルを繰り広げており、1999年と2001年に再来日をしている。

2005年と2008年に、当時の指揮者クリストフ・エッシェンバッハとフィラデルフィア管弦楽団はアジア演奏旅行の際、日本の都市にも立ち寄った。2010年には、首席指揮者のチャールズ・デュトワと共に演奏旅行で訪れている。そのデュトワは現在、NHK交響楽団の名誉指揮者である。2014年に、フィラデルフィア管弦楽団は、新しい指揮者ヤニック・ネゼ・セガン就任の演奏旅行の一環としてアジアや日本を訪問した。

フィラデルフィア管弦楽団は、来日した際には、単に演奏会を行うだけではなく、団員たちは自由時間に、室内コンサートやレッスン指導、リサイタルを行うことがよくある。滞在中は、フィラデルフィア管弦楽団のソフトボール・チーム「火の鳥」と、日本のオーケストラ・チームの間で、ソフトボールの試合が行われ、交流を大いに楽しんでいる。

フィラデルフィア管弦楽団には、2014年現在、日本出身のメンバーが5人いる。バイオリン奏者のヌマザワ・ヤヨイ、オカ・ヒロノ、スコット・ニノミヤ・ユミとピッコロ奏者のトキト・カズオ、そして、ピアニストのタケウチ・キヨコである。バイオリン奏者のミヨ・カーノ、エミー・オーシロ・モラレス、さらに、副主席代理チェロ奏者のユミ・ケンドール、主席ファゴット奏者のダニエル・マツカワという日系人のメンバーもいる。オカとスコットは、1998年2月、長野冬季オリンピックの開会式で、招かれて斉藤記念オーケ

Suntory Hall's tenth anniversary, and again in 1999 and 2001. In 2005 and 2008 then Music Director Christoph Eschenbach and the Orchestra toured Asia, with stops in numerous Japanese cities. The Orchestra's most recent visit to Japan was in 2010 with Chief Conductor Charles Dutoit, who is also currently music director emeritus of the NHK Symphony. In June 2014 the Orchestra returned to Asia, and to Japan, for its inaugural tour with the ensemble's new music director, Yannick Nézet-Séguin.

When The Philadelphia Orchestra comes to Japan, it often does more than give concerts. The Orchestra members' free time is filled with chamber concerts, master classes, and recitals. And no visit to Japan is complete without a boisterous softball game between the Orchestra's "Firebirds" and a team from one of the Japanese orchestras.

There are five Philadelphia Orchestra members who are Japanese: violinists Yayoi Numazawa, Hirono Oka, and Yumi Ninomiya Scott; piccolo player Kazuo Tokito; and pianist Kiyoko Takeuti; and four who are Japanese descendants: violinists Miyo Curnow and Amy Oshiro-Morales; Acting Associate Principal Cello Yumi Kendall; and Principal Bassoon Daniel Matsukawa. Ms. Oka and Ms. Scott returned to Japan for a special honor in February 1998, when they were invited to join the Saito Kinen Orchestra for its performance at the Opening Ceremonies of the Winter Olympic Games in Nagano. The professional and personal ties of friendship between The Philadelphia Orchestra members and their Japanese colleagues and audiences continue to grow while sharing the greatest gift the Orchestra

ストラと一緒に演奏した。

これからもフィラデルフィア管弦楽団
は、音楽を通して、団員の仲間同志そし
て日本の音楽愛好家たちと友情の絆を
育み続けていくであろう。

ダリン・ブリイテング
浜田昌子 訳

can give—its music.

By Darrin T. Britting and Peter Benoliel

If you go: The Academy of Music, 240 South Broad Street, Philadelphia, PA 19102.

Kimmel Center for the Performing Arts, 300 South Broad Street, Philadelphia, PA 19102.

8.4　Shōfūsō: Japanese House and Garden
松風荘：日本の家と庭園

1954年1月29日付けのニューヨークの新聞に、ニューヨーク近代美術館（MoMA）内にあるアビー・アルドリッチ・ロックフエラー・スカルプチャー・ガーデンに、展示用の「日本の家」を建てる計画が発表された。この日は建築材料が名古屋からニューヨークに輸送された日でもあった。そこに至るまでの6ヶ月の間に、根太（ねだ）や梁（はり）から、茶道具や庭石まで、あらゆるものが梱包された700個近い木枠組みの箱が日本からMoMAに送られていた。

「日本の家」は、彫刻庭園の「中庭の家Jシリーズ」の3番目の企画であった。MoMAの建築部門の学芸員であるアーサー・ドレクスラー氏は、日本の建築家、吉村順三氏と協力して伝統的な16世紀様式の家を作ることにした。吉村氏は「書院造り」を設計した。書院造りの名は建物の中央にある、作り付けの机がある書斎に由来している。設計は、滋賀県にある園城寺（三井寺とも呼ばれる）の客間をモデルとしていた。その家は、日本国民に代わって東京の日米協会がアメリカ国民に贈ったものであった。

建物の詳細な模型が作られ、その写真がその後2、3ヶ月にわたり新聞や雑誌に掲載された。家を建てる過程はすべて公開されたため、展示自体と同じくらい大きな教育的効果をアメリカの観客に与えたようである。その家は檜（ひのき）造りで、国の檜林から特別の許可を得て伐採された最良の檜であった。部材にほ

The plan to erect the Japanese Exhibition House in the Museum of Modern Art's Abby Aldrich Rockefeller Sculpture Garden was announced in New York newspapers on January 29, 1954. That was the date the materials were shipped from Nagoya to New York. The preceding six months must have been busy ones, engaged in the collection and fabrication of materials. The first of nearly seven hundred crates arrived about two months later. In them were packed everything from joists and beams to tea sets and garden rocks.

The Japanese House was the third "House in the Museum Garden" in the sculpture garden. The curator of architecture at the Museum of Modern Art, Arthur Drexler, worked with the Japanese architect Yoshimura Junzō during 1953 to realize the concept of creating a house in the traditional sixteenth century style. Yoshimura designed a *shoin* residence, named after the study with a built-in desk that was its central room. The plan was modeled on the Reception Hall at Onjōji (also known as Miidera) Temple in Shiga Prefecture. The house was a gift of the America-Japan Society of Tokyo on behalf of the Japanese people to the American people, as a gesture of friendship and good will.

A detailed model of the structure had been made and photographs of it appeared in newspapers and magazines in New York during the months prior to the opening of

The Japanese House. Shōfūsō—Japanese House and Garden 松風荘 所蔵

ぞ穴があけられ、木製釘でつなぎ合わ
された。庭石は高山の山々の傾斜地か
ら1つ1つ選ばれた。

棟上げの儀式も報道された。儀式は仏
教の僧侶が執り行い、屋根の上には伝
統的な飾りがなされ、床間の前には祭
壇が飾られ、日本の古典音楽が演奏さ
れた。建築に関わったのは22人で、設計
者の吉村順三氏と引き戸に障子紙を貼
った吉村夫人のほか、少なくとも4人の
日本の職人がいた。

この「日本の家」はその後、アーサー・
ドレクサーにより「松風荘」と命名さ
れ、1954年にオープンするとすぐに、

the exhibition at the Museum of Modern
Art. The process of erecting the house may
have had nearly as great an educational
impact upon the American audience as the
exhibition itself, owing to all the publicity.
The house was built of hinoki cypress, the
best specimens of which were obtained, by
special permission, from the national cypress
forests. The framing members were mortised
and fitted together with wooden pegs. The
rocks for the garden were individually
selected from the slopes of the Takayama
Mountains.

The ceremony of the raising of the ridge pole
(*mune-age*) was covered by the press as well.
The ritual was presided over by a Buddhist
priest and involved traditional decorations

263

批評家にも大衆にも好評を博した。松風荘は1954年10月まで公開され、再び1955年4月から10月まで公開された。20万人を超す人が訪れた後、10月16日に解体され、行く先が決定されるまで保管された。

決定を下すのは困難だったに違いない。というのは、その家がフィラデルフィアに移築されるという知らせがニューヨークとフィラデルフィアの新聞に載ったのは、8ヶ月も後のことであったから。1956年6月10日付の『ニューヨーク・タイムズ』紙によると、フェアモント公園が松風荘の移築場所に選定されたということであった。その理由は、並はずれて美しい自然環境を備えていることと、フェアモント公園委員会には歴史的家屋の保存と展示に際立った実績があるということだった。シカゴやワシントンといった都市も競争相手だったが、フィラデルフィアは自然のままの池がある庭がすでに備わっている敷地を提供できる、唯一の都市であった。その庭は元来1908年に仁王門のためにジョン・モリスによって造られたのであった。運悪くその歴史的な山門は1955年5月に火事で焼けてしまい、残った庭は新たな建物が建てられるのを待っている状態であった。松風荘は東京の日米協会の許可を得て、1956年にフィラデルフィアに寄贈された。松風荘は1957年から58年にかけて建造され、1958年10月18日にフィラデルフィアの人々に公開された。松風荘の庭園は造園家、佐野旦斎の設計によるもので、第2次世界大戦後において北アメリカで最初に造られた公共の日本庭園となった。

1976年に、フィラデルフィアで開催された独立200周年記念祭との関連で、大

on the roof, the adornment of an altar in front of the tokonoma post, and classical Japanese music. Twenty-two people worked on the house, including at least four Japanese workmen, as well as the architect, Yoshimura Junzō, and his wife Takiko, who papered the sliding shōji doors.

When the house opened in June 1954, it met with immediate approbation by critics as well as the public. It remained on view until October 1954 and then again from April to October 1955. On October 16, after being visited by over 200,000 people, the Japanese House and Garden were dismantled and stored while a decision was made about what to do with them.

It must have been a difficult decision to make, since it was not until nearly eight months later that an announcement appeared in New York and Philadelphia newspapers that the house would be moved to Philadelphia. According to the June 10, 1956, *New York Times*, Fairmount Park was selected as the permanent site for the house because it provided "an unusually beautiful natural setting and the Commission has an outstanding record of maintaining and displaying historic houses." Although other cities such as Chicago and Washington, DC, vied to be chosen as the permanent location for the Japanese House, Philadelphia was the only city that offered a site already landscaped with an intact pond garden: the garden originally installed by John Morris in 1908 for the Niō-mon. The proposed spot was also near the site of the first Japanese garden in North America from the Japanese Bazaar of the Centennial Exhibition and represented the embodiment of continuous

規模な修理が施された。1982年には松風荘と庭園を維持するために、非営利団体の「松風荘友の会」が結成された。「友の会」は1999年に、120万ドルを拠金し、日本国外で唯一の檜皮葺（ひわだぶき）屋根の総葺き替えを実施した。

世界を舞台に活躍されている現代日本画家、千住博画伯に滝をモチーフとした襖絵20点を寄贈していただき、2007年の松風荘修復工事完了後、一般公開している。

2011年の檜皮葺屋根の修繕後、翌年にはフィラデルフィア市の公園及びレクリエーション部門の協力を得て、1876年に造られた煉瓦の建物2棟を修復、櫻パビリオンと命名し、冬季閉館中の催物及び展示に利用している。

松風荘は1876年から現在に至るまでの日本とフィラデルフィアの友好関係を象徴し、今後も、一般訪問者と研究者のために、日本の伝統的な建築物と庭園を紹介し続けていくことであろう。

チャールズ・エバーズ /キム・アンドリュー 今井元子/小澤悠一 訳

Japanese culture in Philadelphia since 1876.

As fate would have it, the historic Niō-mon temple gate had been destroyed by fire in May of 1955, leaving the old garden available as the site for a new structure. Thus, Shōfūsō Pine Breeze Villa was given to Philadelphia in 1956, with the approval of the America-Japan Society of Tokyo. The house and garden were installed during 1957–58, and opened to the Philadelphia public on October 18, 1958. Shōfūsō's garden, designed by landscape architect Sano Tansai, was the first public Japanese garden constructed in North America after World War II.

A major restoration for the 1976 Bicentennial celebration inspired the founding of the Friends of the Japanese House and Garden (FJHG), a private nonprofit organization that has administered, funded, and preserved the city-owned site since 1982. FJHG raised $1.2 million in 1999 to replace the hinoki roof of Shōfūsō, the only one of its kind outside of Japan.

After visiting Shōfūsō, internationally-renowned contemporary Japanese artist Hiroshi Senju created a series of twenty *fusuma* murals, titled *Waterfall* and inspired by Shōfūsō's water features. This important art installation was put on permanent display by FJHG during an extensive renovation in 2007.

Once they concluded a comprehensive repair of Shōfūsō's hinoki bark roof in 2011, FJHG partnered with Philadelphia Parks and Recreation and preserved the Sakura Pavilion at the Centennial Buildings in 2012, two restored 1876 brick buildings used as year-round space for programming and exhibitions. FJHG most recently conducted an award-winning restoration of Shōfūsō's 1957 pond and garden, a nationally-recognized historic landscape consistently cited for its authenticity.

Shōfūsō is the embodiment of the friendship between Japan and Philadelphia from 1876 to present day and continues to provide a preserved historic Japanese house and garden for the benefit of visitors and scholars alike.

By Charles A. Evers and Kim Andrews

Selected References: Yuichi Ozawa, *Story of Shofuso: A Cultural Bridge between Japan and the United States* (Philadelphia, PA: Privately published, 2010), available at Shōfūsō; Arthur Drexler, *The Architecture of Japan* (New York: The Museum of Modern Art, 1955), pp. 262–86.

If you go: Shōfūsō, West Fairmount Park, enter through Horticultural Drive. Horticultural and Lansdowne Drives, Philadelphia, PA 19131.

8.5 Tea in Postwar Philadelphia: A Widening Circle
茶の湯：広がる茶道の輪

フィラデルフィア市内にあるフェアモント公園の「松風荘」を訪れると、茶道のデモンストレーションや稽古に出合えることがある。抹茶にお湯を注ぎ茶筅（ちゃせん）で点（た）てる。茶の湯、あるいは茶道と呼ばれている。40年近くにわたる熱心な努力が実り、フィラデルフィアには茶道が根付いている。アメリカ独立200周年記念祭の1976年には、ニューヨークと京都の裏千家の教授たちが出席し、松風荘で呈茶が行われた。現在はシャーヴィン・妙子教授（茶名は宗妙）が中心になり、稽古だけでなくフィラデルフィア美術館での講義やデモンストレーションでも大きく茶の湯の輪を広げるきっかけを作っている。

A visit to Shōfūsō, the Pine Breeze Villa Japanese House and Garden in Fairmount Park, often affords an opportunity to participate in a "tea ceremony" demonstration or observe a lesson. This making and serving of a bowl of tea, whisked from green *matcha* powder with "hot water for tea" (*chanoyu*, one name for the Way of Tea, also known as *chadō* or *sadō*), became established in Philadelphia over the course of some four decades through the efforts of dedicated practitioners. A formal tea with Urasenke masters from New York and Kyoto graced the celebration at the Japanese House during the 1976 Bicentennial. Today, the teacher Taeko Shervin (tea name, Sōmyō) is the center of a widening circle of fascination and study that also includes lectures and demonstrations at the Philadelphia Museum of Art.

Brother Joseph Keenan (1932–1999), a member of the Christian Brothers teaching order and a professor at La Salle University, was a specialist in religion and liturgy. Parallels between Japanese ritual tea practice and the Eucharist of the Catholic mass led him to take up tea at the Urasenke Chanoyu Center of New York and to travel to Japan for a year of full-time classes at Midorikai, the school's foreign-language program in Kyoto. Descended from Sen no Rikyū (the person considered to have had the most profound influence on chanoyu; 1522–1591), Urasenke is the largest and most internationally active

Taeko Shervin making tea in Shōfūsō's four-and-a-half mat tearoom. Shōfūsō—Japanese House and Garden 松風荘所蔵

クリスチャン・ブラザーズ修道会に所属していたブラザー・ジョセフ・キーナン(1932 - 1999)は、ラサール大学の教授を務めていた。キーナン神父は宗教学と礼拝法の専門家として、日本の儀式的な茶道とカトリックのミサにおける聖体拝領での共通点に興味を持ち、ニューヨーク市にある裏千家茶の湯センターで稽古を始め、さらに京都に行き、外国人学生専用の裏千家みどり会で1年間学んだ。裏千家は、千利休(1522 - 1591)に始まる数ある流派の中で最大で、海外でも一番普及している。

アメリカに戻ったブラザー・キーナンは、ラサール大学学長を務めていたパトリック・エリス神父を説得し、ニューヨーク裏千家からの教師の協力も得て大学で茶道を正式な授業として教え始めた。さらに当時裏千家のお家元であった千宗室(1923年生まれ、現在は鵬雲斎大宗匠)の協力もあり、日本から大工が来て大学内の小さな建物に茶室を作り、茶道の授業が始まったのであった。この建物は昔、ベルフィールドと呼ばれる屋敷地所の庭管理人の家であった。屋敷自体は、もともと肖像画家のチャールズ・ウイルソン・ピールに始まり、アメリカを代表する文筆家オーエン・ウィスターも住んだ邸宅で、広大な庭があった。1987年9月に茶室開きが行われ、お家元直筆による『賛美感謝庵』の額が入口に掛けられた。

ラサール大学の茶室は、まさしく東洋と西洋の融合で、一階は天井が低く、掛け軸や茶花を飾る床の間の6畳の茶室に水屋もあり、障子越しの光で茶の湯の稽古や初釜が催された。2階は畳敷きながら、壁は昔のままのしっくい作り、さらに

of Japan's several tea schools.

Upon his return, Keenan convinced Brother Patrick Ellis, then president of La Salle, to host a tea school on campus. With the support of the fifteenth Grand Master (*oiemoto*) of the Urasenke School, Sen Sōshitsu, or Hōunsai (b. 1923), a carpenter from Japan converted a small building on La Salle's campus into a proper space for lessons. Once a groundskeeper's house on the Belfield estate—originally owned by the portraitist Charles Wilson Peale and then home to the prominent Owen Wister family—the cottage sat among generous gardens. The tearoom (*chashitsu*) officially opened in September 1987 with the name Sanbikansha-an, "The House of Thanks and Praise," given by Hōunsai. The Grand Master's calligraphy of the name hung inside the doorway, setting the tone for visitors.

The La Salle teahouse was an extraordinary example of east-west hybridity. On the first floor, Japanese materials were fashioned into a low-ceilinged room with an alcove (*tokonoma*) to display a scroll, flowers, and other accouterments of a tea gathering. Light diffused through two paper-covered windows illuminated six rice-straw tatami mats. A kitchen and preparation room (*mizuya*) allowed teachers and students to do regular lessons as well as special seasonal events such as the first tea of the new year. The second floor boasted a room with tatami mats and the original plaster walls and beams of the farmhouse.

La Salle students took academic courses on tea with Brother Keenan while practicing at the tearoom with Taeko Shervin, who, until

Brother Joseph Keenan making tea in the Sanbikansha-an tearoom at La Salle University. La Salle University Archives

she earned full credentials herself, was initially supervised by Yumiko Toyama Pakenham, an instructor from Urasenke New York. Mariko Nishi LaFleur (tea name, Sōshin), who held a master's degree from the Kyoto headquarters of Urasenke, joined the endeavor after moving to Philadelphia in 1990. She also taught popular tea courses at the University of Pennsylvania and Villanova University. After Brother Keenan's tragic death in a hit-and-run accident, La Salle University was unable to sustain the bridges he had built, and they closed the teahouse precipitously in 2007. However, their Connelly Library houses a collection of 250 printed items related to tea.

This is not to say that there is no story of Philadelphia and tea before the 1980s. Shōfūsō's intimate tearoom and large tatami room overlooking the garden compelled practitioners to share the art, and demonstrations were done on occasion even before. The quality of Japanese leaf tea on display at the Japanese Bazaar was noted during the Centennial Exhibition of 1876 in Fairmount Park. Given the impact of Okakura Kakuzō, or Tenshin's, 1906 *Book of Tea*, one can imagine that many Philadelphians plied their Japanese visitors for informal introductions to the actual experience of the "cup of humanity."

Tea lessons continue weekly at Shōfūsō, and annual demonstrations by representatives from Omotesenke and Mushanokōjisenke supplement the program of Urasenke monthly teas. Outdoor tea (*nodate*) features in the

天井は農家風に梁が出ているように仕上げられていた。

ブラザー・キーナンのもと、ニューヨークからのパッケンハム・裕美子が中心となりシャーヴィン・妙子が、ラサール大学の学生たちに授業として茶道を教え始める。さらに京都裏千家のみどり会で教えていたラフレール・真理子（茶名は宗真）も1990年にラサール大学で教え始めた。ラフレールはその後、ペンシルベニア大学とビラノバ大学でもお茶を教え、好評を博した。しかしながら、ブラザー・キーナンが交通事故で亡くなると、ラサール大学は彼が築いた東西の架け

橋となる活動を理解せず、予告なしに2007年に茶室を閉鎖してしまう。幸いなことに大学内のコネレー図書館には、今でも茶道に関する250余の文書が納められている。

1980年代以前、フィラデルフィアには茶道が無かったということではなく、松風荘のこぢんまりとした茶室や、庭に面した15帖の部屋で、茶道の仲間たちが茶道をし、またデモンストレーションも時々行われていた。1876年にフェアモント公園で開かれたアメリカ独立100周年記念万国博覧会には日本の売店が設置され、日本製のお茶が展示されていたことが記録されている。さらに1906年には岡倉天心(覚三)の英語による『茶の本』が出版されることによって、フィラデルフィアの人たちも『カップ・オブ・ヒューマニティー』(後の訳本では、『人情の碗』)と呼ばれる茶道に興味を持ったに違いない。

松風荘では毎週裏千家の稽古が行われているだけでなく、毎月のデモンストレーション、さらに表千家と武者小路千家のデモンストレーションを楽しんでいる。毎春開催される「スバル桜祭り」の期間には、フェアモント公園で野点(のだて)も開かれている。2012年には、フィラデルフィアの裏千家は、京都の裏千家直轄の淡交会として編成された。こうしてブラザー・キーナンが茶の湯の種を播いてから、地道な努力で育ててきたおかげで、ブラザーの元で茶道を始めたモーガン・ビアードとドリュー・ハンソンは、今や地元出身の茶名を持った教師にまで育ったのである。

リンダ・チャンス
山口桂伺郎 訳

Subaru Cherry Blossom Festival of Greater Philadelphia. The region is now served by Chado Urasenke Tankokai Philadelphia Association, directly affiliated with Kyoto Urasenke since 2012. Today Philadelphia has an inaugural generation of locally trained tea teachers, Morgan Beard and Drew Hanson, who first tasted the serenity and discipline of *chanoyu* with Brother Keenan.

By Linda H. Chance

Selected References: Cristeen Taniguchi, "Historical Narrative of Shofuso" (Philadelphia, PA: National Park Service Philadelphia Support Office, 2000); "La Salle Dedicates New Japanese Tea Ceremony House," *La Salle Magazine* (Winter 1987–88): 31-32; Shannon Curley, "Is the tea party over?" *Collegian*, September 19, 2007

If you go: La Salle University, 1900 West Olney Avenue, Philadelphia, PA 19141.

Shōfūsō, West Fairmount Park, enter through Horticultural Drive. Horticultural and Lansdowne Drives, Philadelphia, PA 19131.

8.6　Cherry Blossom Festival: A New Philadelphia Tradition

日米協会とフィラデルフィア桜祭り

花見は奈良時代（710‐794）に宮廷で始まったといわれ、その後、桜の花を愛でることを意味するようになった。宮廷の人々は桜花が盛りを迎えて間もなく散り初めるのを、人生のはかなさにたとえて和歌を詠んだ。江戸時代（1603‐1867）には、花見は一般の人々の間でも行われるようになる。花見の伝統は現代の日本にも受け継がれ、桜の季節が巡ってくるたびに、人々は満開の桜の木の下で弁当を囲み、酒を酌み交わしている。

日本政府は花見の伝統をアメリカにも伝えるため、いくつかの都市に親善のしるしとして桜の木を寄贈している。初めて寄贈されたのは1912年、日本から贈られた3000本の桜がワシントンに植樹された。1926年には、アメリカ独立150周年を讃えるため2600本の桜がフィラデルフィアに寄贈され、フェアモント公園と川沿いに植樹された。満開時には見事に咲き誇る桜は、日本とフィラデルフィアの親善のシンボルとなり、春といえば桜という華やかなイメージがフィラデルフィア市民の間に定着した。

1998年、フィラデルフィア日米協会は当初寄贈された2600本の桜に加え、さらに1000本の桜を植樹するという10年計画を打ち出した。公園に幾重にも広がる淡いピンクの花びらは、フィラデルフィアのスバル桜祭りを美しく彩っている。毎年春には1万2000人を超える人々がフェアモント公園を訪れ、桜の下でピクニック、そして毎年日本から訪れる玉川

The Japanese practice of *hanami*, or flower viewing, is said to have started in the imperial court during the Nara Period (710–794) and over time became synonymous with viewing cherry blossoms, known as *sakura*. Women as well as men at court composed poems comparing the fleeting beauty of the cherry blossoms to the ephemeral nature of life. *Sakura* viewing became a pastime of the common people during the Edo period (1603–1867). Today the Japanese people continue the *hanami* tradition each spring when thousands of people fill Japan's parks to drink sake and picnic under the flowering cherry trees.

The Japanese government helped establish the custom of *hanami* in the United States by donating blossoming cherry trees to several U.S. cities as a gesture of friendship. The first donation took place in 1912, when Japan gave the U.S. government 3,000 *sakura*, which were planted in Washington, D.C. In 1926, in honor of the sesqui-centennial of the United States, the Japanese gave Philadelphia 2,600 flowering cherry trees, which were planted in Fairmount Park and along the river drives. The spectacular blossoms of these trees are an enduring symbol of the friendship between the people of Japan and Philadelphia and have become one of the hallmarks of spring to many Philadelphians.

In 1998 the Japan America Society of Greater Philadelphia (JASGP) embarked on a ten-

The sundial at Fairmount Park.
Japan America Society of
Greater Philadelphia

year program to supplement the original gift of 2,600 trees by planting an additional 1,000 flowering cherry trees. Their beautiful pale pink blossoms now form the backdrop for the Subaru Cherry Blossom Festival of Greater Philadelphia. Each spring, over 12,000 people come to Fairmount Park to picnic under the trees while enjoying traditional Japanese *taiko* drumming performances by the Tamagawa University Drummers and Dancers. Attendees also watch martial arts exhibitions, try their hand at Japanese brush painting, observe ikebana flower arranging demonstrations, learn to play the ancient game of *igo*, and experience modern Japanese arts such as *anime*.

The Subaru Cherry Blossom Festival is the centerpiece cultural project of the Japan America Society of Greater Philadelphia. In 1991, William B. Eagleson, Jr., Philadelphia's newly appointed Honorary Consul General of Japan, proposed to then Ambassador Seki that a Japan America Society be established in Philadelphia. Ambassador Seki was very encouraging, wryly observing that Philadelphia was the only American city to have a major league baseball team but no Japan America Society.

At the time, Philadelphia had several organizations devoted to various aspects of Japanese affairs and interests. These included the Japanese American Citizens League, the Japanese Association of Greater Philadelphia, and the Friends of the Japanese House and Garden, all of which still exist. However, Eagleson sensed a need for an organization to promote greater business and cultural exchange between the two countries, particularly to involve

大学芸術学部による和太鼓と舞踊の公演を楽しんでいる。また、武道演舞、お茶や生け花の実演、書道や囲碁、アニメなどのポップカルチャーなど、さまざまな日本文化に触れることができる。いまや、「スバル桜祭り」は、フィラデルフィア日米協会のプロジェクトのなかでは最大の文化活動となっている。

さかのぼること1991年に、在フィラデルフィア日本国名誉総領事に着任したばかりのウィリアム・B・イーグルソン・Jr.が当時の関大使に対して、フィラデルフィアに日米協会を設立することを提案した。関大使は、フィラデルフィアが全米の中でもメジャー・リーグの球団がありながら、日米協会のない唯一の都市であるという事実を重んじて、協会設立に動

Japanese dancers dressed as maiko perform in the Liberty Place Rotunda, 2004.
Japan America Society of Greater Philadelphia

き出した。当時フィラデルフィアでは各種団体が、日本に関してさまざまな事業やイベントに取り組んでいた。「日系アメリカ人市民同盟」「フィラデルフィア日本人会」「松風荘友の会」などである。これらの団体はすべて現在も活動を続けている。

イーグルソンは、ビジネスや文化交流を推し進めること、特に日本人および日系人の会員が中心であった団体の活動にもっとアメリカ人を巻き込むことが必要だと感じていた。そこでフィラデルフィア国際ネットワークの専務理事であったフレッド・デドリックは、この地域に日本からの投資を惹き付けるために行動を起こす。イーグルソンとデドリックは、当時フィラデルフィアにおける日本人ビジネス界のリーダー的存在であった三菱グループの傘下にあった秦浩一と大村公男に声をかけ、この地で日米協会が果

more diverse people to complement the largely Japanese and Japanese-American memberships of the existing organizations. Fred Dedrick, the director of the Greater Philadelphia International Network, was interested in initiatives to attract Japanese investment to the area. Eagleson and Dedrick started a conversation with the leaders of Philadelphia's Japanese business community, Koichi Hata and Kimio Ohmura, about the role that a Japan America Society might play in the community. By 1994 a bi-national board of directors was formed, initial funding was assured and, most importantly, leadership in the persons of co-chairs Koichi Hata and Peter A. Benoliel was enlisted. Finally, in September of that year, with the help of Dr. Felice Fischer, a founding director, an inaugural ceremony was held at the Philadelphia Museum of Art, attended by

たす役割について模索を始めた。1994
年ごろまでには、日米両国参加の理事
会が結成され、必要資金も確保され、秦
浩一とピーター・A．ベノリエルの2人が
共同チェアマンに就任する。こうして同
年9月にフェリス・フィッシャーの尽力の
もと、フィラデルフィア美術館において
発足式が行われた。式典には関大使の
ほか、当時のフィラデルフィア市長で後
のペンシルベニア州知事となったエド
ワード・G・レンデルも参列した。

発足後20年の今日、フィラデルフィア日
米協会は、この地域に関わる文化、ビジ
ネス、外交関係についての最新情報を
盛り込んだ講義シリーズなど様々なプロ
グラムを通じて、日本とフィラデルフィア
のコミュニティーの交流の場を提供する
という当初の使命を果たし続けている。
また日本の企業に対してフィラデルフィ
ア進出を促すために、フィラデルフィア
市およびペンシルベニア州と密接に連
携しながら、在ニューヨーク日本国総領
事館およびフィラデルフィア市長執務室
をつなげる重要なパイプとなっている。

神戸市は1986年にアメリカ政府の姉妹
都市プログラムにより、親善友好都市と
なったが、2014年にフィラデルフィア日
米協会専務理事であるチューニ・一美
を神戸親善大使に任命した。

アデレード・ファーガソン

モーリス米澤みどり 訳

Ambassador Seki and by Edward G. Rendell, then Mayor of Philadelphia, later Governor of Pennsylvania.

Today, twenty years after its founding, the JASGP continues to fulfill its initial mission of providing forums for the Japanese and Philadelphia business and cultural communities through various programs, including an informative lectures series that brings the latest in Japanese culture, business and government relations updates to the Philadelphia region. The JASGP also works closely with the City of Philadelphia and the State of Pennsylvania to promote Philadelphia to Japanese businesses locating in the United States and has facilitated numerous meetings between the Consul General of Japan in New York and the mayor's office. The City of Kobe, which became Philadelphia's Sister City in 1986 under the U.S. government's Sister Cities Program, appointed JASGP's Executive Director, Kazumi Teune, Kobe's Goodwill Ambassador.

By Adelaide Ferguson

If you go: The Subaru Cherry Blossom Festival spans a few weeks each April. The main event is Sakura Sunday. Visit subarucherryblossom.org and japanphilly. org for more information.

Afterword
あとがき

「フィラ・ニッポニカ」の初版が、1999年にフィラデルフィア日米協会によって出版された際、江戸末期から近代にかけてフィラデルフィアと日本の間には、これほどの交流があったのかという驚きの声があがった。日本人にとって、岩倉具視、津田梅子、新渡戸稲造、有島武郎、野口英世などの名前は非常に親しみを覚える。特に2007年まで五千円札に使用されていた新渡戸と、現在も千円札に使われている野口の顔写真を見たことがない人はいないであろう。

私は1920年代に生まれた両親から、野口英世は当時の初等教育において立身出世をした伝説の人物として教科書に紹介されていたと聞いて育った。学生時代には、有島武郎の本を読みあさったものである。親しい友人の何人かは津田梅子が創立した津田塾大学に進学している。ただひとつ、私を含め多くの日本人が知らなかったことは、日本の歴史に名前を残した多くの人達が、フィラデルフィアに住んでいたという事実である。

初版から現在に至るまでの15年の間、日米両国に住む多くの方々から、追記されるべき人物および教育機関についての情報を提供していただいていた。驚いたことに、情報提供者の多くは、既に論文や本を出版していたということである。苦労することなく改訂版にむけての"資料が自然にフィラデルフィア日米協会に集まって来てくれた"という表現が適切であろう。

When the first edition of Phila-Nipponica was published in 1999, many were surprised to learn that such a number of historically significant exchanges took place between Philadelphia and Japan from the end of the Edo Period into the modern era.

Those educated in Japan know about the accomplishments of Iwakura Tomomi, Tsuda Umeko, Nitobe Inazō, Arishima Takeo, and Noguchi Hideyo. Japanese are just as familiar with Nitobe and Noguchi, who appear on the 5000 and 1000 yen Japanese notes, as Americans are with George Washington and Abraham Lincoln, who appear on their currency. My parents, who were born in the 1920s, learned about the legendary Noguchi, who conquered poverty and became an international figure, in school. While at college, I read all of Arishima's books. Some of my close friends went to Tsuda College established by Tsuda Umeko. One important fact we did not know, however, was that they all had a significant connection to Philadelphia before they became prominent figures in Japanese history.

During the fifteen years after publication of the first edition, many people contacted the Japan America Society of Greater Philadelphia's office to suggest topics that should have been included in the book. To my surprise, many of these informants had already published their own articles or books on the suggested subject. As these

初版では、どちらかというとフィラデルフィアに来た日本人に重点が置かれていたが、この改訂版には、日本のために尽力した地元出身のアメリカ人が追加された。さらに頁数が倍以上になった改訂版では、当時のフィラデルフィアにおける国際的レベルの組織と技術が、後に日本の近代化を推進した多くのリーダーに教育の場を提供していたことが明確に浮かび上がってくる。

戦後に再び緊密となった日米関係のもとで、ビジネス、政治、文化、学術、医学の各分野に従事する数多くの人々がフィラデルフィアと日本の架け橋になってきた。初版と改訂版では、江戸末期から1930年代に活躍した日米の人々を対象としたが、将来、第3版では、戦後から現代に活躍する人たちに焦点をあてたい。既に今の時点で、追記すべき人物の名前が挙がっている。第2次大戦後に巣鴨刑務所で戦犯の世話をしたペンシルバニア大学の精神医学教授アルバート・スタンカード博士と、同大学の医学部出身で、戦後アメリカ政府が設立した「原爆傷害調査委員会」に関与していた北村三郎博士がまず筆頭になるであろう。郊外にある広大なモリス植木園には、ムトウという庭師が作り上げた日本庭園がある。女性として日本初の外務大臣に就任した田中真紀子は、フィラデルフィアの名門校ジャーマンタウン・フレンドスクールに3年間在籍し、1963年に卒業している。1990年に今上天皇の次男である秋篠宮文仁親王に嫁いだ紀子妃殿下は、経済学者である父の川嶋辰彦学習院大学名誉教授が、ペンシルバニア大学博士課程で学んでいた期間、1歳から6歳までフィラデルフィア市内にあるリー・スクールに通っていた。

recommendations trickled into our office one by one it became apparent that a second edition of Phila-Nipponica was in order.

In the first edition, the emphasis was on Japanese who came to Philadelphia. In this edition, we included more Philadelphians who made contributions to Japan. The crucial role that Philadelphia played during the period of Japanese modernization will become clearer to readers. Philadelphia's advanced industry and technology illustrated possibilities for Japan, and its first class educational institutions trained many of the pioneers who built modern Japan.

Even as we were putting the finishing touches on this edition, we continued to uncover others whose valuable contributions deserve to be memorialized. Professor of Psychiatry Albert J. Stunkard, M.D., late of the University of Pennsylvania's Perelman School of Medicine, who cared for Japanese war criminals in Sugamo Prison, and Dr. Kitamura Saburō, a 1930 University of Pennsylvania and 1936 Penn Medical School graduate, affiliated with the Atomic Bomb Casualty Commission, which studied the effects of the bomb under a U.S. government mandate to withhold treatment, are the first ones on the list. Y. Muto, the gardener, reappears with another pair named Morris, John and Lydia, who had Muto design two gardens now preserved in the Morris Arboretum. The Japanese politician Tanaka Makiko, who served as Japan's first female foreign minister in the cabinet of Koizumi Jun'ichirō, graduated from Germantown Friends' School in 1963, and provides another example. Finally, Kawashima Kiko, who married the second son of the current

21世紀に入ってからは、長い間、限られたアメリカ人たちの間でしか認識されていなかった日本文化は、アニメや日本食に代表されるように、アメリカ文化の一部になってきている。日本語を勉強する学生数も、日本がアメリカに次ぐ経済大国になるとともに飛躍的に増加してきた。「寿司」はアメリカ人の会話の中に頻繁に登場し、寿司レストランは全米のあらゆる都市に存在し、今やパーティーなどには不可欠のメニューのひとつとなっている。 フィラデルフィア日米協会が1998年より始めた"桜祭り"には毎年数万人が参加するが、ほとんどが地元のアメリカ人で、特に20代から30代の若者であることは、まさにこの現象を反映しているといえる。

最後に、非常に短い準備期間にもかかわらず、快く「フィラ・ニッポニカ改訂版」に貢献しくださった30数名にのぼる著者、編集者、翻訳者の皆様に心より御礼を申し上げたい。まさにグループでやり遂げた快挙であった。

チューニ一美

2014 年 11月

emperor of Japan, lived in Philadelphia from the ages of one to six while her father, Kawashima Tatsuhiko, an economist, worked on his doctorate at the University of Pennsylvania. Kiko attended the Lea School in West Philadelphia. Princess Kiko went on to have three children with Prince Akishino, contributing to the stability of the imperial household.

I am sure that there are many others who deserve to be included and we will certainly introduce them in the third edition, which seems inevitable given the depth and variety of connections between Philadelphia and Japan.

I would like to extend my utmost appreciation to all those who contributed to this second edition.

Kazumi Teune

November 2014

Contributors
貢献者リスト

Editors-in-Chief	Linda H. Chance	Associate Professor Department of East Asian Language and Civilizations University of Pennsylvania
	TetsukoToda 戸田徹子	Associate Professor Faculty of International Humanities Josai International University 国際人文学部 城西国際大学 准教授
Contributing Editors	Adelaide Ferguson	Director Japan America Society of Greater Philadelphia
	Masako Hamada 浜田昌子	Associate Professor Japanese Studies Program Institute for Global Interdisciplinary Studies Villanova University
Managing Editor	Kazumi Teune チューニ　一美	Executive Director Japan America Society of Greater Philadelphia フィラデルフィア日米協会 専務理事
Authors	Kim Andrews	Executive Director Shofuso Japanese House & Garden
	F. Michael Angelo	Archivist and Special Collections Librarian Thomas Jefferson University
	Toshio Asakura 朝倉稔生	Professor Emeritus, Pediatrics University of Pennsylvania
	Peter A. Benoliel	Chairman Emeritus Quaker Chemical Corporation
	Steven M. Berzin	Attorney, financial services and former Executive Vice President New York City Economic Development Corporation
	Darrin T. Britting	Associate Director for Publications and Content Development The Philadelphia Orchestra
	Frank L. Chance	Associate Director for Academics Center for East Asian Studies University of Pennsylvania
	Denise Connerty	Assistant Vice President, International Affairs Temple University
	F. Hilary Conroy	Emeritus Professor of Far Eastern History University of Pennsylvania

Fredrick R. Dickinson	Professor Department of History University of Pennsylvania
Benjamin Duke	Trustee and Professor Emeritus , International Christian University (Japan)
William B. Eagleson, Jr.	Former Honorary Consul General of Japan
Charles A. Evers	Architect
Felice Fischer	Luther W. Brady Curator of Japanese Art Philadelphia Museum of Art
Williams Higgins	Principal Financial Analyst School District of Philadelphia
Masaharu Imai 今井雅晴	Professor Emeritus Tsukuba University (Japan) 筑波大学名誉教授
Gwendolyn Clara Watkins Kiefer	Whitney Family descendant
Kyoko Kinoshita 木下京子	Project Associate Curator East Asian Art Philadelphia Museum of Art
Akira Kitade 北出　明	Former Director Japan National Tourism Organization 元国際観光振興機構 コンベンション誘致部長
Matsumoto Shin'ichi 松本晋一	Dentist, Matsumoto Dental Clinic 松本歯科医院　歯科医
Masayoshi Matsumura 松村正義	Professor Emeritus, Teikyo University (Japan) 外交史家、元帝京大学教授
Martin Meyerson	President Emeritus, University of Pennsylvania
Matthew Mizenko	Associate Professor Japanese and East Asian Studies Ursinus College
Taiken Murakami 村上泰賢	Tozenji 東善寺住職 小栗上野介顕彰会理事
Mira Nakashima	George Nakashima Woodworkers
Chieko Nishikawa 西川知恵子	Former Board Member, Kashiwa Welfare Fellowship 元柏朋会幹事
A. Hirotoshi Nishikawa	Past President and current board member, Philadelphia JACL (Japanese American Citizens League)
Fernanda H. Perrone	Curator of the William Elliot Griffis Collection Rutgers University
Diana Franzusoff Peterson	Manuscripts Librarian & College Archivist Haverford College

279

	Frederik L. Schodt	Translator, interpreter, and award-winning writer based in San Francisco
	Jeffrey A. Sheehan	Associate Dean, International Relations The Wharton School, University of Pennsylvania
	Quincy Williams	Former Board Member, Japan America Society of Greater Philadelphia
	Ohtsuka Kenji 大塚兼司	President , Irwin School (Japan) アルウイン学園 玉成高等保育学校 理事長
	Sumiko Enbutsu 圓佛須美子	
	Hideo Watanabe 渡辺英男	Assistant Professor Department of Languages and Cultures William Paterson University
Translators	Mark Bookman	Fulbright Research Fellow in Japan
	Nanako M. Hoch ホーク菜々子	Japanese Instructor Harrisburg Area Community College
	Hanae Nakamura 中村英惠	Japanese Instructor Lower Merion School District; Harriton High School
	Minako Kobayashi 小林美奈子	Japanese Instructor East Asian Studies Haverford College
	Midori Yonezawa Morris モーリス米澤みどり	Lecturer Department of East Asian Languages and Civilizations University of Pennsylvania
	Keijiroh Yama-Guchi 山口桂伺郎	Interpreter
	Samuel Malissa	Ph.D. Candidate Yale University
	Motoko Imai 今井元子	
	Sumiko Imai 今井澄子	
	Fujiko Hara 原不二子	
	Masako Iino 飯野正子	Professor Emeritus/Past President, Tsuda College (Japan) President, Fulbright Foundation 津田塾大学名誉教授・前学長 フルブライト財団理事長
	Paul Schuble	Research/Admin Assistant Research Institute of Telecommunications and Economics
Copy Editors	Masako Kaida 甲斐田雅子	Editor, New York Japion 『NYジャピオン』編集者

	Richard Showstack	
	Mark Swirsky	
Assistants	Nora Casper	Japan America Society of Greater Philadelphia
	Aaron Dilliplane	フィラデルフィア日米協会
	Yaritza Hernandez	
	Elaine Maulucci	
	Kazue Nomoto 野本和恵	
	Maki Takeuchi 竹内真希	
Designer	Matthew Meyer	

63803330R00157

Made in the USA
Charleston, SC
13 November 2016